101 DISCOVERIES

★ ★

LONDON EH TO ZED

FOR CANADIAN VISITORS TO LONDON

CHRISTOPHER WALTERS

DUNDURN
TORONTO

Editor: Cheryl Hawley
Design: Courtney Horner
Cover Design: Sarah Beaudin
Printer: Webcom

Library and Archives Canada Cataloguing in Publication

Walters, Christopher, 1964-, author
London eh to zed : 101 discoveries for Canadian visitors to London
/ Christopher Walters.

Includes index.
Issued in print and electronic formats.
ISBN 978-1-4597-2986-5

1. London (England)--Guidebooks. I. Title.

DA679.W26 2015   914.2104'86   C2014-908131-6
                                              C2014-908132-4

1   2   3   4   5   19   18   17   16   15

We acknowledge the support of the **Canada Council for the Arts** and the **Ontario Arts Council** for our publishing program. We also acknowledge the financial support of the **Government of Canada** through the **Canada Book Fund** and **Livres Canada Books**, and the **Government of Ontario** through the **Ontario Book Publishing Tax Credit** and the **Ontario Media Development Corporation**.

Visit us at
Dundurn.com | @dundurnpress | Facebook.com/dundurnpress | Pinterest.com/Dundurnpress

Dundurn
3 Church Street, Suite 500
Toronto, Ontario, Canada
M5E 1M2

TABLE OF CONTENTS

FOREWORD

"When a man is tired of London, he is tired of life," Samuel Johnson famously wrote. Young Christopher Walters, the author of this distinctive and original guide to London, has wonderfully updated Dr. Johnson: "When a Canadian is tired of London, he is not only tired of life, but has also given up on his historical soul."

I say "young" Mr. Walters because that is how he still seems to me, although it has been more than three decades since he first walked into my life — in London, not surprisingly. He was still a university student on the lam during the summer holidays during his undergraduate career in Canada. I was the West European bureau chief for the *Globe and Mail* and occupied a plummy suite of offices in Temple Chambers, just off Fleet Street, which was still the world-famous "street of shame" as the satirical magazine *Private Eye* dubbed the once-famous thoroughfare of newspaper and magazine premises and beer-soaked pubs.

The bureau secretary came into the office and told me I should see this "kid" in the outer office who was looking for some sort of work. He had clearly worked his charms on the secretary because I tried to get her to tell him to go fly a kite, but she stood her ground.

"He's cute," she said. "He'd be fun to have around here."

"Oh great," I said. "He's cute. Shall we have him stand outside the office like a cigar store Indian...?"

And that's when it hit me!

My older sister was about to deposit her two preteen sons on my wife and me before she could join us for a holiday in Britain and I hadn't a clue what to do about or with them. Suddenly, as if on a mission from the deity, young Mr. Walters presented himself and I had the gushing secretary usher him into my office. After discovering that he was a lot more than "cute" and had a genuine interest in history and journalism and politics, I asked him if he would ever consider being a very special tour guide for my nephews, who were at a perfect age to discover storybook London. He agreed, I think primarily because he had been pounding the pavement for awhile and this was the first tangible offer of *anything.*

It's entirely possible that some of the first insights into this useful and clever book were germinated with the nephews. Certainly, they would come back each day and regale my wife and me about how enthusiastic Chris was about all the places they went to. We noticed one special trait that still runs strong in the Walters's file: he can transform the seemingly ordinary and almost forgotten into the memorable, whether it's down in the crypt of St. Paul's Cathedral, where some unlikely Canadians are memorialized, or in the ornate and sleepy rooms of the Reform Club on Pall Mall, where much of Canada's initial constitutional makeup was formulated.

Canadians sometimes have an unfortunate tendency to forget or trash their history when it becomes either inconvenient or complicated, but it is their history that has crafted the wonderful country we each cherish today. However, and from wherever, our families came to be in Canada — from First Nations to the most recent immigrants — several centuries of it were intimately tied up in the two mother countries of France and the United Kingdom. To understand better what we have become it is good to know from whence we came, and the surviving emblems and monuments and edifices with Canadian links sprinkled about London have a unique and often important story to tell.

And they are told here very well and very wittily by young Mr. Walters.

John Fraser

INTRODUCTION

I miss England. It took a lot of our history with it when we cut it adrift.
— Canadian journalist Charles Lynch[1]

Fresh out of university in Britain and flat broke, I landed a job as a tour guide for visiting American high-school students in London. After their initial disappointment with my Canadian accent — by the crestfallen look on their faces I think they were expecting the actor Hugh Grant to show them around — we set off as intrepid if similarly sounding North Americans to explore the city's popular attractions: Westminster Abbey, the Tower of London, and, with some coercion on their part and hearing loss on mine, an occasional dance club in Leicester Square.

As I prepped for my new job by reading up about London, I was struck by how oddly *American* it all seemed. Guidebooks frequently mentioned U.S. figures like John Harvard or Captain Smith of Pocahontas fame. There were prominent statues of George Washington, Abraham Lincoln, Ike, and FDR. The house of Benjamin Franklin, a U.S. ambassador to Britain, bore an historic blue plaque, as did the house of John F. Kennedy, the son of one. There was an America Square, an American Church, and even a Little America.

Whether out of genuine curiosity or simple politeness, my students occasionally asked me about Canadian landmarks. Apart from

Canada House in Trafalgar Square, I was hard pressed to identify any. My charges were as bemused as I was befuddled. After all if they knew anything about the "North" in their America, it was the fact Canadians remained loyal to Britain in the American Revolution and still bore the queen on our coinage as a reward. Yet there were no statues to our leaders in the capital of the Mother Country.

My unease with this national neglect only grew, living and working in London over many years. But while Canadians may not be represented by bronze statues or blue plaques at every street corner, I discovered we are not completely absent. It all depends on how you look at things. As Canada marks its 150th birthday in 2017, I felt it was high time to address a century-and-a-half neglect and create a new guide to an old city written especially for Canadian visitors.

But in preparing this book I kept in mind two realities. One is that many Canadians seem to enjoy British history these days. The popularity of TV shows like *Downton Abbey* and *The Tudors* is evidence of this. The second is that sites of Canadian interest are scattered throughout London and beyond. I had to find a way to weave in some local history and at the same time present the sites of Canadian interest in a way that didn't have readers crisscrossing an infernally large city.

I decided to group my discoveries into seven armchair walks — one for each day of the week — and present a brief history of each area visited. To fill in the inevitable gaps that existed, I decided to look more broadly at who and what should be featured. I settled on people, places, events, objects and even architecture that had some interesting link to Canada. This included iconic figures who had left their indelible marks in London like media tycoons lords Black and Beaverbrook. On occasion physical landmarks eluded me so I had to identify interesting features that could otherwise act as prompts. Thus while the Victorian wards of Guy's and St. Thomas's Hospital on the south side of the River Thames have no real link to Canada, they do serve to recall a nineteenth-century medical student from Canada who studied there and became a notorious serial killer known as the Lambeth Poisoner.

Organizing this book by walks also allowed me to indulge unashamedly in the enjoyment of being a guide again, identifying the quirky and often more memorable side of history, and putting to paper my personal conviction that if one looked at London a little differently, one could find a city full of discoveries about Canada and the people who are fortunate to call it home.

My rolled and dog-eared *London A to Z* street guide was my faithful Jean Passepartout around the city and the inspiration for the title of this book. In telling these 101 stories about Canada's links to London, I am struck by how little human nature has changed since Confederation. What frustrated Canada's first diplomats to London in the 1880s still does today. What Britain's Lord Derby said to reassure a nervous Chancellor of the Exchequer in the 1860s could be the words of Prime Minister Stephen Harper to his next finance minister: "Relax. They give you the figures."

— *Reform Club, London*

WALK 1:

TWO ROYAL PARKS

With all the things to see and do in London, it's easy to overlook the city's parks. Lakes and trees, after all, like British weather, are not big draws for Canadians. But put this bias aside, if only for a couple of hours. This walk through Green Park and St. James's Park is a delightful way to ease into London gently after an overnight flight and make some surprising discoveries about Canada along the way.

This walk begins at Hyde Park Corner Tube station and ends at Trafalgar Square. The distance is about 1.4 miles (2.3 kilometres) with two sets of stairs en route. As Constitution Hill and the Mall are closed to vehicles on Sundays, this is an ideal day to take this walk.

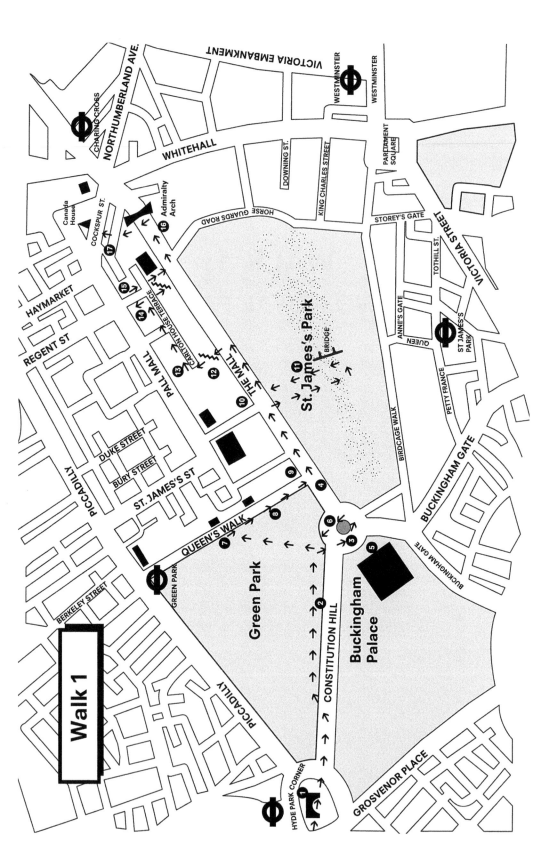

DISCOVERIES

1. Apsley House: Wellington to the Rescue
2. The Canada Memorial: A Splash in the Park
3. Victoria Memorial: Canada's Queen
4. The Mall: The Chameleon Laurier and the Queen's Jubilee
5. Buckingham Palace: The King's Canadian Brother
6. Green Park: Canada's Golden Gates
7. Spencer House: *The Death of General Wolfe*
8. Stornoway House: Lord Durham's Indigestion
9. Lancaster House: Trendy Trudeau Makes an Exit
10. Marlborough House: The End of Empire
11. St. James's Park: The Most Loathsome Bird in Britain
12. Carlton House Steps: Two Kings and a Queen
13. Carlton Gardens: *Le Général* Oversteps His Welcome
14. Franklin Monument: An Absent Husband
15. Edward VII Monument: Our Oversexed Rex
16. Cook Monument: The Ramparts of Quebec
17. Spring Gardens: Rupert's Land

A SHORT HISTORY OF THE AREA

St. James's Park is the oldest of London's five royal parks. It takes its name from St. James the Less, a medieval hospital for lepers once located where St. James's Palace is today. When King Henry VIII (1491–1547; reigned from 1509) confiscated the hospital for a hunting lodge, he enclosed the adjoining 91-acre (37-hectare) fields for his two favourite manly pastimes: hunting deer and jousting in armour.

The Stuart kings that followed the Tudors were a less macho bunch and altered St. James's field for more genteel pursuits. King James I (1566–1625; reigned from 1603), for example, added a menagerie that included exotic birds, crocodiles, and a wild elephant tamed with a gallon of wine every day.' Tennis courts, a medicinal herb garden, and an alley for an Italian game called *palla a maglio* or Pell-mell soon followed. It was around this time that the park first opened to the public. Two major alterations changed the park's look and feel dramatically. The first was by King Charles II (1630–85; reigned from 1660) who acquired a courtly taste for French gardens during his exile in France. Upon his return to London, he hired the Frenchman André Le Nôtre (1613–1700) to recreate his famous gardens of Versailles with neat rows of trees, manicured shrubs, and a central canal.

The second major change occurred when a more romantic style of gardens came into vogue in the time of King George IV (1762–1830; reigned from 1820). John Nash (1752–1835), a Regency architect and renowned dandy behind many of London's best-known streetscapes, redesigned the park to more like we see today: winding paths, unexpected vistas, and a fairy-tale lake that could be right out of a Black Forest fable.

But if St. James's Park was the beautiful princess, nearby Green Park was the homely half-sister. Rustic, plain, and oddly shaped, it was neither popular nor much admired. For good reason: legend says the park was once the burial ground for the lepers of St. James's Hospital, which may explain why it has remained largely untouched in marked contrast to its Cinderella-like sibling.

Close to palaces and Parliament, both parks have always been popular with diplomats and politicians. In the 1700s, however, the parks attracted an even shadier crowd. Green Park was notorious for high-waymen and St. James's for the sex trade. Although the gates to St.

James's were locked at 10 p.m., keys could be had for two a penny. "At night, I strolled into the park and took the first whore I met," wrote the diarist and man-about-town James Boswell (1740–95). "She was ugly and lean and her breath smelled of spirits."[2]

THE WALK

Although this walk takes us through two of London's most charming parks, our starting point is a little less so. Hyde Park Corner is a combination Underground Station, traffic roundabout, and pedestrian maze. Look for Exit 2 when making your way up to street level. A tunnel with murals that recall the Battle of Waterloo (1815) brings us to a park-like green. The impressive assortment of memorials here tells us we've arrived in a once-imperial city.

Look north across Piccadilly to the colonnaded house of light-brown stone. This is Apsley House, or "Number One, London" as it was sometimes known. Its address is fitting enough to begin any walking tour of London — even more so a Canadian one.

Robert Adam, a neoclassical architect, built the house in 1771–78 for Henry Bathurst (1714–94), Lord Apsley, whose son would later become secretary for the colonies and lend his name to a city in New Brunswick and a streetcar route in Toronto. Although the address is actually 149 Piccadilly, Apsley House acquired the name Number One, London, owing to the fact it was the first house along a toll road into the city. Once part of a row of Georgian monster homes, this grand old dame now stands in splendid isolation on this busy corner of Hyde Park.

Arthur Wellesley, 1st Duke of Wellington. After the War of 1812 he wanted a permanent way to defend British North America from the United States. He called the sprawling territory "all frontier and nothing else."

Of interest to us is the third owner of Apsley House, Field Marshal Arthur Wellesley (1769–1852), 1st Duke of Wellington.

Wellington was a British military commander, administrator, diplomat, and prime minister (twice). He was also a dogmatic Tory who earned the nickname Iron Duke not for his steadfast conservatism, which he had in spades, but for securing Apsley House with iron shutters in the 1830s to shield it from protesters demanding the vote. The duke was many things, but not a democrat.

Wellington is best known for leading a military coalition which defeated the French dictator Napoleon Bonaparte (1769–1821) at the Battle of Waterloo in Belgium. But the British commander left his military mark in Canada as well.

During the War of 1812 (1812–14) between Britain and the United States, Wellington bolstered Canada's defences by sending 15,000 troops to Canada. After the war, he ordered the construction of military structures that survive to this day. One of these is the Rideau Canal, a man-made waterway between Lake Ontario and the Ottawa River snaking 124 miles (202 kilometres) through mosquito-infested swamps. The remarkable owner of Apsley House is our first discovery for Canadian visitors to London.

Apsley House: *Wellington to the Rescue*

The War of 1812 convinced the Duke of Wellington that Canada wouldn't survive another conflict with the United States. Canada simply lacked the resources of its bigger neighbour across a long, indefensible border. The duke called the sprawling territory "all frontier and nothing else."[3]

With Napoleon exiled and Europe once more at peace, Wellington turned his considerable talents to the permanent defence of Canada. With his good friend Charles Lennox (1764–1819), 4th Duke of Richmond and governor general of Canada, he hatched an elaborate plan to build or improve a series of military forts that stretched across the territory's eastern flank. These included the Halifax and Quebec citadels as well as Fort Lennox near Montreal, named in honour of Richmond after he was bitten by a pet fox in Canada and died horribly from rabies. The Rideau Canal to move troops more easily through the wooded landscape was the cornerstone of the plan. Without Wellington's support, it would never have been built. His influence and political sleight of hand helped ram through Parliament the costliest project in the whole British Empire.

Fortunately for Canadians, Wellington's defensive system was never needed: the War of 1812 was the last war fought on Canadian soil. Far from serving any military purpose, the canal proved infinitely more valuable for recreational boating in summer and as the world's largest skating rink in winter. So tip your toques to the duke — and the poor British taxpayers who footed the bill — the next time you skate the Rideau Canal with a Beavertail pastry in hand.

Today, Apsley House is home to the Wellington Museum, which displays the duke's extensive collection of paintings, porcelains, and other artifacts from his eventful life and career. If you visit the museum, descend back into the pedestrian underpass and look for Exit 1. Consider purchasing a combined ticket at the museum that also gives you access to Constitution Arch (1827–28). It's a place from which you can get a wonderful treetop view of the parks we'll visit — and a peek into the queen's backyard in nearby Buckingham Palace if you are inclined to be nosey.

Before we set off, we should say a word or two about the assortment of imperial-looking monuments on the green. The equestrian statue immediately in front of Apsley House is by J.E. Boehm (1888). It is of the duke himself, in bronze rather than iron, bestride Copenhagen, the horse on which he rode into battle. Wellington is the only non-royal to have two equestrian statues in London; the other is in front of the Royal Exchange in the city's financial district.

To its right is the Memorial to the

Trivia: *In 1815, during a ball hosted by the duke and duchess of Richmond in Brussels, Wellington learned Napoleon's army was nearby. "Napoleon has humbugged me, by Gad!" he said to his friend. "I must fight him here," and pointed to a place on a map called Waterloo.[4]*

Machine Gun Corps by Francis Wood depicting a naked David holding Goliath's sword. It is the smaller of two nude bronzes in the area (the other being of Achilles in Hyde Park). Locals say when Queen Mary first saw this monument in 1925, she remarked: "I thought it might have been larger." To which a nearby wit quickly replied: "It's just the cold, ma'am."

The most spectacular monument on the green, hot or cold, is undoubtedly the just-noted Constitution Arch, also known as Wellington Arch, designed by the Victorian architect Decimus Burton (1800–81). In recent years, two other monuments have graced the green. These are the Australian War Memorial (2003) by Peter Tonkin and the New Zealand War Memorial (2006) by John Hardwick-Smith and Paul Dibble. The first consists of a wall of Australian green granite that curves around the southwest corner of the green and is etched with names of towns and villages in Australia that sent men and women to two world wars. The other comprises sixteen bronze timbers set into the grass, each bearing Maori symbols and sayings such as: "We are the hull of a great canoe." Both illuminate the great human cost of war and are dramatic and moving in their simplicity.

Now, let's make our way through Constitution Arch to Green Park, keeping in mind the cars and what the elderly but still proud duke said here after a Good Samaritan once helped him across the busy street: "I do believe that if it weren't for me, that fellow would have been run over." Today, we have the benefit of traffic lights.

Entering at the wedge tip of Green Park, let's make our way along the gravel pathway that follows Constitution Hill. At the entrance we pass the Memorial Gates (2002), four pillars of Portland stone commemorating the nearly five million men and women from Africa, India, and the Caribbean who fought alongside Britain in two world wars. Beyond this and to our left is the Bomber Command Memorial. Continue under the stately sycamore trees. It is not long before we see a low, red-granite shape emerging indistinctly from behind them on our left. With a respectful nod to the English war poet Rupert Brooke (1887–1915), we now find ourselves in "some corner of a foreign field" that will be forever Canada.

The Canada Memorial: *A Splash in the Park*

Designed by Montreal sculptor Pierre Granche (1948–97), the Canada Memorial is a water fountain shaped like a truncated pyramid honouring the Canadian men and women in two world wars. Unlike other war memorials, this one commemorates participation rather than sacrifice. It was unveiled by the queen in 1994 and is the only Canadian war memorial in Britain.

As water flows gently over the fountain's red-granite surface inset with bronze maple leaves, the sky and trees reflect back creating the impression of leaves floating down a stream. It's an iconic image designed to tug the heartstrings of every Canadian. A few metres away, a compass face points west in the direction of Halifax from where Canadians in both wars embarked. The inscription reads: "From dangers shared, our friendship prospers." Yet despite the monument's relatively modest size, its troubles have been surprisingly big.

From the day it was unveiled, the little memorial has been beset by problems. First, leaves (from park sycamores rather than Canadian maples) clogged the water pump, leaving the monument as dry as a prairie summer. Then, when the plumbing did work, officials became so alarmed about children playing in the moving water that they posted warning signs like the Selfish Giant to stay away. They even considered fencing it. But the bigger problem was who would pay for its upkeep.

That's because the man behind the memorial was former Canadian newspaper baron Conrad Black (b. 1944), Baron Black of Crossharbour. Alas, when the good lord became a convicted felon, responsibility for the monument fell into limbo and no one — not even the many names engraved so immodestly on its granite compass — came to its rescue. "If I wasn't preoccupied with other things," Black said before handing over his shoes and belt to authorities, "I would raise or contribute a fund adequate to assure its maintenance."[5] Finally, in 2007, the Canadian government agreed to step in. Maybe because of these failings, rather than in spite of them, this modest little memorial is *thoroughly* Canadian.

> **Trivia:** *On Parliament Hill in Ottawa, Queen Victoria's statue watches un-amused over MPs and senators as if to say of their constant misdemeanours: "To err is human, to forgive is not government policy."*

Within sight of the Canada Memorial are Buckingham Palace and its vast Victoria Memorial (1911) by the Sir Thomas Brock (1847–1922). Let's make our way there next before returning to discover some more sites of Canadian interest in Green Park.

Victoria Memorial: *Canada's Queen*

Glancing up at the marble statue of Queen Victoria beneath a golden representation of Victory, you'd be forgiven if you thought the queen-empress towered majestically over her Canadian subjects like a giant west coast totem. In fact, she was plump, stood only five feet tall, and spent much of her life in seclusion mourning a dead husband and arranging her children's royal marriages. Yet in many ways, this small and humourless woman was, and remains, Canada's queen, present at the creation and an enduring part of our national character, myth, and psyche.

Victoria was born on May 24, 1819, with little expectation of a monarch's crown. When she died in 1901 after more than sixty years wearing it, Canadians honoured her memory by making her birthday a national holiday — still celebrated with beer and fireworks in Ontario to the bemusement of other provinces. More enduring perhaps is her influence on the names of buildings, parks, streets, and other features across the country. Her name was even disguised in long-forgotten dead languages. John Campbell (1845–1914), Marquis of Lorne and governor general of Canada, renamed Pile O' Bones, Saskatchewan, "Regina," Latin for queen. It not only pleased early Canadian gazetteer-makers faced with another place called Victoria but the old gal herself, who just happened to be Lorne's mother-in-law.

Victoria instilled the faraway colony and later country with a sense of order, deference to authority, and national do-goodness. Some even called her the Mother of Confederation for signing the country's first constitution in 1867, the British North America Act. Queer as it may be, Canada's founding queen even graced our last three-dollar bill.[6]

> **Trivia:** *In 1791, Prince Edward Augustus, Duke of Kent, took command of a regiment in Quebec. Abandoning his French mistress, he returned to England in 1801 and fathered Princess (later Queen) Victoria. Prince Edward Island bears his name, as does Quebec City's Kent Gate.*

Stop here a moment and look down the grand ceremonial avenue known as the Mall. Over the years this beautiful area of London has seen its fair share of pomp and pageantry, but perhaps none so vast nor as extraordinary as the colourful parade held for Queen Victoria in 1897 to celebrate her Diamond Jubilee.

The Mall: *The Chameleon Laurier and the Queen's Jubilee*

In 1897, Queen Victoria celebrated sixty years on the throne. Throughout London, colourful flags with the insignia VRI for *Victoria Regina et Imperatrix* ("Victoria, queen and empress" in Latin) festooned windows and doorways along a winding procession route that led from here to St. Paul's Cathedral. From all around the British Empire, dignitaries came to celebrate this magnificent occasion.

Sir Wilfrid Laurier (1841–1919), Canada's new prime minister, led the colonial procession. The first French Canadian to be prime minister, he held "the highest place of any man of the queen's dominions," and was living proof of the variety of peoples and cultures who lived harmoniously in Victoria's realms. In court dress and newly knighted, Laurier sat with his wife in an open carriage, escorted by the Governor General's Foot Guards in a colourful procession. It paraded down the Mall and took the salute in the open square in front of Buckingham Palace (there was no Victoria Memorial then), where the queen herself joined it. The grand parade then marched up Constitution Hill, and down Piccadilly and Fleet Street to St. Paul's Cathedral where the old queen, moved by the adulation, was seen to shed a tear.[7]

As dazzled as Laurier was by the pomp, he knew there was no such thing as a free lunch — not even at Buckingham Palace. Britain wanted to bind Canada into the empire more closely, especially in terms of military defence. Laurier was fearful that the country would be drawn into a war in South Africa that was looming on the horizon.

So he kept his cards close to his chest, smiling and talking like an ardent imperialist but never committing to anything. He maintained this stance throughout his years as prime minister: a policy historians have called the "everlasting no."[8]

Trivia: *While visiting Queen Victoria at Windsor Castle, Sir John Thompson (1845–94), Canada's fifth prime minister, suffered a heart attack and died. The queen was horrified and sent the Canadian's corpse home on a warship painted black.*

Behind the Victoria Memorial is Buckingham Palace, not to be confused with the headquarters of the National Research Council in Ottawa, which some say is a scaled down replica of it. Over the years, the palace has welcomed royals and royal pretenders, but perhaps none so unusual as a pretend Canadian.

Buckingham Palace: *The King's Canadian Brother*

Not long after King George VI (1895–1952; reigned from 1936) came to the throne, an unusual visitor from the former colonies came to see him. No, it wasn't the king's Australian speech therapist, who helped him overcome his debilitating stutter, but Grey Owl (1888–1938), a tall Ojibwa from Canada with a drawn face and hawk-like nose. Grey Owl's books and films about life in the wilds of Canada were immensely popular in Britain in the 1930s and his rustic, regal stature gave him a lot of leeway when it came to addressing the king.

Contrary to royal protocol, Grey Owl insisted that the king and his family be seated before he entered the palace's audience chamber. He then surprised King George by greeting him with the words "Peace, brother." But the king was more amused than affronted by this strange Canadian in leather moccasins and sporting an eagle feather in his hair. So much so that for the next three hours, he and the queen and their two young daughters (the current queen and her late sister Margaret) listened intently to what Grey Owl had to say about Canada's northern animals and peoples. At the end of the lesson, Grey Owl held out one hand to the king and placed the other on his royal shoulder, saying: "Good-bye brother. I'll be seeing you." He then departed as majestically as he had arrived.

Years later it was revealed that Grey Owl was one of the world's greatest hoaxers: he wasn't an Ojibwa at all but a British immigrant named Archibald Belaney from Hastings, East Sussex.[9]

If your visit to London happens to occur between mid-August and late September, you may be able to venture inside the palace. If there is one thing Canadians like, it's the chance to snoop at an open house. This hasn't always been possible for people like us. Following the queen's *annus horribilis* (horrible year in Latin) in 1992, the palace was opened to paying visitors to help defray the costs of refurbishing Windsor Castle, damaged by fire. Mind you, some visitors are disappointed they don't run into Her Majesty on the visit. "At least when you go to Disneyland," complained one, "Mickey Mouse is there."

Queen Victoria's 1897 Diamond Jubilee was celebrated in Britain and in Canada.

Here's to Queen Victoria, dressed in all her regalia/With one foot in Canada, and the other in Australia.

— CANADIAN POET UNKNOWN[10]

Now let's turn back to the ornate, iron and gilt gates which we passed a few minutes ago on the edge of Green Park. These are the Canada Gates, though it's easy to miss the connection if you don't scrutinize the stone and ironwork carefully.

Green Park: *Canada's Golden Gates*

The Victoria Memorial comprises not only the grand marble statue of the queen-empress but also a series of ornamental gates that encircle it. These gates represent South Africa, Australia, Newfoundland, and many other former colonies of Britain. Canada, the empire's eldest daughter, paid the equivalent of about $3 million to be part of this sprawling homage to its late queen.[11]

Naturally, we got our money's worth. The Canada Gates are the most elaborate of any found here. They were produced by a group of artists associated with the Arts and Crafts Movement known as the Bromsgrove Guild. Their notable skills also grace the gates of nearby Buckingham Palace and the *Lusitania*, though it famously sank in 1915.

Only the coats of arms of six provinces made it onto the original gates. That's because the cut-off date for inclusion was 1903 and at the time Saskatchewan and Alberta were not yet provinces. British Columbia, on the other hand, was so new it hadn't got around to the important things like designing a coat of arms. The gates remained unfinished until 1982 when the crests of the missing provinces were

All hail Queen Victoria: The Victoria Memorial as seen through Canada's equally grand golden gates in Green Park.

finally placed on the stone pillars.[12] Newfoundland, which was not part of Canada when the gates were built, has a column nearby. It has the dubious distinction of being the only colony in the British Empire to gain independence from Britain and then lose it again. Nunavut, Yukon, and the Northwest Territories still wait for full self-government and their place of honour on the gates.

Victoria's eldest grandson, Germany's Kaiser Wilhelm II (1859–1941), attended the official unveiling of the memorial in 1911. Willy didn't like the English much but was loyal to his English grandmamma, even though he believed in the last years of her reign that it was high time the old woman died. Few at the ceremony could have guessed that Britain and Canada would be at war with Germany three years later, making Wilhelm the most vilified man in Canada and throughout the British Empire.

Two other places of Canadian interest in Green Park bear brief mention before we set off down the Mall.

The first is Spencer House, located midway up Queen's Walk on the park's eastern edge. Completed in 1766 and faced in Portland stone, it is one of the last surviving aristocratic town homes in the area and is considered by many to be the most important. It once belonged to the family of Diana (1961–97), Princess of Wales, born Lady Diana Spencer.

The Canadian connection to Spencer House is found in the green-and-white dining room on the first floor overlooking the park. Above the fireplace is the iconic painting *Death of General Wolfe* (1771) by the American painter Benjamin West (1738–1820). It's displayed between two other historical paintings by West, *The Death of the Chevalier Bayard* (1772) and the *Death of Epaminondas* (1773). It's hard to think of *Wolfe* as part of a set, but this one is. The paintings were all commissioned by King George III to depict heroic deaths in history.

Hold on, some of you might say, isn't West's most famous painting in Canada? Indeed it is, in not *one* but *two* places: Ottawa's National Gallery of Canada and Toronto's Royal Ontario Museum. The painting at Spencer House may belong to the royal collection, but it isn't the original. And therein lies the rub of our next discovery for Canadian visitors to London.

Spencer House from Green Park. Once the home of the family of Diana, Princess of Wales, it now conceals a Canadian connection.

Spencer House: *The Death of General Wolfe*

King George III was not a connoisseur of art, but as the saying goes, he knew what he liked and he liked what he knew. And what he liked were historical paintings with a moral purpose. So when the king encouraged the young West to paint classical scenes depicting courage, he reasonably expected to see some brave men in togas.

But that wasn't what West had in mind. He planned to paint a modern example of bravery featuring soldiers in contemporary dress. Sir Joshua Reynolds (1723–92), the leading painter of his day, is said to have thought this rather vulgar and advised the king against buying it. Although the king didn't like Reynolds much, he valued his opinion when it came to art. He dutifully told West he wasn't interested.

It didn't matter. The precocious West produced his painting anyway, vulgar modern dress and all, and the *Death of General Wolfe* turned out to be an astonishing artistic success. People flocked to view it. Even the elderly and infirm William Pitt (1708–88), 1st Earl of Chatham, the politician who had ordered the assault on Quebec, came to see what all the fuss was about. He alone seemed unimpressed by the tableau and wondered why the death of a common and presumably expendable soldier had everyone in the painting looking so sad.

Yet for the vast majority, the painting was unquestionably a *tour de force* or what one contemporary historian has described as "a stupendous piece of drama; brilliance and gloom, victory and death, saintly sacrifice and inconsolable sorrow set side by side."[13] But more problematically, it wasn't the king's. When a wealthy aristocrat snatched it up instead, the king had no choice but to commission a copy to adorn his wall. And a slightly smug West was only too happy to oblige.[14]

In 1991, Spencer House was host to an event with another Canadian connection. Lord Black, then proprietor of London's *Daily Telegraph* among other newspapers owned by his Chicago-based Hollinger International Inc., threw a party here. And not just any party. Over 200 guests attended the splashy event, including former-British prime minister Margaret Thatcher (1925–2013). With flights, hotels, and food, the entire event was estimated to cost Hollinger's beleaguered shareholders a cool $2.5 million.[15]

> *Empires die of indigestion.*
>
> — NAPOLEON BONAPARTE

A few yards along Queen's Walk toward the Mall is another house of Canadian interest. Look for the stately white building with a corner turret. This is Stornoway House (13 Cleveland Row), now an office but once an elegant private home that boasted fourteen bedrooms, six reception areas, and a ballroom.[16] Although heavily bombed during the Second World War, the exterior remains largely unchanged from 1817 when it was occupied by John Lambton (1792–1840), 1st Earl of Durham. Durham's little known but landmark report in 1839 was the first to propose a form of government in Canada in which the governor was responsible to an elected legislature (called "responsible government"). This was the first tentative step toward political independence in Canada and ultimately the breakup of the British Empire.

Stornoway House: *Lord Durham's Indigestion*

Even Lord Durham's friends thought he was an odd choice to investigate the rebellions in Upper and Lower Canada in 1837–38. Cultured, handsome, and fabulously rich, he was also dyspeptic, high strung, and notoriously vain. But his strong liberal ideas — he was popularly known to his fellow Whig politicians as "Radical Jack" — made him apparently the ideal man to show Britain was serious about change in the Canadian colonies.

Yet despite Durham's promise to be the *humble* instrument of authority, his arrival in Canada was anything but. Mounted on a white horse, in full regalia and accompanied by an orchestra, his lavish landing could have shamed a sultan. To the delight of his political opponents in the opposition Tory Party, moreover, he quickly overstepped his authority and returned home *post-haste*.

But it was back in London where Durham ultimately proved the right man for the job. Keen to restore his name, in late 1838 he sat down to write his *Report on the Affairs of British North America* — perhaps at a desk overlooking this very spot in Green Park.

"He worked incessantly," his wife reported, and his health, which was always frail, grew worse by the day. By February 1839, his report calling for responsible government in Canada to prevent future rebellions was finished and, practically speaking, so was he. Durham died soon afterward from consumption (tuberculosis). "I would fain hope I have not lived in vain," he said. "Whatever the Tories say, the Canadians will one day do justice to my memory."[17]

Durham's report fundamentally changed how Canada would be governed. But if his report was far-sighted, it was a bit nasty too. Durham believed Canada's problem of "two nations warring in the bosom of a single state" could only be solved by assimilating French Canada. He remains so vilified for these views that his portrait had to be removed from an outdoor display in Ottawa as late as 2008.

Trivia: *In 1924, the Canadian-born newspaper baron William Aitken (1879–1964), 1st Baron Beaverbrook, took up residence at Stornoway House. It was bombed in 1940.*

Stornoway House overlooking Green Park was once home to John "Radical Jack" Lambton, Lord Durham, the man who first proposed responsible government for Canada.

Now, let's turn onto the Mall and walk eastward, with St. James's Park on our right. Immediately on our left is the first of an assortment of park-side palaces. This is Lancaster House, a fine Italianate home built in 1825–27 for Frederick, Duke of York, the second son of King George III.

Modest and understated Lancaster House isn't, especially inside. Its ornate main rooms on the second floor are accessed by a spectacular staircase that was once the scene of a brief but surprising Canadian event.

> *There is no need for any nation, however great, leaving the empire because the empire is a commonwealth of nations.*
>
> — Lord Rosebery, 1887

Lancaster House: *Trendy Trudeau Makes an Exit*

In 1968, Pierre Trudeau (1919–2000) replaced Lester Pearson (1897–1972) as Canada's fifteenth prime minister and came to London to attend his first Commonwealth prime ministers' summit. The clubbish nature of the English-speaking organization of Britain's former colonies at first perplexed the dashing French Canadian from Montreal, as did the odd assortment of African and Caribbean leaders dressed in their trademark safari suits. Some, like Cyprus's Archbishop Makarios (1913–77), had been part of struggles for independence. Wearing black robes and a stovepipe mitre, the bearded giant towered over Trudeau and made the French Canadian a bit uneasy. He even wondered if the archbishop was hiding hand grenades under his garments.

As a reception at Lancaster House broke up, Trudeau left the state-room and headed toward the opulent staircase. Spying the press gathered in the foyer below, he decided to make an exit that would play to the cameras and set him apart from the old warriors he had just left upstairs. He leapt onto the banister shouting *"Olé"* and slid down its length as guests watched in disbelief. "It burnished his reputation as a swinging bachelor," the Commonwealth secretary-general later said, and earned the young prime minister the nickname "Trendy Trudeau" in the British tabloid press.[18]

A few steps beyond is St. James's Palace, the official seat of the royal court since 1698. We'll say a bit more about the palace on our next walk.

> *The sun never set on the British Empire, and never rose on the Commonwealth.*
>
> — Historian Max Beloff

Next to it behind a garden wall and row of colourful flags is Marlborough House, once home to the first Duke and Duchess of Marlborough. Today, it is home to the Commonwealth Secretariat, the headquarters of the association of about fifty-three former British colonies — give or take an expelled dictatorship or two.

Marlborough House: *The End of Empire*

As Canada and other colonies in the British Empire matured and gained independence, they surprised just about everyone by agreeing to form a family-like association — *and we all know what families can be like.*

It was unquestionably an odd group. Yet in the beginning the members of the British Commonwealth got along relatively well, fought wars together, and were for the most part still, well, very British. That began to change in the early 1960s, however, when the new members from Africa and the Caribbean demanded more say in running Commonwealth affairs. For starters they insisted on dropping the prefix "British" from the group's name and demanded to be treated as equals. At a conference in 1966, they went so far as to turn the table completely on Mother Britain by badgering its prime minister, Harold Wilson (1916–95) so much he shouted back: "You're treating Britain like a bloody *colony!*"[19]

Canada's relationship to the Commonwealth has always been up and down — sometimes enthusiastic but sadly more often not. Much has depended on the personal whimsies of each Canadian prime minister.

Pearson, a winner of a Nobel Peace Prize, was a pragmatist who wanted to keep republics such as India in the association in order to keep them out of the hands of Soviet Russia and China. John Diefenbaker (1895–1979) made the fight against racial discrimination his *cause célèbre* but in the process divided the organization. "Your policies are not only wrong but dangerous," he told South Africa's apartheid leaders. They called him a vicious fellow and walked out.[20]

Trudeau, after his initial perplexity with the grouping, fell in love with it and was soon wearing safari suits himself. Brian Mulroney (b. 1939), took up Dief's old cause and led efforts to end apartheid in South Africa — often straining his relationship with his Conservative idol Thatcher.

Another influential but less well-known Canadian was the Commonwealth's first secretary-general, Arnold Smith (1915–94). He was a career diplomat and a former ambassador to the Soviet Union. In 1965, Smith took charge of the Commonwealth Secretariat and had to skilfully manoeuvre it through family quarrels and its own rocky years of independence. Fearing the place was bugged by MI5, Britain's security agency, he held confidential discussions in the garden. Despite this, he wrote in his memoirs, "Historians will consider the Commonwealth the greatest of all Britain's contributions to man's social and political history."[21]

Before we leave Marlborough House, let's take quick note of two small monuments here. On Marlborough Road, opposite the Friary Court of St. James's Palace, is a bronze fountain to Queen Alexandra (1844–1925) by Alfred Gilbert. The Princess Diana of her day, Alexandra

Trivia: *Of the fifty-three or so countries that comprise the Commonwealth, the queen is head of state in sixteen of them, including Canada. She is the world's only international monarch.*

was the long suffering wife of the philanderer King Edward VII (1841–1910; reigned from 1901). A once-popular hotel in Winnipeg bore her name, as does an historic theatre in Toronto.

Inset into the garden wall at the corner of Marlborough Road is a tablet to Queen Mary (1867–1953), consort of the next king, King George V (1865–1936, reigned from 1910). Like Alexandra, Mary spent her widowhood in Marlborough House. It was here that Mary learned that her eldest son, the dashing King Edward VIII (1894–1972; reigned briefly in 1936), would marry the woman he loved, Wallis Simpson (1896–1986). Canadians liked Edward — he owned a ranch in Alberta — but they disliked the idea of Queen Wallis. She was not only twice divorced, but *American.*

At the junction of Marlborough Road and the Mall, let's turn and head into St. James's Park for one of the most romantic views in London. From the bridge over the duck pond you can see Buckingham Palace at one end and Downing Street and the Italianate Foreign and Commonwealth Office at the other. If you need a rest, you can sit in an inviting park deck chair. Be warned, however, ever-vigilant park collectors habitually appear out of nowhere to collect payment for these. If you hear familiar honking, it's probably the noise of a few Canada geese nearby. Lucky ones at that.

11. St. James's Park: *The Most Loathsome Bird in Britain*

"Should there ever be a prize for Britain's most hated bird, then surely it would go to the Canada goose," wrote a British newspaper journalist in 2008, echoing the thoughts of many park visitors with do-do on their shoes.[23] The birds are Britain's shame the writer went on: park potatoes who lounge around all day long and produce nothing but offspring and excrement.

Yet the story of how these unwelcome Canadians got here is as old as the park itself.

The Canadian geese of St. James's Park arrived here not as migrant tourists but as gifts from early explorers in the New World around

1665. These explorers knew King Charles II appreciated his birds, be they feathered or frocked, and thought these specimens would be a nice addition to his park menagerie. But if these noisy, honking, and untidy pooping machines from Canada weren't bad enough, over the years their British descendants have evolved into creatures far more slothful, living on public handouts. After eating an endless supply of white-bread crusts, they are now fatter, lazier, and almost flightless compared to their Canadian cousins.

Moreover, without natural predators, their numbers exploded. From the original few imports, the flock in Britain grew to some 80,000 breeding adults. With their population at an all-time high and their popularity at an all-time low, park officials in the 1990s took action. Hundreds of the birds were despatched in a controversial cull that outraged animal rights campaigners and sparked the creation of the Canada Goose Conservation Society. Yet in the end, clean footpaths triumphed over dirty water fowl and today only a lucky few of these old world cousins of *Branta Canadensis* survive in beautiful and tidy St. James's Park.

Now, let's head back to the Mall and continue east. On our left at the staircase is a memorial to King

Trivia: *On average, a Canada goose poops every three minutes.*

George VI and his long surviving widow, Queen Elizabeth (1900–2002), known after 1952 as the Queen Mother.

The statue of George VI was placed here after his death in 1952 and was joined by one of his wife in 2009. The bronze reliefs set into the stairs depict the two scenes most fondly associated with the queen: horse racing and her visit during the Second World War to London's heavily bombed East End. After a bomb hit Buckingham Palace, she famously remarked that she could now look East Enders in the face.

George VI was a shy and dutiful man with an irreproachable character and strong sense of decency. He also had a look of perpetual weariness in his eyes. As the second in line to the throne, young "Bertie" was never groomed to be king. He only got the job after his older brother, Edward, abdicated to marry Wallis Simpson. Despite his debilitating stutter, the new king became a popular wartime monarch — much aided and abetted by his charming and savvy wife.

In 1939, the royal couple visited Canada — the first reigning monarch and his consort to do so — and became the best loved. Much of that adoration was due to the queen. Her energy, easy manner, and sense of humour compensated for the king's awkwardness. Their royal tour on the eve of war also solidified an important bond.

Once asked why he decided to fight in the Second World War, a Canadian soldier replied: "I saw the queen when she was in Canada and I said if there is ever a war, I'm going to fight for that little lady."[24]

Carlton House Steps: *Two Kings and a Queen*

After months of planning, the *Empress of Australia* finally steamed up the St. Lawrence to Quebec City, accompanied by a flotilla of warships. Along the shoreline, bonfires were lit to greet the royal passengers. On shore, dressed in ceremonial court uniform, was Canada's prime minister, William Lyon Mackenzie King (1874–1950): "Welcome, Sire, to your Majesty's realm of Canada," he said with a practised bow.

Over the next month, the king and queen travelled some 3,000 miles (5,000 kilometres) across Canada and back again onboard a special train kitted out with every convenience, including air conditioning and a post office. No matter what hour their whistle stops took place, crowds came out to see them. At one stop in the prairies, 8,000 people cheered their arrival. "How many people live here?" asked a journalist accompanying the royal couple. "Nobody," came the reply. In Ontario, the royal couple unveiled the National War Memorial in Ottawa and descended a mine in Sudbury. In Vancouver, they opened Lion's Gate Bridge.

No less memorable was an event in Doaktown, New Brunswick. Travelling by car from Newcastle to Fredericton, the royal couple stopped at a private home for tea. Measures had been taken to provide comfort for the queen and her ladies in waiting but none for His Majesty. When the error became obvious, George VI was escorted outside where he is said to have relieved himself next to the Miramichi.[25]

Throughout the visit, Canada's prime minister was the royals' constant companion. Accustomed more to jeers than cheers, King revelled in their popularity. To ensure he alone shared the limelight, King told Canada's governor general, John Buchan (1875–1940), 1st Baron Tweedsmuir, he had no official role on the tour. When the royals asked after their vice-regal friend, King said he was regrettably indisposed — and went on smiling for the cameras.

After the war, George VI witnessed many dramatic changes, including personal ones. With India's independence he lost the much-coveted title of emperor. But the humiliations didn't stop there. To ensure that the monarch would have no legal or constitutional role over the new British Commonwealth, Canada suggested the king become "the symbol of the free association and, *as such*, Head of the Commonwealth." To which a perplexed and wounded king is said to have replied, "What exactly am I to do, *as such*?"

King George VI and his wife Queen Elizabeth undertook a royal tour of Canada in 1939. If Prime Minister W.L. Mackenzie King could have squeezed into a photograph, he would have.

Now, let's ascend the Carlton House steps. Immediately at the top on our left is 2 Carlton House Terrace, currently the home of Britain's foreign minister but once home to Field Marshal Horatio Kitchener (1850-1916), 1st Earl of Kitchener, a controversial military leader who died when his ship struck a mine. With his trademark moustache and stern features, Kitchener was an imperial man if there ever was one. We best know him as the glaring face on the recruiting posters of the First World War that challenged the patriotism of any man who refused to serve king and country. So high were anti-German feelings in Canada during the war that Berlin, Ontario, was renamed after him.

What am I going to do at a "fair"?

— CHARLES DE GAULLE ON BEING

INVITED TO EXPO '67

Across the street is a statue you wouldn't expect to find in London: that of Charles de Gaulle (1890–1970), leader of the Free French Army and president of France from 1959–69. It is by the British sculptor Angela Conner. After the fall of France in 1940, de Gaulle came to London and broadcast patriotic speeches from nearby. In Canada, he is remembered for his other stirring words or, perhaps more correctly, just one word — "free."

Carlton Gardens: *Le Général Oversteps His Welcome*

General Charles de Gaulle didn't want to visit Canada but Quebec's new premier, Daniel Johnson Sr. (1915–68), convinced him to come to see Expo '67, the world's fair in Montreal. "*Mon Général*, Quebec needs you. It is now or never," Johnson said, and de Gaulle reluctantly agreed.[26]

French Canadians went crazy for de Gaulle. Greeted by crowds at every turn, his tour of Quebec recalled his triumphant return to Paris during the Second World War (or, as noted by some suspicious English Canadians, a certain dictator's liberation of the Sudetenland); a fact that did not sit well in an Ottawa already uneasy with the president's views on Quebec's independence.

In Montreal, so many people clamoured to see the French president that he was obliged to stand in his car for the last 50 kilometres of his ride. At Montreal's city hall, he was surrounded by separatist placards: "*France libre.*" "*Québec libre.*" "*Le Québec aux Québecois!*"

Montreal's mayor, the federalist Jean Drapeau (1916–99), didn't want de Gaulle to speak to the assembled crowd and tried to usher him inside. "No, it is to them, the people cheering me, that I want to speak," de Gaulle said, walking up to a radio microphone that had hastily appeared on the balcony to the mayor's chagrin. Looking out across the crowds, de Gaulle went further in his support of an independent Quebec than he had ever gone publicly. His one word too many, "*Vive le Québec libre (free),*" made him an instant hero to *indépendantistes* and *persona non grata* to everyone else.[27]

Crowds of well-wishers greet French president Charles de Gaulle at Expo '67 in Montreal. He went home for saying one word too many.

Walk past the gardens of the old Carlton House that once stood here and admire the prettiest backs in all of London. They belong to three private gentlemen's clubs: from left to right, the Reform, the Travellers and the Athenaeum. We'll say a bit more about two of these on our next walk.

Just beyond the gardens of the Athenaeum Club and largely hidden by trees is an 1866 statue by Matthew Nobel of Sir John Franklin (1786–1847), probably the best-known explorer of Canada's Arctic. He died while searching for the elusive Northwest Passage. Franklin's heroic story is partially about an aging sailor's quest for self-redemption. But it is also about a woman's unwavering commitment to her husband after he was presumed lost. The bronze on the plinth may be that of Sir John, but the monument is really a tribute to the perseverance of Lady Jane, his wife.

Franklin Monument: *An Absent Husband*

In May 1845, when Sir John Franklin set out in HMS *Erebus* and *Terror* to Canada's north from the River Thames, all the stars seemed aligned in his favour. He was an accomplished Arctic explorer and national hero, and his ships were the best equipped for their time. In addition to modern screw propellers for ploughing through pack ice, Franklin's cargo included some 8,000 tins of non-perishable food — enough for his crew of 129 to last three years.

But after being spotted by whalers in Baffin Bay, Franklin and his crew were never seen again. We now know that he met his maker in 1847 near King William Island and that technology, perhaps as much as the harsh Canadian conditions, was a factor in his death: the iron propellers rusted quickly and lead from the solder of the food tins may have poisoned his crew. But at the time, his disappearance captured the public's imagination around the world and prompted thirty search attempts to Canada's north over twelve years. No one was more responsible for these searches than Lady Franklin herself.

One of several London memorials to Sir John Franklin, the lost explorer of Canada's Arctic. His disappearance in 1845 sparked thirty search parties, many encouraged by his wife.

Armed only with pen, paper, and a strong Victorian sense of duty, Lady Franklin never forgot her "absent husband" and appealed to everyone for help in finding him — British politicians, naval officials, even the U.S. president. Between 1850 and 1857, she even outfitted five ships at her own expense. Her wealthy father grew so alarmed over her efforts, he disinherited her.

Of all the expeditions galvanized by Lady Jane's efforts, only four managed to shed any light on the mystery of her husband's fate, and only one came back with conclusive evidence he was dead. For her "zeal and self-sacrifice," the widow Franklin was awarded the Royal Geographical Society's founder's medal in 1860 — the first woman to receive the prize.

At Waterloo Place, head down the Duke of York steps and back into the Mall and St. James's Park. Before we do, let's pause at the nearby equestrian statue of King Edward VII (1841–1910, reigned from 1901), *imperitor rex*, the last monarch commemorated on our walk. Edward

> **Trivia:** *On a trip to Canada in 1827, Sir John Franklin visited Ottawa and laid the first stone in the third lock of the Rideau Canal.*

was Queen Victoria's eldest son and great-grandfather to the present monarch. In 1860, as a young Prince of Wales and heir to the throne, he was the first member of the royal family to make an official visit to Canada, starting a trend that continues to this day.

Edward VII Monument: *Our Oversexed Rex*

Albert Edward, Prince of Wales, lived large and lived well. Denied much of a role by his domineering mother, Queen Victoria, he drank, gambled, and womanized like a royal rebel without a cause. In 1863, he finally settled down and married the beautiful Princess Alexandra of Denmark. The two and their circle of friends became known as the "Marlborough House Set" after the London residence where the young royals lived.

Married life didn't slow Edward down for long, however, and his extra-marital affairs became legendary. The library of Marlborough House, with its door hidden by fake books, was one of his favourite trysting places. (To keep their virtue, women had to appreciate Edwardian puns: the latch was concealed beside a book called *On the Door* by John Locke.) When good living meant Edward could no longer do up the last button of his waist coat, men's fashion simply followed suit.

In 1860, at the younger and slimmer age of eighteen, Edward made the first royal visit to Canada and enchanted women wherever he went. In Montreal, known then as it is now for its dynamic nightlife, the prince partied like it was 1899. Yet Mama was never far from the fun. In Halifax, he visited the home of her father and plucked her a rose from the garden.

In Montreal, he dedicated the first railway bridge across the St. Lawrence River to her. Even in sleepy Cobourg, Ontario, he couldn't escape her presence. The impressive new courthouse he opened was called Victoria Hall.

After only nine years on the throne, Edward was succeeded by his son, King George V (1865–1936; reigned from 1910). Like his father, George ruled over a quarter of the world's population; but the empire was in its twilight. On his deathbed George's last words were reputedly: "How goes the empire?" But some say what he really asked was: "What's on at the Empire?"— a local theatre in Leicester Square. A less noble finale to the age of empire perhaps, but no less poignant.[28]

Trivia: *An equestrian statue of Edward VII by Thomas Brock stands in Toronto's Queen's Park. The 1919 bronze originally stood in New Delhi, India, but was saved from the scrap heap after India's independence.*

Ahead of us on the way back to St. James's Park is a bronze statue of Prince Frederick Augustus, Duke of York (1763–1827) on a tall column of pink granite. It is by the British sculptor Sir Richard Westmacott.

Frederick was the second and favourite son of King George III, and commander-in-chief of the British Army. Although a popular soldier, his

Who's who and who's blue: Queen Victoria and her family in 1887. Edward, Prince of Wales (top), visited Canada in 1860. The queen's son-in-law, the Marquis of Lorne (left, fourth row) was governor general of Canada from 1879 to 1883. His wife, the queen's daughter Princess Louise, didn't take to Canada and stayed home most of the time. Prince Arthur, Duke of Connaught (middle, fourth row), was governor general of Canada from 1911 to 1916. As a young man in 1870 he fought Fenian raiders in Canada.

military career came to an abrupt end over accusations that his mistress sold commissions in the army. He spent the rest of his life building homes he couldn't afford (like Lancaster House) and avoiding debt collectors at his

Trivia: *When New Brunswick became a colony in 1784, the loyalist town of Ste. Anne's Point was renamed Frederick's Town in honour of the Duke of York. It was shortened to Fredericton in 1785.*

door.[29] Despite these human failings, Upper Canada's Lieutenant-Governor John Graves Simcoe (1752–1806) admired the duke so much he named his military garrison on Lake Ontario after him in 1793. The name York didn't stick for long and reverted back to its Indian name Toronto in 1834.

Descend the steps back into the Mall and turn left.

Head toward Admiralty Arch, built in 1911 as the southern entrance to the processional route leading up to the Victoria Memorial. On our right along the Mall is a statue of Captain James Cook (1728–79), again by Thomas Brock. Cook was one of Britain's greatest explorers and most skilled ocean navigators. The 1914 bronze shows him resting in front of a capstan on a coil of rope. Sly observers have remarked it's an elegant pose on a plinth but a dangerous one on a sailing ship. Cook is mostly remembered for his travels in the Pacific and along Canada's west coast, but the legendary seaman cut his teeth in eastern Canada. It was while leading Wolfe down the St. Lawrence River to Quebec in 1759 that Cook first caught the attention of admiralty brass.

Cook Monument: *The Ramparts of Quebec*

At the start of the Seven Years' War (1756–63), the St. Lawrence River was uncharted and dangerous. There were no published maps of the river into the heartland of French Canada and whatever records existed were unreliable. Beyond the Saguenay, submerged shoals and under-water channels confounded the ablest of seamen.

For the French, this was a good thing. They relied upon these river dangers as a natural buffer against an invading navy. After 150 years of settlement in Canada, the river had both served and protected Quebec well. Colonel Louis-Antoine de Bougainville (1729–1811), a young French army officer in Canada and future explorer, shrewdly called the river "Quebec's most effective rampart."[30]

Cook joined the Royal Navy in 1755 and swiftly advanced to become master of the sixty-four-gun *Pembroke*. He arrived in Canada as part of a naval force that captured the French fort of Louisbourg in Nova Scotia. He then spent the following winter in Halifax awaiting spring orders to attack Quebec.

Maybe it was the excitement of uncharted waters, or simply the boredom of a long Canadian winter, but Cook busied himself learning everything he could about the river. When spring came and the fleet set off, it was Cook's ship that carefully led the British armada to Quebec, taking soundings and marking the way with buoys.

On the morning of June 27, 1759, General Louis-Joseph de Montcalm (1712–59) looked out from his stone fortress high on the cliffs and was astonished to see the British fleet gathered in the nearby basin. Resigned to his inescapable fate, he wryly predicted that a good map of the river would be published soon.[31]

Turn left before you reach Admiralty Arch and head across the concourse next to the British Council. On either side is a soulless warren of gray buildings and back streets. This street is known as Spring Gardens, named for a pleasure garden that once occupied a strip of land from here back to Waterloo Place.

In Shakespeare's time, Londoners came to Spring Gardens to enjoy promenades, outdoor music, and dancing around a water fountain. When King Charles II came to the throne, he sold off part of the garden to his cousin Prince Rupert.

Around this time Rupert acquired another piece of property from his royal cousin, but not in London. He became the first governor of the Hudson's Bay Company and with the title acquired most the territory west of the Great Lakes for the exclusive use of his private company. The area known as Rupert's Land bore this name right up until 1870.

Trivia: *In May 1670, Charles II granted Prince Rupert and his associates the exclusive right to be the "true and absolute Lordes and Proprietors" of most of the lands west of the Great Lakes to the Pacific Coast and north to the Arctic Ocean.*

Spring Gardens: *Rupert's Land*

Ruprecht von Wittelsbach (1619–82) was a prince without a throne —
or even a home for that matter. His parents were the king and queen of
Bohemia, but after fleeing their country after an early uprising became
known ever after as the Winter King and Queen. Their departure was
so sudden, in fact, they almost left their baby, Rupert, behind.

As a young exile, Rupert came to England to support his uncle
King Charles I (1600–49; reigned from 1625) in the English Civil War.
Talented and courageous, Rupert became a skilled military leader —
though some say his exploits bordered on insanity. At 6'4", he was
definitely a hard man to ignore. He also happened to be the best tennis
player in all of England.

Unfortunately for Rupert, neither war nor tennis made him very rich.
So in 1665, when two wild French adventurers from Canada named
Pierre-Esprit Radisson (1636–1710) and Médard Chouart des Groseilliers
(1618–ca.1696) proposed a new route to the fur territory of North
America via Hudson's Bay, the prince saw a way at last to make money.
In return for an exclusive right to the region, Rupert promised the king
the pelts of two elks and two black beaver every year. Evidently short of
these things, the king accepted and the Hudson's Bay Company was
born with Rupert at its helm.

Many of the first meetings of the company were held in Spring
Gardens. Without an office, the seven distinguished men Rupert
assembled for the company ran its affairs from his home. To his bitter
disappointment, however, he never made a penny from the Canadian
fur trade and died here poor in 1682. Among the chief mourners at his
funeral were his fellow members of the Hudson's Bay Company — and
his tennis coach.

Nowadays, Spring Gardens, the street, leads not into any delightful
garden at its terminus but to a more modern necessity: the Trafalgar
Square Car Park. Head to nearby
Trafalgar Square, with Canada
House in front of us, where our
walk ends.

Trivia: *The busy seaport of Prince
Rupert, B.C., is named for Prince
Ruprecht von Wittelsbach.*

WALK 2:

ST. JAMES'S AND PALL MALL

If you frequent gentlemen's clubs in Canada, you might raise a few eyebrows. Not in London. Gentlemen's clubs here are about table talks not table dances. They are grand sanctuaries from a bygone era full of leather-bound books and armchairs where well-heeled Victorians first invented the idea of social networking. For over 300 years, the historic neighbourhood of St. James's has been home to many of these clubs and their colourful club characters — some gentlemen, some not — including a few with links to Canada.

This walk starts at Green Park Tube station and ends at Trafalgar Square. The walking distance is about 1.2 miles (1.9 kilometres).

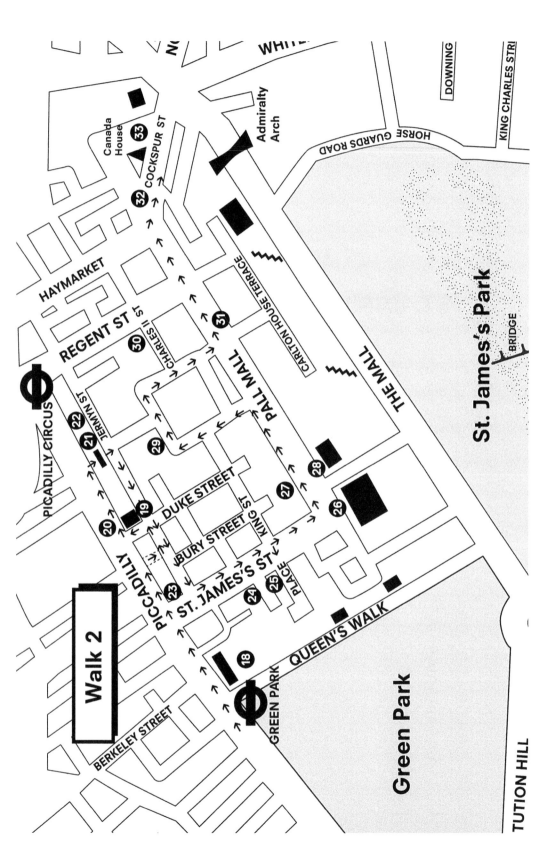

DISCOVERIES

A SHORT HISTORY OF THE AREA

St. James's is a fashionable commercial quarter bordered by Piccadilly to the north, Haymarket Street to the east, and royal parks both south and west. Like the adjacent royal park, this area takes its name from St. James's Palace, built for King Henry VIII (1491–1547; reigned from 1509) and official court of the monarchy since 1698.

Once royals settled in the area, ambitious courtiers soon followed. One of the first was Henry Jermyn (1604–1684), Earl of St. Albans, who saw promise in the vacant fields north of the palace. Jermyn was always looking for ways to advance himself, socially or financially. Like today, urban development was the way to accomplish both.

The centre of Jermyn's new housing development was St. James's Square, an elegant enclave designed for well-to-do courtiers keen to live near the palace. The gamble paid off handsomely for Jermyn and it wasn't long before his square was the most desirable address in London and he a wealthy man.

In the 1700s, palace courtiers gave way to other members of society equally interested in advancement. These were wealthy landowners, military men, merchants, and politicians. This was the notorious age of gin, gossip, and gambling and the stakes were often very high: women lost their reputations from whispers and men their fortunes at cards.

Coffee was another vice of this immoral age. Its importation into Britain around this time started a craze that has never been kicked. Coffee stimulated creativity, commerce, and even dissent.[1] In time coffee houses evolved into private clubs. But many suspected the Ethiopian bean led to crime as well as revolution. Brazen highwaymen robbed coaches in Pall Mall and thieves snatched wigs and pickpocketed churchgoers in their pews. The area's decline was so great that one aristocrat called it an "abyss of fog, sulphur, fever, cold and all the excretions on this side of the Styx."[2]

Today, that fog has lifted and respectable St. James's is home to fashionable retailers, auction houses, private capital firms, and others seeking the cachet of a smart London address. Private gentlemen's clubs still dominate the area, though many have come and gone with time and taste. The Macaroni Club was one of these. It was formed in 1764 by foppish young men who had visited Italy, wore their hair long, and ate only pasta. But fashions and fads never last long, and neither did the Macaroni.[3]

THE WALK

Leaving Green Park Tube station, let's make our way east along the south side of Piccadilly past the gates to Green Park and the multitude of hawkers who gather here daily to sell double-decker bus tours. If you only have a few hours to see London, these popular tours are a great way to get your bearings; just don't expect the guides to identify any sites of *Canadian* interest.

The imposing Ritz Hotel is immediately on our right. A faded tribute to France's *belle époque*, the hotel was built in 1905 by the Swiss hotelier César Ritz (1850–1918) using the

> *This America's sweetheart business must stop. She's my sweetheart.*
> — DOUGLAS FAIRBANKS TO REPORTERS, 1920[4]

latest construction techniques. Perhaps a greater innovation was Ritz's insistence that all his rooms be equipped with private bathrooms — undoubtedly a big draw for the über-rich tired of passing each other in the hallways on their way to their baths.

One of many famous guests at the Ritz was Canadian-born Mary Pickford (1892–1979), a silent-film star, who honeymooned here in 1920. Pickford was the first actor to rise to global stardom because of movies. In fact, many say she created the age of celebrity that endures to this day.

The Ritz Hotel: *The World's First Movie Star*

Gladys Louise Smith was living proof that that practice makes perfect. Hailing from a working-class Irish family in Toronto, she began her career at age seven performing in vaudeville for Canadian soldiers. From then on, she was constantly on the stage: first with a touring company in Buffalo and then in New York City where she adopted the name "Mary Pickford" and went on to star in the pioneering films of D.W. Griffith (1875–1948). By the time she was twenty-two, she had some twelve million fans worldwide who saw her films every day.[5]

In 1920, Pickford divorced her first husband and secretly married the American film idol Douglas Fairbanks (1883–1939). It was a match made in heaven, or at least Hollywood's version of it. With her golden curls and feisty determination, Pickford was dubbed "America's sweetheart"

In 1920 thousands of fans blocked Piccadilly to see the famous newlyweds Mary Pickford and Douglas Fairbanks at the Ritz Hotel.

and Fairbanks the "All-American boy." Word of the marriage of these two Hollywood royals made headlines around the world. But it wasn't until the newlyweds arrived in London that they realized just how famous they were. The *New York Times* called their honeymoon "the most conspicuous in the history of the marriage institution."[6]

At the Ritz Hotel where the couple stayed, the scene was pandemonium. "Outside our window we saw them, thousands and thousands of them, waiting day and night on the streets below, for a glimpse of us," recalled Pickford later. Her British fans snarled traffic so badly on Piccadilly that even King George V (1865–1936; reigned from 1910) got stranded in his limousine.[7]

Pickford's fame was truly global. That's because silent films were cheap to produce, easy to distribute, and understandable in any language. But if filmgoers made her a huge star almost overnight, they unmade her just as quickly too. In a few years her stardom faded, replaced by more sexually charged screen idols. In the 1930s, Pickford retired from show business, divorced Fairbanks, and withdrew into seclusion. For the most part, the world's first global movie star lived the rest of her life in obscurity.

At the corner of St. James's Street, cross over and continue northeast along Piccadilly for about 100 metres (328 feet). Descend into fashionable Jermyn Street through the ornate Piccadilly Arcade.

Jermyn Street is London's best-known shopping area for high-end clothing, second only in reputation to Savile Row's suit-makers. At the foot of Piccadilly Arcade, a statue of the Regency dandy George "Beau" Brummell (1778–1840) greets us. The inscription reads: "To be truly elegant one should not be noticed." Brummell was a London *bon vivant* who spent so much on clothes and gambling that he died badly in debt. It's a warning to the wise that nothing comes cheap on Jermyn Street.

Another *bon vivant* of Jermyn Street, though not as well-known, was General John "Jack" Hill

> **Trivia:** *Mary Pickford lived at 211 University Avenue, Toronto. The site is now the city's Hospital for Sick Children. A plaque unveiled in 1973 honours the former home of the world's first movie star.*

(ca.1680–1735). He was a fun-loving army officer who was well connected at court. When he took part in a disastrous bid to capture Quebec forty-eight years before the more famous Major-General James Wolfe (1727–59), those connections came in very handy.

Jermyn Street: *General Hill's Misadventure*

In 1711, Europe's two squabbling sisters — Britain and France — were once again at war. This was the War of the Spanish Succession or Queen Anne's War as it is sometimes called. Urged on by American colonists, the British government decided to strike against France by capturing its fortress stronghold at Quebec. But the expedition would be perilous and costly, and needed the blessing of none other than Queen Anne (1665–1714; reigned from 1702) herself. To win her over, the government proposed Hill to command the army.

Like many military men of the period, Hill owed his success more to his connections than his capacities. One of his early patrons was the influential Sarah Churchill (1660–1744), 1st Duchess of Marlborough. When her influence faded at court, Hill plucked another ace from his fashionable sleeve: his own sister Abigail. She became the queen's intimate confidant. Under Abigail's persuasion, Anne agreed to the dangerous plan. Along with Hill would go the scarcely more talented Admiral Sir Hovenden Walker (ca.1656–1728) in charge of the navy. The two set off to Canada with high hopes and 5,000 of Britain's best fighting men — but the attack was an unmitigated failure.

Strong winds, dense fog, and a weak knowledge of the St. Lawrence River made havoc of the expedition. Eight ships foundered on a rocky shoal called Egg Island 500 kilometres (310 miles) from Quebec City and some 900 men drowned. Hill and Walker abandoned their mission and beat a hasty retreat home to face a cool reception. "Was it expected that I should have commanded wind and weather?" Walker demanded.[8] He fought accusations of cowardice but not so much the well-connected Hill. Promoted to major-general, he continued his drinking and good living in Jermyn Street until it was too much for him, and died a worn-out bachelor here in 1735.

Continuing east on the north side of Jermyn Street to Duke Street, we come to the landmark retail store Fortnum & Mason (181 Piccadilly).

Renowned for its window displays and enticing jams, jellies, and teas, this venerable old store dates to around 1707 when William Fortnum, a footman to Queen Anne, began selling groceries to St. James's rich. Fortnum got his start by melting down the discarded ends of palace candles and making new ones with his sidekick Hugh Mason. The Art Nouveau light sconces on Piccadilly may look like something out of Walt Disney's *Beauty and the Beast* but no doubt pay tribute to Fortnum's entrepreneurial spirit as lamplighter to the queen. Turn left and walk up Duke Street to Piccadilly. If you go in by the side entrance, you'll avoid the crowds but miss more of the wonderful display windows on Piccadilly.

Despite its Englishness inside and out, Fortnum & Mason is the crown jewel of a British food empire with Canadian roots. In 1951, the financially troubled store was purchased by the Canadian billionaire W. Garfield Weston (1898–1978). Weston was a canny businessman who had created a huge multinational food and retail company from his father's small bakery business in Toronto. He owed his success to adopting modern bread-making techniques and knowing what his customers liked. When a journalist once marvelled how his machinery blew excess icing off the biscuits, Weston replied: "Oh no, it's blowing the profit on." His father, George, was even cannier. "People will eat horse shit if it has enough icing on it," he once remarked.[9]

It was the billionaire Weston who installed the four-ton clock above the main entrance of the store. On the hour, the store's namesakes, Messrs. Fortnum and Mason, appear from behind bronze doors and bow to each other in a hokey but charming glockenspiel. If you arrive at the right moment, cross Piccadilly to see the show.

In 1971, a meeting took place here between the billionaire Garfield and his son Galen (b. 1940) that changed Canadian eating habits forever. It also solidified a food-and-fashion dynasty in Canada that endures to this day.

Fortnum & Mason: *The Royals of Retail*

Like the fall of the Roman Empire, the cracks of Garfield Weston's food empire started in the provinces. In the late 1960s, Weston-owned Loblaw grocery stores in Canada were losing truckloads of money. For the aging bread man, the barbarians were at the gate. In 1971 he called his son Galen into his office at Fortnum & Mason to decide the fate of the Canadian enterprise. He gave his son a year to turn Loblaw around or close it down.

Galen wasn't exactly the ideal grocer's son. A tall, handsome, and outgoing socialite with a penchant for polo, his only connection to the Canadian food chain was stocking shelves there during his summer holidays. But he had learned a few tricks at his father's knee and took over as CEO, moving to Canada with his Irish model wife, Hilary Frayne (b. 1942). It would certainly prove a safer place than Ireland: the Provisional Irish Republican Army had once tried to kidnap Galen to ransom him for cash.

Weston decided to take the Canadian food chain upmarket and hired an old university roommate Dave Nichol (b. 1940), as the company's president. Like Banting and Best, it was a fruitful collaboration. They revamped stores, adopted a new red-and-orange logo, and introduced fancy products under the President's Choice label. If Garfield the father brought sliced bread to Britain, observers say Galen the son brought balsamic vinegar to Canada.

Today, Canada's royal family of retail owns Loblaw, Real Canadian Superstores, Holt Renfrew, and T&T, the largest Asian grocery chain in the country. And the dynasty seems to be going strong with the fourth generation. Galen Jr. (b. 1972) is Loblaw's current president, as well as geeky TV spokesperson.

After stocking up at Fortnum's, continue along Piccadilly past Hatchard's, London's oldest booksellers (187 Piccadilly). Set back from the street a little farther on is St. James's Piccadilly church.

St. James's Piccadilly, dating to 1676, is the oldest building in the area. It was financed by Henry Jermyn himself and designed by the architect Sir Christopher Wren (1632–1723). Some say its modest scale allowed churchgoers to hear not only the sermons in the pulpit but the gossip in the pews.[10] Although badly damaged during the Second World War, the church

Trivia: *In 2004, Galen Weston Jr. and his sister, Alannah, opened a club of their own in Toronto: the Spoke Club targeted trendy, creative types.*

was restored with its original woodwork by master carver Grinling Gibbons (1648–1721).

Adjoining the parish is a peaceful former churchyard whose gravestones have been lost to time and the need for patio stones — like the ones you're probably standing on. Nowadays, a social worker in a green trailer offers drop-in counselling to London's homeless. A few of these find refuge inside, so be prepared.

Inside St. James's Piccadilly four large windows on both sides make it surprisingly bright. Under the second window along the Piccadilly side is a memorial to Loyalist Guy Johns(t)on (ca.1740–88) of Guy Park, New York. He was a bombastic Irishman who was forced to abandon his home and flee to Canada during the American Revolution. For this and much more, he vowed revenge against the United States.

Johnson Memorial: *A Loyalist's Curse*

In 1755, Guy Johnson arrived in pre-Revolutionary Boston without a shilling in his pocket but a good family connection to bank on: his relative, the prosperous and well-known Sir William Johnson (1715–74), superintendant of the Mohawk Indians in upper New York province. Before Bostonians could say "Bill's your uncle," the spendthrift Johnson was so badly in debt that Sir William had to rescue him with a chequebook. It didn't seem to bother the older Johnson: Guy married one of Sir William's daughters in 1763 and became his trusted aide, even taking over Sir William's Indian duties after his death.

Johnson's gift for words and Irish bravado made him genuinely popular with the Mohawks, who named him *Uraghquadirha* or "Rays of the Sun Enlightening the Earth."[11] As the American Revolution gathered steam, Johnson worked hard to keep the Mohawks loyal to Britain but was forced to flee to Montreal with his family when fighting broke out near his Mohawk Valley home in 1775. Further tragedy struck nearly within sight of Canada when Johnson's exhausted wife died at Oswego, New York.

Distraught, Johnson vowed revenge against the American patriots who had caused him so much grief. With the help of the Iroquois leader Joseph Brant (ca.1743–1807), he was put in charge of Canada's Indians and eventually made good his curse by leading devastating raids on the American frontier from Fort Niagara. In 1783, he returned to London to seek restitution for lost property in New York but died here uncompensated and unvalued, "broken in health, spirit and estate."[12]

By the third window along the same side is a memorial to Sir Colin Campbell (1776–1847), a one-time lieutenant governor of Nova Scotia. A Scot from a military family, Campbell served under the Duke of Wellington and admired his commander so much he named his son after him. Although Campbell was offered the governorship of Tobago as a reward for military service, he passed up the tropical paradise for "the beautiful and interesting" Nova Scotia. His term from 1834–40 in the feisty colony, however, would prove anything but idyllic.

22

Campbell Memorial: *Against the Tide in Nova Scotia*

When Sir Colin Campbell landed in Nova Scotia as the province's new governor in July 1834, he knew how to win over a crowd: hosting picnics and parties and bravely visiting areas hit by cholera. But it didn't take long before the conservative Scot started to ruffle a few feathers, especially with the province's elected assemblymen who wanted a greater say in how Nova Scotia was governed. Unfortunately for a man like Campbell, the assembly's grievances were beyond his comprehension. He didn't know it yet but he was battling a tide as strong as the Bay of Fundy's. It was called democracy, or the reform movement.

One of Campbell's political rivals was the fiery Joseph Howe (1804–73), a newspaperman and leading Reform politician who later opposed Confederation. Howe and his supporters disliked Campbell so much they lobbied London for his dismissal. Mind you, not every Nova Scotian shared their view. Perhaps fearing the end to his picnics and parties, many Nova Scotians petitioned for Campbell to stay.

The matter came to a head when Canada's governor general, Sir Charles Poulett Thomson (1799–1841), arrived in Halifax to settle the stalemate. Thomson, a Reformer himself from the British Whig party, took the side of Howe and the assembly against Campbell. "The time has gone by when these North American provinces can be governed in the old system," he said.[13] Sir Colin was sent packing to Sri Lanka and returned to London in 1847, old and feeble-minded.[14]

Just beyond the fourth window is another plaque. It is a memorial to a physician named Sir Richard Croft. If it weren't for Croft, Queen Victoria might not have been Canada's first queen. Croft was a royal obstetrician to Princess Charlotte, the only child of King George IV (1762–1830; regent from 1811–1820; reigned from 1820). When Charlotte gave birth in 1817, Croft botched his bedside care so badly that both mother and child died. Without an heir, the crown passed to the king's niece, the young princess Victoria.

> I dined alone at the St. James's Club among diplomats and old prints — rather dreary.
>
> — CANADIAN DIPLOMAT CHARLES RITCHIE, 1942[15]

Exit the church on Jermyn Street and partake in some retail therapy or head back along Jermyn Street in the direction from which we came: St. James's Street.

We now find ourselves on St. James's Street in the heart of London's clubland. This elegant but busy street and its sibling Pall Mall are the principal addresses of many of London's best-known gentlemen's clubs. At one time there were more than 200 such establishments in London. Today fewer than a quarter of them survive.

The area's oldest and most preeminent is White's Club (37–38 St. James's Street), just up a little toward Piccadilly. Its origins go back to White's Chocolate House, founded in 1693, though the present clubhouse dates from about 1787.

If you look behind the iron railing of White's, you will see an odd set of steps that don't lead anywhere. That's because the club's door was moved right in 1811, perhaps in keeping with the club's politics.[16] The central bay window was an ideal spot where Brummell, our dandy of Jermyn Street, could play cards and keep his eye on the fashions of unsuspecting passersby.

Among the portraits on the walls of White's is one of distinguished club member Field Marshal Sir Harold Alexander (1891–1969), 1st Earl Alexander of Tunis. It's by the English portrait painter Sir Oswald Birley. Alexander was a decorated war hero and the last of a vanishing breed: the gentleman soldier. He was also Canada's last British governor general from 1946–52.

White's Club: *The Gentleman's General*

Harold Alexander was a handsome, fastidious soldier whose shoes and manners bore equal polish. Born into an Anglo-Irish aristocratic family, he always dreamed of being a painter. But like many of his generation, those dreams were upended when he enlisted in the First World War. By 1937, he had climbed in the ranks to become the youngest general in the British Army, known to everyone simply as "Alex."

Even in the face of adversity, Alex was always a gentleman. Confronted by the German *blitzkrieg* (lightening war) in the Second World War, he was ordered to evacuate his army from France. Although British prime minister Winston Churchill (1874–1965) had given him permission to surrender, he defended the evacuation at Dunkirk to the last man. "Is anyone there?" he called out along the beaches in English and French before getting into a boat and leaving himself.[17] Although he later won battles in North Africa, the Middle East, and Italy — often at the head of Canadian troops — some say he might have been a greater commander if he had not been so nice a man, and so deeply a gentleman.[18]

When peace came, Canada asked if Alex would be the country's next governor general. He had expected another job in the army but Churchill told him Canada was a much more important post.[19]

As governor general, Alexander proved as popular with Canadian civilians as he had been with his troops. But he also found the time at last to pursue his long-delayed passion to paint. He studied art, befriended Canadian artists, and took along his easel just about everywhere he went around Canada. Such was his fondness for the country that he added Baron Rideau of Ottawa to his title when he was granted an earldom in 1952.

Not every club member could claim to be as much a gentleman as Alexander. Drinkers and gamblers were legion at White's. Jonathan Swift (1667–1745), the satirist and author of *Gulliver's Travels*, was certainly no fan. He shook his fist every time he walked by the place and called it "the common rendezvous of infamous sharpers [swindlers] and noble cullies [pals]."[20]

Unhappy shareholders of Hollinger International might do the same. That's because Conrad Black (b. 1944), Baron Black of Crossharbour, was a member here. He joined with the help of Peter Carington (b. 1919), 6th Baron Carrington, a former Conservative foreign secretary. Black offered Carington a lucrative directorship on the board of the *Daily Telegraph* and like magic Black was tucking into his sherry trifle at the members' table. "He is a very generous man," Carington said sheepishly of his new patron and fellow club member.[21]

Let's leave White's now and walk farther down St. James's Street.

The 1960s office tower in the plaza behind Boodles club (28 St. James's Street), is the headquarters

The statue of Earl Alexander of Tunis, Canada's last British governor general, in the Wellington Barracks on the west side of St. James's Park. It was erected in 1985.

of the weekly news magazine *The Economist*. It was created in the turbulent 1800s to advocate for free trade and put an end to the imperial trading system that gave preference to imports from colonies like Canada.

Despite its serious name, the magazine has a whimsical streak. In 2003, *The Economist* put a moose sporting sunglasses on its cover and called Canada cool for its economic success and boldness in social matters like the legalization of gay marriage and possible decriminalization of marijuana. This was under Prime Minister Jean Chrétien (b. 1934). A year and a half later, the magazine changed its tune and called Chrétien's successor, Paul Martin Jr. (b. 1938), "Mr. Dithers." The name persisted even if Mr. Dithers didn't.

Across the street opposite is another gentlemen's club: Brooks's (60 St. James's Street). It was founded in 1764 for members of the more liberal Whig Party. A wit once compared it to a duke's country house — with the duke lying dead upstairs.[22]

Whigs sympathized with the patriots in the American Revolution and the lead plant containers outside the door recall the date 1776. One of the club's prized possessions is said to be a book that lists the wagers of early members. One entry for £50 was placed in 1777 by club member General John Burgoyne (1722–92) or "Gentleman Johnny" to his friends. Burgoyne wagered he would defeat the Americans by attacking with an army from Montreal and be back at the club in time for Christmas. Alas, the boastful Burgoyne wasn't cut out for backwoods warfare. His Canadian attack failed and he lost his army as well as his shirt.[23]

Canada's Vincent Massey (1887–1967) was a member here. Massey succeeded Alexander as governor general of Canada and was the first Canadian to hold the vice-regal post. But not everyone noticed the difference. Massey was such an imperialist some people didn't think he was quite *Canadian* enough.

Trivia: *Vincent Massey gave his collection of modern British art to the National Gallery of Canada. Prime Minister W.L. Mackenzie King was unimpressed. "You cannot possibly like those dreadful pictures Vincent and Alice buy," he said.*[24]

Brooks's Club: *Which King's Man?*

Vincent Massey was a small, cultivated lawyer from an Ontario family made rich from selling farm tractors across the British Empire. After helping secure a Liberal victory in 1935, he was appointed as Canada's high commissioner in London by a grateful Prime Minister William Lyon Mackenzie King (1874–1950). King would soon regret his decision.

For Massey, the London job was a dream come true. Educated at Oxford University, he adored everything British: their manners, tastes, and traditions. He knew every duke by name, one diplomat observed, and was friendly with all the royals — dubbed a real king's man. For some, his British reverence and clubbable, upper-class manner was just a little *un-Canadian*. One governor general thought him a bit "too Balliol" (after his Oxford college) while the Canadian journalist Charles Lynch joked he made English toffs (aristocrats) feel inferior.[25]

It may have been the reason King kept his old Liberal friend on a short leash in London. King was as much an anglophobe as Massey was an anglophile. King knew Brits, he once warned his high commissioner, and they needed to be watched.[26] Inevitably, the high costs of living in London also strained their transatlantic relationship. King refused to buy an official residence for Massey in London or even to bombproof Canada House on Trafalgar Square during the Second World War. As a result Massey had to live in rented digs and authorized the embassy's improvements himself.[27]

Their relationship was never more tested than when King visited London in 1946. Inside Canada House, the prime minister found photographs of the king and queen prominently on display but his own hidden behind a door. He never forgave Massey for the sleight.[28]

Opposite King Street is St. James's Place on our right. Number 10 was once a small hotel. Oscar Wilde (1854–1900) lived here in 1893–94 at the height of his success. Much of his *An Ideal Husband* was penned here.

A flamboyant *fin-de-siècle* writer and advocate of the decorative arts, Wilde was celebrated and loathed in equal measure. He lived a self-fulfilling prophecy to be famous and, if not famous, notorious. In reality, he was both.

Canadian prime minister W.L. Mackenzie King is greeted in London by his anglophile high commissioner, Vincent Massey.

Wilde chose this tucked-away hotel in St. James's Place to elude the prying eyes of society while he wrote, sipped German white wine (hock) and soda, and conducted his discreet — and at the time criminal — relations with other men. Without any luck. In 1895, he was arrested at the Cadogan Hotel (75 Sloane Street) in London's Knightsbridge area and put on trial. An eyewitness testified Wilde often entertained young men of "quite inferior station" here in St. James's Place. This testimony helped seal Wilde's fate and send him to prison to do hard labour.[29]

Trivia: *In 1887, Oscar Wilde is said to have sat for a portrait by the Canadian painter Frances Richards. "What a tragic thing it is," Wilde mused. "This portrait will never grow older but I shall." His novella soon followed, called* The Picture of Dorian Gray.[30]

As our walks don't take us into Knightsbridge, we'll use this spot to recall Wilde's relationship with Canada's Robert Baldwin Ross (1869–1918), a lover and lifelong friend of Wilde's who was with the writer at the time of his arrest. John Betjeman (1906–84), a British poet laureate, later imagined the moment in his poem "The Arrest of Oscar Wilde at the Cadogan Hotel":

> *More hock Robbie — where is the seltzer?*
> *Dear boy, pull again at the bell!*
> *They are all little better than* cretins,
> *Though this* is *the Cadogan Hotel.*

10 St. James's Place: *Oscar Wilde's Canadian Friend*

Robert Baldwin Ross was the youngest son of John Ross (1818–71), a well-respected attorney general in Upper Canada, and Elizabeth Baldwin, daughter of the Canadian Reformer Robert Baldwin (1804–58). When the elder Ross died after an illness in Toronto, the family moved to London. Despite spending only a few years in Canada, the youngest Ross never lost his Canadian heritage or his accent.[31]

Short with boyish features, "little Robbie" was not particularly handsome but there was something about his mischievous face that endeared him to Wilde. How they met is not known for certain but it may have been through a Canadian painter and neighbour in Chelsea named Frances Richards (1852–1934). In any case, when Ross was a student at Cambridge University, the two were possibly lovers.

Ross's unashamed homosexuality and aesthetic lifestyle (like Wilde, he wore his hair long) made him unpopular at the university, where he was bullied and dumped in a college fountain. As a writer later in Edinburgh and London, he remained a devoted friend to Wilde. When others deserted the playwright at his trial, Ross stood by him, even dangerously doffing his hat to the humiliated playwright in public.

On the day of Wilde's arrest, Ross urged the distraught playwright to flee to France for safety. Wilde didn't heed his advice. "The train is gone, it's too late," he said in defeat. After Wilde's imprisonment and death, Ross managed Wilde's estate and erected a headstone at the writer's grave in a Paris cemetery. In due course, he even joined Wilde there.[32]

At the foot of our street is St. James's Palace. Dwarfed by grander buildings, its Tudor scale can be a bit underwhelming. While it is still the official seat of the monarchy (known as "the Court of St. James's"), in practice all sovereigns since Queen Victoria (1819–1901; reigned from 1837) have lived in the more impressive digs around the corner. Little of the original Tudor palace survives except for the entrance, some reception rooms, and the Chapel Royal within. Today, it is mostly used for offices and charitable functions.

Many royals are associated with St. James's Palace. Queen Mary (1516–58; reigned from 1553), who was elder half-sister to Queen Elizabeth I and better known to us as "Bloody Mary," died here in 1558 and King Charles I (1600–49; reigned from 1625) spent his last few hours in the chapel praying before walking to his execution in nearby Whitehall. Other monarchs were born here including King Charles II (1630–85; reigned from 1660), his brother King James II (1633–1701; reigned 1685–88) as well as Queen Anne.

Across from Friary Court on Marlborough Road is the Queen's Chapel, built in 1623 by the architect Inigo Jones (1573–1652). It is used as a Chapel Royal or special church of the monarch. Two such Chapel Royals are found in Ontario: the Queen's Chapel of the Mohawks in Brantford and Christ Church, Chapel Royal of the Mohawks in Deseronto. They honour the special links between the sovereign and the Mohawk people who remained loyal to Britain during the American Revolution.

St. James's Palace was also the birthplace of Sir Albert Grey (1851–1917), 4th Earl Grey, governor general of Canada from 1904 to 1911. Grey was raised at the palace and came from a prominent political family (his grandfather was the prime minister who inspired the name of tea made with Bergamot). He wasn't a royal, just the son of parents who worked for them.

If Canadians recall Grey at all, it is for the trophy in Canadian football that bears his name. While his cup fostered Canadian nationalism in sport, however, it had the unintended effect of dividing Canada from the empire Grey loved.

St. James's Palace: *Grey's Cup Runneth Over*

Albert Grey was a crusader who believed almost religiously in the British Empire. While others gave their lives for the cause, he gave his hair: in India he suffered severe sun stroke and was left bald for the rest of his life.[34] As Canada's governor general, he was a fervent promoter of imperial schemes — many of them crazy — which often put him at odds with just about everyone including prime ministers Sir Wilfrid Laurier (1841–1919) and Sir Robert Borden (1854–1937).

"I doubt Albert's level-headedness," the outgoing governor general confided to his wife on learning of Grey's appointment, "and an enormous amount of harm may be done here by any impetuous action and want of judgment." History would prove these words prophetic in an odd way. It centred on a $48 trophy.

In 1823, William Ellis invented a game in Rugby, England, by picking up a soccer ball and running down the field with it. (His tombstone says he had a fine disregard for the rules.) "Rugby" quickly spread with immigration to Australia and New Zealand and along with cricket became the main sport of the British Empire. Canada embraced the game too and introduced it to the United States in 1874. Not long afterward the Americans changed the rules again, eliminating the scrum for a ball passed to a quarterback, and football was born.

In 1909, when Grey donated his cup for amateur rugby football in Canada, the game was a bit of an odd hybrid: neither rugby nor modern Canadian football. But Grey's cup accelerated the game's unique evolution. As more and more amateur clubs across Canada vied for his trophy, it spurred the creation of a common rulebook. Before long rules on forward passes, snap backs, interference, and even how many Americans could play on a team created a new game that drove a sporting wedge between the empire with its fondness for Ellis's rugby and Canada with a national game of its own.[35]

Now let's leave one game for another as we look down one of

> *Walking through St. James's Park I encountered that gypsy woman whom I have seen telling people's fortunes. I decided to try mine. She took my hand, looked at it, and instantly said: "They will never make a gentleman of you."*
>
> —Canadian diplomat Charles Ritchie, April 1969[36]

London's most fabled streets: Pall Mall. The name comes from a medieval Italian game *palla a maglio* (ball to mallet), which King Charles II loved to play here in an alley bordered by elms.

Opposite us on Pall Mall is the Parisian-style office of the Quebec Government (59 Pall Mall). At one time many provinces had buildings in London to promote trade but now only Quebec House remains.

In 1981, an angry Quebec Government made a last-ditch effort to stop the patriation of Canada's constitution from Britain. If old soldiers never die, then the ghost of René Lévesque (1922–87) may still haunt this place.

Lord Grey, governor general of Canada from 1904 to 1911. His trophy for football divided Canada from the British Empire — in sport at least.

59 Pall Mall: *Quebec's Last Stand*

When René Lévesque failed to win special recognition for his province during constitutional negotiations in the early 1980s, Quebec's chain-smoking premier set his sights on London. His front gunner in the British dogfight was his government's agent-general in London Gilles Loiselle (b. 1929). He was told to do everything in his power to stall the vote in Britain's parliament that would allow the constitution to be sent home to Canada.

The battle brought lobbyists from all sides of the issue to London to stuff hungry parliamentarians with food and propaganda.[37] Loiselle was a tough man to beat. A former journalist with Radio-Canada and federal cabinet minister, he knew his pinots from his clarets and spoke equally well the queen's English and the French of Molière. He was the kind of Péquiste, someone said, who liked to taunt Prime Minister Pierre Trudeau (1919–2000) with being an English snob, but was no stranger to pretentiousness himself.[38]

Loiselle knew the best way to a politician's heart was through his stomach. He also knew that the real power in Britain's parliament rested with its backbench MPs. With one of the best chefs in town, a wine cellar, and a hefty hospitality budget, Loiselle wined and dined some 250 parliamentarians to explain Quebec's grudges with Trudeau and his government. "I have never seen the booze flow with such abandon," a columnist observed in the *Sunday Times*.

As pleasurable and intoxicating as it must have been, Loiselle's "lobbying *à la carte*" ultimately failed. Much to Lévesque's horror, Britain passed the Canada Act with little objection in early 1982, severing Canada's last legal ties to Britain and paving the way for the creation of the country's new constitution, which didn't include Quebec.

Embittered and betrayed, Lévesque famously muttered: *"Trudeau m'a fourré"* (Trudeau fucked me). He was to die from heart failure a few years later.[39]

Before we leave Quebec House, note the marks on the façade on either side of the blue *fleur-de-lys*. At one time, two poles jutted out over the sidewalk for the flags of Canada and Quebec. In 1995, the Quebec Government quietly removed the Canadian flag in a public assertion of its independence abroad.

Tucked out of sight across the street is Marlborough House. Having discovered some of its occupants on Walk 1, we'll now say a word or two about the owners for whom the house was originally built: John and Sarah Churchill, 1st Duke and Duchess of Marlborough.

Britain's original power couple, the Marlboroughs were distant ancestors of Winston Churchill and leapt to fame and influence during the reign of Queen Anne. Marlborough's victory over the French at the Battle of Blenheim (1704) in the War of the Spanish Succession (1701–14) made him a national hero and very, very rich.

Pluck up the courage and poke your head through the gateway. Sir Christopher Wren designed the

> Lévesque's agent-general in London is losing no time in popularizing his provincial government. On Saturday night, he had all the chauffeurs in for a drink.
>
> —CANADIAN HIGH COMMISSIONER PAUL MARTIN SR., NOVEMBER 1977[40]

original redbrick house especially for the duchess. She disliked the ornamentation of Blenheim Palace, her other home near Oxford, and wanted something "small, plain and convenient" in the heart of London.

Despite their tremendous wealth, the Marlboroughs were fanatically frugal; after landing his troops in Holland, the duke loaded up his navy ships with bricks to take advantage of the free transportation home. When it came to his job as a governor of the Hudson's Bay Company, he similarly profited from his military connections.

Marlborough House: *Churchill Collects His HBC Rewards*

Granted a royal charter in 1670, the Hudson's Bay Company is one of the oldest incorporated merchandising companies in the world. But in the first fifteen years of operation, it failed to make a penny for its owners.

In 1685, before he became Duke of Marlborough, John Churchill agreed to become the third governor of the HBC. At thirty-five, he was handsome and courteous, a rising military star, and very well connected in Parliament and at court. It was for these reasons that the company sought him out for the governorship. The company's second governor and Churchill's immediate predecessor had been utterly incompetent: a neglectful and ineffective man who even refused to sign everyday business papers. He would prove an even less successful king.[41]

Churchill, to the contrary, was a man of action. Using his control over Britain's military, he directed the navy to help protect supply ships from French raiders sailing in and out of the trading posts in Hudson Bay. He also ensured the company's monopoly to trade furs was formalized with an Act of Parliament. As a result of these and other efforts, the HBC finally became profitable under Churchill's watch and paid generous dividends — the company's first.

Such was the company's gratitude that it named the Churchill River after him in what later became Manitoba.[42]

Walk along Pall Mall to St. James's Square. Across from the entrance to this square once stood the Conservative Carlton Club.[43] In October 1922, Andrew Bonar Law (1858–1923), a New Brunswicker by birth, was returned as leader of the Conservative Party by backbench MPs here. Shortly afterward, his party won a general election — making him the only British prime minister born outside the United Kingdom. Tory backbenchers to this day are known as the 1922 Committee in reference to these historic events it is said.

Now let's head north into St. James's Square. At one time the most fashionable quarter in London, nowadays it's hard to imagine it as a refined residential square.

Working our way around to the top, we pass the East India Club and private London Library to come to 10 St. James Square. This was the home at various times of three British leaders: William Pitt (1708–78), 1st Earl of Chatham, Edward Smith-Stanley (1799–1869), 14th Earl of Derby, and William Gladstone (1809–98). For now, we'll just consider the first of these.

Chatham House: *The Year of Victories*

William Pitt ranks as one of Britain's greatest leaders. At the height of the Seven Years' War (1756–63), he became secretary of state and leased 10 St. James's Square. From there he directed a series of bold military manoeuvres in North America that would change the continent forever.

Pitt was a political outsider known as the Great Commoner. Energetic, brilliant, and a champion of trade, he was also highly unstable: at times so melancholic he couldn't bear to see anyone. He was also relatively poor and is said to have kept his rooms so cold that the visiting prime minister, the Duke of Newcastle, once had to climb into a bed just to stay warm.

Pitt's plan to win the war called for a series of surprise attacks on French fortresses overseas at Louisbourg, Quebec, and elsewhere to reduce the power of France. One by one, these strongholds fell and 1759 became known the *Annus Mirabilis* ("Year of Victories" in Latin). When Fort Duquesne on the Ohio River was taken, British soldiers honoured their leader by renaming it Pittsburgh.

The other part of Pitt's winning strategy was to put his trust in bold, young military men like Major-General James Wolfe. Wolfe is said to have dined with Pitt here on the eve of his departure for Quebec. After dinner Wolfe stood up, flourished his sword, and struck the table with it in a show of bravado. Pitt may have wondered about Wolfe's sanity but no doubt saw the fearless qualities he was looking for in a military leader. He may also have recognized Wolfe was dying of tuberculosis and had nothing to lose from the venture. "Good God," Pitt said afterward, "that I should have entrusted the fate of our country to such hands."[44]

Today, Britain's Royal Institute of International Affairs occupies the building, now known as Chatham House, after the earldom bestowed on Pitt. The term "Chatham House Rule" was coined here in 1927 and simply means discussions are "not for attribution." While the term is often pluralized, Chatham House's web site reminds us that there is — and has only ever been — *one* rule.

Continue around the square. To our right at the top of Duke of York Street is the parish church of St. James's Piccadilly we visited earlier. The bronze equestrian statue in the central square portrays King William III (1650–1702; reigned from 1689). It depicts the moment before the horse stumbled on a molehill, ultimately causing the king's death. During the Second World War, the Canadian diplomat Charles Ritchie (1906–95) brought a girlfriend here. Their canoodling was interrupted by a passerby who warned them of an unexploded bomb in the park.[45]

Circling around the square, we come to Charles II Street. Just beyond at the corner of Regent Street is British Columbia House (1 Regent Street), once home to the province's agent-general in London.

Prince Arthur (1850–1942), Duke of Connaught, laid the cornerstone of the building. He was the seventh of Queen Victoria's nine children and Canada's most

Trivia: *Colonel Reuben Wells Leonard (1860–1930) was a wealthy Ontario businessman, who gave money to purchase 10 St. James's Square and named it in honour of his hero William Pitt, Earl of Chatham.*

royal governor general when he served in the post from 1911 to 1916. A career military man, he had defended Canada against Fenian raiders in 1870 and, into his nineties, was ready to take up arms again to fight the Nazis in the Second World War. Connaught also laid the foundation stone of Canada's new parliament buildings in 1916.

British Columbia House: *A Room with a View*

British Columbia House was the brainchild of John Herbert Turner (1833–1923), a provincial politician known for extravagance when it came to spending the public purse. As finance minister, he never balanced a budget and ran up the province's debt sevenfold by the time he left office. His opponents called his style of fiscal management "Turnerism" — like socialism or communism. When he sued once for libel, he lost.

If profligacy wasn't bad enough, Turner frequently used his position and influence to feather his own nest. This got him into hot water so many times his government sent him to London as the province's representative in 1901 to escape further controversy. But it was hard for the old dog to learn new tricks and he was soon bent on spending again, this time constructing a permanent symbol of his much beloved British Columbia in London.

Turner bought an old hotel on Regent Street and had it redeveloped by one of London's pre-eminent architects of the day, Sir Reginald Blomfield. Not only was the result a fine building with the flourishes of a hunting lodge in the Rockies, it also came with a penthouse apartment with an equally fine view over London's parks. Unfortunately, Turner's luck finally ran out just as he was about to move into his new digs. In 1915, another agent-general was named by the province and Turner never had the chance to enjoy the beautiful apartment — or the view.

Continuing back in St. James's Square, a plaque at number 31 tells us that this was the site of Norfolk House, once home to the Duke of Norfolk and later site of the First Allied Force Headquarters from

1942–44. Operation Overlord, the code name for the invasion of Europe in the Second World War, was planned here.

In movies like *Saving Private Ryan*, you would be forgiven for thinking D-Day was a purely American enterprise. But Canadians shared in every aspect of the operation and were assigned Juno Beach, one of the toughest of the five assault beaches in Normandy. Despite strong German defences and resistance, Canadians penetrated farther inland than any other Allied division during the first day. The enormous cost of over a thousand Canadian lives was half of what Allied planners had expected.

Less august battles also unfolded here. In 1937, Canada and other Commonwealth countries met at Norfolk House to plan the coronation of King George VI. An issue arose over what to wear to the event. Canadian officials in Ottawa balked at the idea of donning stockings and knee breeches — official court dress — though, not surprisingly, the anglophile Vincent Massey, Canada's high commissioner, didn't. "I wish to goodness some of my fellow countrymen wouldn't have an almost religious antipathy to knee-breeches," he said.[46] But sensing a wind of change, the British backed down. "We don't want to break up the empire for the sake of a pair of trousers," one said.[47]

Let's leave St. James's Square now and return to Pall Mall. Directly across from us are two Italianate masterpieces of architecture: the Travellers Club, built in 1832, and the Reform Club, built in 1841 (102 and 104 Pall Mall). Sir Charles Barry (1795–1860), Britain's leading architect, designed both of them. Classical, confident, and elevated above street level, the pair exude the ideals of democracy and respectability but with a hint of superiority. When the old Tory rulers of Toronto set out to build Osgoode Hall for their law society, they modelled it in the manner of these clubs. "It expressed the cult of pretensions of the English upper class," an architectural historian has written. "It was a trend in English society and the builders of Osgoode Hall were trying to emulate it."[49]

> I lunched on gammon at the Travellers club and afterwards read a pornographic book in the library. It is the most beautiful room in London. We used not to have any sex in the club library but now it is everywhere, like petrol fumes in the air.
>
> —CANADIAN DIPLOMAT CHARLES RITCHIE, JANUARY 1969[48]

In popular culture, the Reform Club is best known as the place where Phileas Fogg took his wager to circumnavigate the globe in Jules Verne's *Around the World in Eighty Days*. Our interest, however, lies not so much with fiction as foundation. That's because the club was founded in 1836 by a group of political reformers who wanted democratic changes in Britain and places like Canada. Long before there was a Preston Manning (b. 1942) or his Alberta Reform Party, these early reform ideas took root in Canada and led to its independence.

In the late 1600s, England had a parliament but not really a democracy. Members were either landowning aristocrats or later simply bought their seats in voterless ridings called pocket or rotten boroughs. But revolutions in the United States and France, as well as simmering discontent in Britain, fuelled a desire to broaden the definition of who could vote. In 1832, a parliamentary group of Whigs and Radicals united to pass the Great Reform Act — the first step toward democracy in Britain.

Similar ideas spread to Canada where a growing number of merchants were disenchanted with the rule of British governors and their Tory friends. Rebellions in Upper and Lower Canada in 1837–38 led by William Lyon Mackenzie (1795–1861) and Louis-Joseph Papineau (1786–1871) respectively signalled the need for change. As we learned on Walk 1, Britain sent one of its leading Reformers to find a solution: John "Radical Jack" Lambton (1792–1840), 1st Earl of Durham. He was a founding member of the Reform Club and advocate for greater self-government in Canada. A portrait of his handsome figure still watches over members dozing in the afternoon sunshine in the upstairs gallery.

Durham isn't the only early club member with ties to Canada. Beside his portrait in the upper gallery is one of Sir Charles Poulett Thomson. Thomson was a Whig and fiscal reformer who succeeded Durham as governor general of Canada. His mission was to unite Upper and Lower Canada as part of his predecessor's plan.

Reform Club: *Chicken à la King*

Charles Edward Poulett Thomson wasn't an aristocrat but he ached to be one. The son of a timber merchant, he admired the upper classes and went out of his way to behave like a proper gentleman. His father's ego may have been partially to blame. In 1820, John Thomson added Poulett to the family name, lending it a double-barrelled air of aristocracy. "He is very good humoured, pleasing and intelligent," said a contemporary of the younger Thomson, but he is "the greatest coxcomb I ever saw, and the vainest dog."[50]

Like many young men unable to succeed elsewhere, Thomson ran for Parliament. Mocked cruelly in the House of Commons as an effeminate bore, he had a talent for numbers and surprised everyone by becoming the *de facto* head of Britain's Board of Trade. In 1839, he was asked to be governor general of Canada to implement Durham's recommendation to unite Upper and Lower Canada. Thomson accepted on one condition: he be ennobled as an aristocrat if he succeeded.

Marrying Upper and Lower Canada was easier said than done, however. Frustrated with colonial bickering at every turn, Thomson soon regretted the deal he had struck back in London. He wrote in despair: "I would not stay here if they made me Duke of Canada." Quebeckers never took to him — they called him *le poulet* (the chicken) — and Torontonians were not much fonder. They only agreed to unite with Lower Canada when Thomson offered to pay off their debts. To their wounded civic pride, however, he chose Kingston, Ontario, as the new capital of the united Province of Canada, claiming Toronto was "too far and out of the way."

With his mission accomplished, Thomson at last sought out his coveted reward. But when he suggested the title "Lord St. Lawrence," his superiors balked, believing it a bit too grand. Favouring something farther and more out of the way, they made him Lord Sydenham and Toronto instead.[51]

At the foot of Regent Street, we reach an open space known as Waterloo Place. On our left is the Guards Crimea Memorial by John

Henry Foley and Arthur George Walker. It commemorates the more than two thousand British soldiers who died fighting Russia in the Crimean War (1853–56). On the south side of the monument is a

bronze statue of Florence Nightingale (1820–1910), "the lady with the lamp." Nightingale enlisted thirty-eight women to provide care to the sick and wounded in the Crimean War and broke a longstanding taboo against women on the front lines.

Whether in the flesh or in bronze, it seems she had a knack for providing comfort. Early in the Second World War, Vincent Massey and his wife, Alice, were crossing Waterloo Place when they heard the whistle of a German bomb and dove for cover. When they stood up and brushed themselves off, they found themselves at the foot of Nightingale's statue. Massey wrote it was a comforting symbol he always remembered.[53]

Although no Canadian military units fought in the Crimean War, a number of Canadians enlisted individually. Lieutenant Alexander Dunn (1833–68) was one of these and became the first Canadian to win the Victoria Cross, the highest military award in the British Empire. He received it during the doomed charge of the Light Brigade in 1854. A monument erected in St. Paul's Cemetery in Halifax in 1860 to commemorate two other Canadians in the Crimean War is said to be one of the oldest war memorials in the country.

Let's cross now to the south side of Pall Mall at Waterloo Place. Continuing on, we come to

Maritime names: In 1784, New Brunswick was named after King George III, who was also Duke of Brunswick. Charlottetown, Prince Edward Island, was named after his homely wife, Charlotte of Mecklenburg-Strelitz (1744–1818).

Haymarket, with the New Zealand High Commission's midcentury skyscraper on the corner.

Where Pall Mall divides right and left into Pall Mall East and Cockspur Street stands an equestrian statue, by Matthew Coates Wyatt, of the hatless King George III (1738–1820; reigned 1760–1811), America's last British king and, practically speaking, Canada's first. Cross over here at the traffic light.

George III came to the throne in a blaze of glory after the final conquest of Canada in 1760. The exit of his elderly grandfather George II blazed in a different way. He died from a stroke brought on by his exertions on the toilet.

As the king who lost the American colonies, history has been unkind to George III. What is often overlooked is that he was a hardworking and dutiful king who was forced to increase taxes on American colonists to pay for the war against the French in

Canada. He is also remembered for his madness — later diagnosed as *porphyria*, a disorder of the nervous system — which landed him in a straightjacket in 1811 and his ne'er-do-well son on the throne as regent. Poor George III spent his last years out of his mind: deaf, blind, and bearded, playing the harpsichord and talking of men and women long since dead.[54]

Although Roman Catholics had limited rights in Britain, George III was a realist when it came to Canada. By signing the Quebec Act of 1774, he recognized the authority of the Catholic Church in Quebec, as well as the use of French civil law. In doing so, he helped lay the foundation for the Canada we have today. While the

An equestrian statue of King George III stands on Pall Mall East. Perhaps the first and finest likeness of the mad king (above), however, was found down a Montreal well.

Quebec Act won the loyalty of French Canadians, it infuriated the Americans. They called it one of the crown's "intolerable Acts" provoking their revolution.

King George III Monument: *Le pape du Canada*

In Montreal's McCord Museum is a fine marble bust of King George III dated 1765 — carved by the noted British sculptor Joseph Wilton (1722–1803) and believed to be the first likeness of the new king. How it got there is one of the city's most remarkable tales.

In 1765, after a fire devastated part of Montreal, a wealthy British merchant and philanthropist named Jonas Hanway (1712–86) led a fundraising drive in London to help rebuild the city. He sent over two fire pumps to help the stricken city, as well as a gift slightly less useful in terms of putting out fires. In fact, it may have helped start one: a fine marble bust of King George III.

The bust was displayed on a pedestal in Montreal's Place des Armes. In 1775, only two years after it was unveiled, it was defaced with tar and adorned with a bishop's mitre and rosary made of potatoes. Written on the rosary's cross was: *Voilà le pape du Canada et le Sot Anglois* (Here is the pope of Canada and the English sot).

The vandalism outraged Montrealers and accusations of who was responsible flew from every quarter: French Canadians blamed English-speakers, Protestants blamed Catholics, and even some Jews were fingered. But the vandals were never caught. Then, in 1776, after the bust was cleaned up and returned to its public place, it disappeared for good after marauding American Revolutionaries attacked the city. For fifty years the whereabouts of George's head was a mystery, until 1834 when workers found it in an old well in the square where the American soldiers had presumably tossed it — still remarkably well preserved in its own facial mud pack.[55]

Keep now to the right and follow Cockspur Street for a few more metres until we reach the heavily colonnaded steps of Canada House. It was designed by the neoclassical British architect Sir Robert Smirke

Salada tea man Peter Larkin greets Queen Mary and King George V at the opening of Canada House in Trafalgar Square in 1927. The king is said to have admired Larkin's office more than his own.

(1780–1867), who also designed the British Museum. This is Canada's most prominent piece of foreign real estate, popular with both Canadian backpackers and — more often than not — protesters against the oil sands and annual seal hunts. It is a fitting place to end our walk through London's clubland as it was once a club itself. That it now belongs to Canada owes much to a self-made man people called the Tea King of America or "Lord Salada."

33 Canada House: *A Club of One's Own*

Peter Larkin (1855–1930) was a tall and dapper millionaire who rose from humble origins to head the largest tea empire in North America. He owed the success not only to his special blend of Sri Lankan and Indian tea but to the discovery that foil packaging kept it fresh longer. In 1890, he created the Salada Tea Company and made a fortune promoting his drink through the new medium of mass marketing.

In 1921, Larkin arrived in London as Canada's fifth high commissioner. He carried with him an important mandate from Prime Minister William Lyon Mackenzie King: find a home suitable to represent Canada in the city.

Larkin's long search at first centred on Trafalgar Square, known informally then as "Little Canada" with many Canadian banks and railway and insurance offices located there. He immediately set his sights on the prominent but financially ailing Union Club. Its membership had once included the *School for Scandal* playwright Richard Brinsley Sheridan (1751–1816), the wealthy businessman Cecil Rhodes (1853–1902) and the author Charles Dickens (1812–1870), though Dickens died the day he was elected a member. But in a city known for high-priced lawyers, the club made a fatal mistake that may have precipitated its decline: it barred lawyers from joining. And no one likes to buy an expensive club lunch more than an expensive club lawyer.

While the Union Club bickered over the sale, Larkin did consider other buildings. British Columbia House was a good choice but the province's man wouldn't give up his apartment and view. Another deal fell through when Nova Scotia's agent-general wanted a hefty finder's fee. "I am quite sick of this endeavour to obtain a home for ourselves in London," Larkin wrote in frustration to his prime minister.

When the Union Club finally agreed to sell Larkin faced his last hurdle: what to call the impressive building. Although "Canada House" was the most obvious name, Mackenzie King didn't think the term "house" quite grand enough. In deference to his wishes, only the name Canada was engraved above the door. When King George V opened the building in 1925, he is said to have told Larkin that his office was the finest in London, better than his own.[56]

We now find ourselves in Trafalgar Square, where our walk ends.

WALK 3:

TRAFALGAR SQUARE
AND WHITEHALL

There's something theatrical about this part of London even if it isn't known for West End shows. Trafalgar Square appears like an outdoor opera set from behind the curtain of Admiralty Arch, while in Whitehall grandees cast in bronze seem poised to launch into plummy soliloquies like actors in the wings. Parliament, too, is known for its occasional dramas. Make no mistake about it; this area is London's theatre of state.

This walk begins at Embankment Tube Station and ends at Parliament Square (nearest Tube stop: Westminster.) Walking distance is about 1.2 miles (2 kilometres).

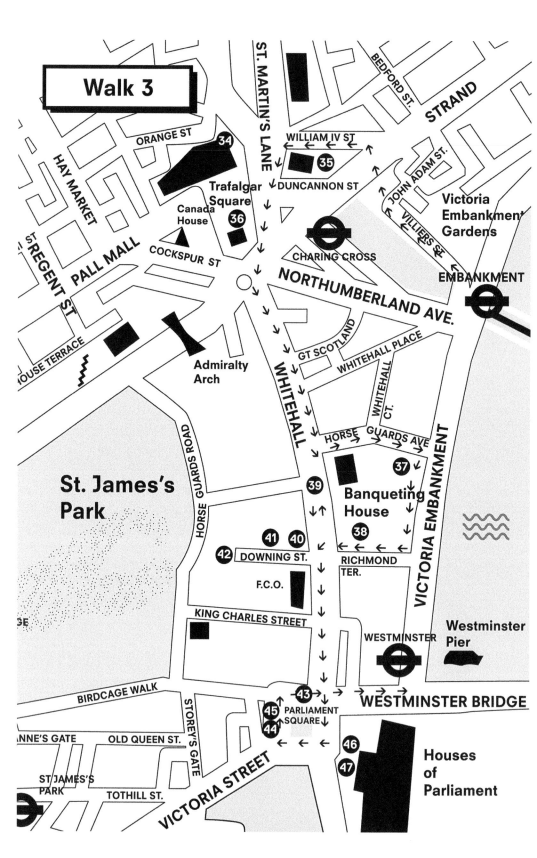

DISCOVERIES

A SHORT HISTORY OF THE AREA

In medieval London, the village of Charing Cross lay just outside the Tudor palace of Whitehall, a ramshackle maze of buildings and court-yards dating from 1514 and sandwiched between the River Thames and St. James's Park. The origin of the name Charing is a matter of dispute. It may take its name from either French (*chère reine* for dear queen), a reference to Queen Eleanor (1241–1290), wife of King Edward I (1239–1307; reigned from 1272), whose funeral cortege rested here for the night, or more likely from Anglo-Saxon (*cerr*) meaning a turn or bend in the river. In either case, the village lay on an important ancient road that ran from the city of London through Whitehall Palace to Westminster Abbey.

From its earliest days, Charing Cross has been associated with demonstrations and dissent. In Tudor times, this is where dangerous rebellions gathered and, during the English civil war and its aftermath, where beheadings took place. It's ironic today that Trafalgar Square continues to be a site of protest for anyone with a modern axe to grind, so to speak. In the 1800s, demonstrators included anti-machine Luddites and suffragettes; in the century that followed they were Welsh miners, Irish nationalists and just about everyone else.

Whitehall Palace, on the other hand, was a place where swords and dissent were forbidden. It was originally occupied by Cardinal Thomas Wolsey (ca.1475–1530), an influential mover and shaker in the Tudor world who lived lavishly for a man of the cloth: his "fayre house," made of white stone, stretched over 22 acres (nine hectares) from Northumberland Street to Downing Street. When Wolsey fell from favour for failing to convince the Pope to grant a divorce to King Henry VIII (1491–1547; reigned from 1509) in 1529, the king confiscated Whitehall and the rest of Wolsey's property. Perhaps to impress his subsequent five royal wives, Henry made numerous home improvements to Whitehall, including the addition of tennis courts, galleries, a bowling alley, and a cockpit. When he finally stopped building, the palace was said to contain 2,000 rooms. In one of these an exhausted Henry Tudor died in 1547.

Trafalgar Square is a much more recent addition to the area. Once a royal stable yard, it was cleared for a public square in 1830 by John Nash (1752–1835), the architect behind Regent Street and St. James's Park. Nash didn't live long enough to see it completed, however, and the lion's share of the work fell to his successor, the architect Sir Charles Barry (1795–1860). Barry battled city officials to lower the elevation of the square to make the National Gallery appear larger and more grand. He battled against the blight of Nelson's column too, but lost.[1]

THE WALK

Exit Embankment Underground Station on the side of Villiers Street. To our right hidden from view is Victoria Embankment Gardens, a lovely if often crowded place to relax near the river when the weather cooperates. The Victoria Embankment runs 1.5 miles (2.4 kilometres) from Blackfriars Bridge to Westminster Bridge. It was designed from reclaimed land in the 1860s by Sir Joseph Bazalgette (1819–91) to accommodate one of London's first major sewers. The York Watergate found in the park was constructed in 1626 and was once a private entranceway on the edge of the old riverbank. A weathered crest on it is that of the local Villiers family.

George Villiers (1592–1628), 1st Duke of Buckingham, was a court favourite associated with two successive monarchs: King James I

> A great sleepiness lies on Vancouver as compared with an American town; men don't fly up and down the street telling lies, and the spittoons in the delightfully comfortable hotel are unused....
>
> — RUDYARD KIPLING, 1899

(1566–1625, reigned from 1603) and his son King Charles I (1600–49, reigned from 1625). King James famously bragged "Christ had his John, and I have my George."[2] Villiers lived in a house that once stood here. The narrow lane that runs alongside the subterranean Gordon's Wine Bar is Watergate Walk, once a waterfront promenade.

Walk up Villiers Street, a busy commercial area lined with food shops for city commuters. In 1889–91, Rudyard Kipling (1865–1936), the Nobel Prize-winning poet and author of *The Jungle Book* and other stories, lived at number 43 (at the time number 19), above what was then Harris the Sausage King. Although Kipling married an American, he preferred Canada to the U.S. He visited Vancouver three times but failed miserably at the local pastime: real estate speculation.

Trivia: *In 1922, Rudyard Kipling devised the initiation for professional engineers in Canada, known as the "Kipling Ritual." During the ceremony, new graduates are presented with an iron ring to symbolize humility and pride in their profession.*

At the top of Villiers Street we come to the Strand, which runs from Trafalgar Square to the west and to Fleet Street in the historic City of London to the east. The Strand is the Old English name for shore. On our left, in the forecourt of the railway station, is the ornate cross that gives the area its name.

Cross over the Strand by Charing Cross at Duncannon Street. Ascend the pedestrian walkway past a ghoulish monument to Oscar Wilde (1854–1900) and turn left on William IV Street at the Post Office. At the next corner is a 1920 marble memorial by Sir George Frampton to the British nurse Edith Cavell (1865–1915), who was shot during the First World War for helping British and Allied soldiers escape German-occupied Belgium. The execution of the patriotic Cavell (rhymes with gravel) enraged the Allies. Many newborn girls were named Edith as a mark of respect (among them the French singer Edith Piaf). In Canada we did one better and named a mountain after her (Mount Edith Cavell in Jasper National Park).

Just beyond Cavell's monument is the National Portrait Gallery. It opened in 1896 and displays the faces of Britain's most accomplished men and women. Originally, only the portraits of those who had been dead ten years or more were displayed, but in the permissive 1960s this and many other rules were relaxed. Today, you'll find more current celebrity faces here than on a magazine rack at Chapter's. For this reason some unkind locals have dubbed it "Madame Tussaud's for the middle classes."

The gallery houses some 160,000 portraits, though thankfully for those with limited time only a portion are on view. Many of the figures portrayed played a part in Canada's history. It's a shame visitors have to come halfway around the world to see them here rather

Trivia: *Sir Christopher Ondaatje was born in Kandy, Sri Lanka, and emigrated to Canada when he was twenty-two. He took to winters like Maurice Richard to ice and won gold for Canada at the 1964 Innsbruck Winter Olympics in the team bobsled event. He went on to make his fortune in finance.*

than in our own national portrait gallery. With luck, someday this may change.

Just beyond the gallery's revolving front doors is the Ondaatje Wing. It's named not after the Canadian novelist Michael Ondaatje (b. 1943) but his older brother and gallery benefactor, the financial tycoon Sir Christopher Ondaatje (b. 1933).

Now every country arguably has its own Mona Lisa or defining painting. In Britain, the equivalent is found here in the National Portrait Gallery. In 1856, Francis Egerton (1800–57), 1st Earl of Ellesmere, donated his famous portrait of the playwright William Shakespeare (ca.1564–1616). It's known as the Chandos portrait or

Will the real Bard please stand up? The Sanders portrait of William Shakespeare is the Canadian contender in the great "battle of wills" to find a likeness of the famous playwright.

simply as "NPG1." For years, this pirate-like figure with a gold earring was believed to be the truest painted likeness of the Bard. But in 2002 a rival from Canada appeared on the scene to rattle Britain's Shakespeare establishment. It challenged mainstream opinion about who Shakespeare was — or, perhaps more accurately, the notion that we will ever really know.

National Portrait Gallery: *Move Over Will Shakespeare*

Nobody knows if Shakespeare ever sat for a portrait, but as a successful and wealthy poet and playwright in Elizabethan England, it is possible, nay probable, that he did. Of the likenesses that exist, only a line drawing published in his complete works and a plump funeral bust in Stratford-upon-Avon are thought to be the most credible as they were likely supervised by people who knew him. The trouble is both are cartoonish and lack depth. Lovers of Shakespeare crave more.

Thus the search for a portrait of Shakespeare began. Over the years, a number of contenders have emerged from flea markets and family estates. Of these, six portraits are thought to be the most worthy as they can be traced back more or less to the poet's lifetime. None, however, is categorically the real McCoy.

The world of Shakespeare went topsy-turvy in 2002 when Lloyd Sullivan, a retired engineer and part-time bus driver from Ottawa, Ontario, went public with an old family heirloom: a painting dated 1603 known as the Sanders portrait of Shakespeare. Sullivan says this likeness was painted by his ancestor John Sanders. The painting came to Canada from Britain in 1919. Unlike the other portraits, his doesn't depict a balding, accomplished gentleman but rather a young, rakish man with reddish-brown hair and a wry, knowing smile.

While detractors say the image is much too young to be the Bard in 1603, when he was thirty-nine and middle aged for the times, the painting has caused a lot of fuss. First, it has a long family history and can be traced to Shakespeare's lifetime. Uniquely among the main contenders, it also comes with a label. This is of similar age to the portrait and uses the spelling "Shakspere," which the Bard himself used. It is also dated 1603, a fact confirmed by tests. Researchers have also linked Sullivan's family to the Bard's, suggesting a plausible reason for the Sullivans to possess such a portrait in the first place.

But perhaps the oddest argument in favour of the Canadian contender is the sitter's left ear. If the line engraving of Shakespeare found in his published works is the accepted lifetime likeness, then Shakespeare had attached earlobes. Sullivan's Canadian portrait shows this. The Mona Lisa of the NPG doesn't.[3]

Leave the National Portrait Gallery and follow the crowds down St. Martin's Place to Trafalgar Square.

To our left on the southeast side of the square is the colonnaded church St. Martin-in-the-Fields, designed by the Scottish architect James Gibbs

Shakespeare was a savage who had some imagination. He has written many happy lines; but his plays can only please in London and in Canada.

— French philosopher François-Marie Voltaire, 1765

(1682–1754). Gibbs trained to be a priest in Rome but switched to more earthly pursuits after he fell in love with baroque architecture. In 1709, he came to London to practise his trade and was mentored by the extraordinary architect Christopher Wren (1632–1723).

Look at St. Martin's and you'll see an ornate, wedding-cake steeple set on top of a Roman temple. Gibbs was as famous for his steeples as he was for where he put them. Before Gibbs, steeples were usually attached to churches at the side or front. But St. Martin-in-the-Fields is interesting for another reason: it's the most copied church in Canada and the United States.

In 1728, Gibbs published his design for St. Martin-in-the-Fields and other churches in a celebrated work called *A Book of Architecture*. It was a sort of emblem of respectability with British settlers in North America. But these migrants didn't just display the book on their coffee tables for visitors to admire. They built what was in it.

One of these settlers was likely Governor Edward Cornwallis (ca.1712–76), the founder of Halifax, Nova Scotia, who came to Canada in 1749.[4] Certainly, St. Paul's Church in Halifax, which dates from 1750 and is the oldest surviving Anglican church in Canada, was heavily influenced by Gibbs's book. So too were the Charlotte County Court House in St. Andrews, New Brunswick, and many other buildings in Canada. But the most striking copy of St. Martin-in-the Fields can be found in the heart of French Canada. If visitors to Quebec City think the Cathedral of the Holy Trinity seems oddly out of place, it was designed to be.

Imitation, they say, is the best form of flattery: St. Martin-in-the-Fields by the architect James Gibbs is the most widely copied church in North America.

St. Martin-in-the-Fields: *A Church for All Seasons?*

After the fall of New France, Canada's new British rulers wanted their citizens to embrace Protestantism. But the more pressing need to keep French Canadians loyal during the American Revolution delayed their religious zeal. With the war lost, in 1793 they forged ahead with their plans and created an Anglican diocese for Upper and Lower Canada based in Quebec City.

The man chosen to head the new diocese was a proud and uncompromising Norfolk vicar named Jacob Mountain (1749–1825). In 1793, he was consecrated bishop at Lambeth Palace in London and sent to Quebec. When he discovered to his horror that his new congregation worshipped in a Roman Catholic church amid "crucifixes, images and pictures of saints," he set about quickly building his own.[5]

Mountain determined that nothing about his new Anglican cathedral — workmen, materials, nor design — would be French. So he built the most English church he could lay his fingers on: Gibbs's St. Martin-in-the-Fields.[6] But it was French Canadians who enjoyed the last laugh. St. Martin's may have been a symbol of Quebec's new rulers, but it was poorly designed for Quebec's winters. Maybe if Mountain had followed the building codes of the *Ancien Régime* and kept the pitch of his new roof to a steep angle, he might have saved his cathedral some trouble. No sooner was his cathedral finished when he had to redo the roof to keep it from collapsing from the weight of snow. It was a lesson French Canadian builders — but evidently not London architects — knew only too well.

When Mountain died in 1825, he was buried under the chancel of his beloved cathedral. His epitaph said he was the "Founder of the Church of England in the Canada," but in many ways Wren's epitaph in St. Paul's Cathedral would have been equally fitting: "If you seek his memorial, look around you."

Now let's head into Trafalgar Square, the vast tribute to Britain's sea power, keeping to the left side. At one time you would have dodged traffic to do this but in 2003 a large pedestrian terrace was created in front of the National Gallery as part of a redevelopment of the square.

During an earlier redevelopment in 1939, Barry's original red-granite fountains, admired by Londoners for a hundred years, were removed and re-gifted to Canada. They now splutter 1,400 miles (2,200 kilometres) apart: one in Regina and the other in Ottawa.

Nelson's column dedicated to Vice-Admiral Horatio Nelson (1758–1805), 1st Viscount Nelson, who died at the Battle of Trafalgar, towers in front of us.

Although a naval genius, Nelson was rash, cruel, and famously short-tempered. He was also very hot-blooded. "Pray do not let your fascinating Neapolitan dames approach too near him for he is made of flesh and blood and cannot

resist their temptation," a naval official once warned the wife of the British ambassador in Naples to no avail.[8] It was a pattern of destructive behaviour that may have first manifested itself in Canada.

Nelson Monument: *Fair Canada, and Fairer Mary Simpson*

In April 1782, Nelson was ordered to escort a convoy of ships to resupply the British garrison at Quebec City. He didn't want to go. Small, thin, and often unwell, the young Nelson worried the cold North Atlantic climate would do him more harm than good. He was right. When his fleet arrived in Newfoundland, the cold, thick fog penetrated to his very bones with a numbing chill. Compounded by scurvy, his health deteriorated.[9]

Quebec City, however, offered a welcome respite from damp St. John's. On his arrival inland, Nelson wrote to his father: "Health, that greatest of blessings, is what I never truly enjoyed until I saw Fair Canada. The change it has wrought I am convinced is truly wonderful."

Nelson's change of heart wasn't just due to a change in the weather. At a garrison ball, Nelson set sights on young Mary Simpson, the daughter of the provost-marshal of Quebec. Simpson was a striking girl, attractive and well-educated and about two years Nelson's junior. It wasn't long before this flesh-and-blood man was ready to abandon the Royal Navy for the woman he loved. "I find it utterly impossible to leave this place without waiting on her whose society has so much added to its charms and laying myself and my fortunes at her feet," he reputedly said.[10]

It's folly but fun to imagine what might have happened if Nelson, who ultimately vanquished Napoleon at sea in 1805, had followed his heart and settled in Canada. Would we now be standing in Trafalgar Square or *Place de l'Empereur*? Alas, no wedding bells chimed for Nelson and his Quebec City belle. While ascending the steep streets from Lower Town to propose to her, Nelson was persuaded against his folly by a friend. He gave up his pursuit and sailed with his ship before the ice set in on the river. He never saw his first love, Mary Simpson, again.[11]

Before we leave Trafalgar Square, let's fast forward to the twentieth century. As a young correspondent for Radio-Canada, the future premier of Quebec, René Lévesque (1922–87), stood here to report on the coronation of Queen Elizabeth II in June 1953. Before the state coach passed on its way to Westminster Abbey, Lévesque filled five hours of radio time for French listeners back home. "What followed was one of the great performances in the history of radio," he recalled. "Never had so much work been done for so little."[12]

Now let's make our way down the left side of Whitehall.

At the Banqueting House follow Horse Guards Avenue down to the River Thames, past the modern Ministry of Defence building completed in 1951. After a short walk we arrive back at the Victoria Embankment. Excavated in the grass behind the ministry are the Whitehall Palace steps that once led down to the river. It is believed that Cardinal Thomas Wolsey went down steps like these when he abandoned his home for King Henry VIII in 1529. So too did the executioner of King Charles I in 1649 with his axe.[13]

Near the Whitehall steps is a bronze statue by the sculptor Sir William Thornycroft of Major-General Charles Gordon (1833–85). This nineteenth-century British hero holds a bible under one arm and rests his foot on a cannon. Gordon was a half-mad Christian soldier with icy blue eyes and wildly eccentric beliefs. His statue originally stood in Trafalgar Square but now languishes here largely forgotten, but not by us.

Trivia: *Field Marshal Sir Garnet Wolseley was the inspiration behind Gilbert and Sullivan's "model of a modern major general." A statue of Sir Garnet stands across Whitehall in Horse Guards Parade.*

In early 1884, Gordon was sent to evacuate Egyptian forces loyal to Britain in Sudan. He was supposed to accomplish this mission peacefully but things didn't go according to plan. When he and his forces became trapped by rebels in Khartoum, he took up arms to defend the city rather than abandon it. British voters called out for his rescue and the government reluctantly agreed.

Now what you might ask has Canada got to do with a wayward crusader in faraway Africa? Prime Minister Sir John A. Macdonald (1815–91) wondered that too. When Britain called for soldiers across the British Empire to rescue Gordon, Canada's "Old Tomorrow" declined to get involved. But that didn't stop some citizens from going.

To rescue Gordon, the British Government appointed Field Marshal Sir Garnet Wolseley (1833–1913), at the time the most famous soldier in Britain and widely believed to be the only man up to the task. That's because some fifteen years earlier, Wolseley had led a dramatic 620-mile (1,000-kilometre) expedition up the Red River in Manitoba to put down Louis Riel's rebellion at Fort Garry (now Winnipeg).

Wolseley believed the fastest route to Gordon was by another river, the Nile — and the only people who could get him there were the hearty voyageurs he had relied on so ably in Canada. The fact the two rivers were very different didn't concern him. "Water is water," he said blithely. The Gordon Relief Expedition to Africa in 1884–85 would become the first overseas expedition undertaken by Canadians.

Gordon Monument: *Canadians to Khartoum!*

The hardy Canadian voyageurs who had paddled Wolseley up the Red River in 1870 were, by 1884, a vanishing breed. The railroad had put many out of work and those who had kept paddling Canadian rivers were getting a bit long in the tooth. "The Red River men naturally are rather past their prime," responded an official in Ottawa to Wolseley's request for his old crew. Instead, the official advertised for lumbermen who worked on the Ottawa, Gatineau, and Saguenay rivers: "Good boatmen to accompany English Expedition up the Nile, to steer boats through the rapids and do all necessary portaging," it said.[14]

For the boatmen, the opportunity of a six-month contract and foreign adventure to Africa was too good to pass up. Within a month, some 400 volunteers were on their way to Egypt, including one as old as sixty-four. They hailed from Ottawa, Winnipeg, Trois Rivières, Sherbrooke, and the Kahnawake territory on the St. Lawrence River. At the helm was thirty-seven-year-old Frederick Denison (1846–96), a wealthy Toronto lawyer, politician, and veteran of the Red River Campaign. "What with Canadian men, Canadian officers, Canadian clothing, and the best Canadian tobacco, Gordon is safe," proclaimed the *Hamilton Times*.[15]

But for all his confidence, Wolseley had badly misjudged the situation. For starters, the cataracts on the Nile came in quick succession and the current was so strong the men rowed for hours without advancing. Nor were Denison's men the cheery voyageurs who had paddled to Fort Garry singing songs. They were a rough and argumentative lot and it wasn't long before many got fed up and went home, leaving only a handful to haul the boats the rest of the way. This little group struggled for three months longer until the terrible news reached them: upriver Khartoum had fallen and Gordon was dead.

A year after it had begun, what remained of the Gordon rescue expedition returned home. Denison and his men were feted as heroes and Wolseley, like many military embarrassments, was promoted. Inside, however, he knew his status as Britain's modern major-general was not only tarnished but over.

Walk through the gardens and return to Whitehall via Richmond Terrace.

In the middle of Whitehall is the memorial to the Women of the Second World War (2005), which echoes the Cenotaph a bit farther

---

The Dominion of Canada supplied us with a most useful body of boatmen. Their skill in the management of boats in difficult and dangerous waters was of the utmost use to us in our long ascent of the Nile.

— Major-General Sir Garnet Wolseley[16]

---

down the street. However, unlike the Cenotaph, this memorial isn't decorated with flags but with the uniforms and working clothes worn by women. On our immediate left in front of the Ministry of Defence is Raleigh Green, where a statue of Sir Walter Raleigh (ca.1552–1618) can be found. A number of other statues here continue our military theme.

Trivia: *Sir Walter Raleigh, the famous pirate and privateer under Queen Elizabeth I, raided St. John's, Newfoundland, in 1618, on his way to the West Indies. He plundered food, ammunition, and men for his ships.[17]*

Our interest is a 1980 bronze statue of Field Marshal Bernard Montgomery (1887–1976), 1st Viscount Montgomery of Alamein, wearing his characteristic military beret. The statue is by the Croatia-born artist Oscar Nemon (1906–85) whose statue of Winston Churchill stands near Toronto's City Hall.

As an outstanding but difficult military leader, Montgomery was the man every soldier loved to hate. In the Second World War, he led Canadian troops in Italy, Sicily, and France. His admiration for Canadian soldiers,

British General Bernard Montgomery, or "Monty" to his troops. He was so austere he could have been a monk.

however, was matched only by his contempt for their commanders.

Montgomery Monument: *Monty's Hit Parade*

General Bernard Montgomery, or "Monty" as he was popularly known, was so austere he could have been a monk. But he was also vain, nasty, and an outright liar — attributes which ruled out a career in the church, in theory at least. Instead, he joined the army and rose right to the top. When he took charge of South-Eastern Command during the Second World War, he put Canadian soldiers on a strict physical regime — and their commanders too. He gave the boot to those who didn't live up to his expectations.

"I hope to be sending Price back to you," Montgomery wrote slyly to Ottawa about one Canadian commander and former dairy farmer who didn't make the grade. "He will be of great value in Canada where his knowledge of the milk industry will help on the national war effort."[18]

Monty was particularly disenchanted with Canada's General Andrew McNaughton (1887–1966). He believed the assertive McNaughton lacked the necessary mettle and experience in the field and is thought to have colluded with his colleague Field Marshal Sir Alan Brooke (1883–1963), 1st Viscount Alanbrooke (whose statue stands nearby) to have Ottawa recall the Canadian. Instead, a badgered McNaughton retired in 1943.

But Montgomery got more than he bargained for next. McNaughton was replaced by General Harry Crerar (1888–1965), a Canadian who had more battle experience than McNaughton — and more pluck. Crerar may have been "no ball of fire" in Monty's eyes but he knew at least what he was up against. An officer had warned him Monty was "an efficient little shit."[19]

Predictably, it wasn't long before that efficiency hit the fan. When Crerar declined a meeting with Montgomery in order to attend a memorial ser-vice at Dieppe, Montgomery flew into a rage. He called Crerar's absence insubordination. But the Canuck wouldn't be bullied. "There was a powerful Canadian reason why I should have been present at Dieppe that day," Crerar said with the full backing of the Canadian Government. "In fact, there were 800 reasons — the Canadian dead buried at Dieppe Cemetery."[20]

Walk a few steps back up Whitehall toward the Banqueting House. Near to it is a controversial equestrian statue by Alfred Hardiman of an equally controversial equestrian general. This is the hatless Field Marshal Sir Douglas Haig (1861–1928), 1st Earl Haig, commander-in-chief of British and Empire troops in the First World War. His command included some 620,000 Canadian soldiers, about one in ten of

I fear he thinks he is a great soldier and he was determined to show it from the moment he took over command at 1200hrs on July 23. He made his first mistake at 1205 hrs; and his second after lunch.

— British General Bernard Montgomery on Canadian General Harry Crerar[21]

whom never returned from the war. If Haig died a military hero, it wasn't long before his detractors accused him of incompetence causing the loss of untold lives in France.

General Douglas Haig, supreme commander of British and Canadian troops in the First World War. One in ten Canadian soldiers never came home.

Haig Monument: *All the King's Men*

Douglas Haig was a twentieth-century general schooled in nineteenth-century warfare. As a young cavalry officer, he had fought in Sudan and South Africa and unfailingly believed that men and horses could beat machine guns. To many, this belief epitomized his failure to grasp the realities of modern warfare.

For Canadians, Haig was both hero and villain. While he sometimes supported the able Sir Arthur Currie (1875–1933), the leader of the Canadian forces, the two men were often at odds over how Canadians should be deployed. This was particularly true over the third Battle of Ypres, also known as Passchendaele.

In July 1917, Haig launched a third offensive against the enemy near the Flemish town of Ypres. The aim was to break the well-defended German line and then use cavalry to rush for the Belgium coast. The battle forever cast Haig as a commander who was stubborn, aloof, and insensitive to human loss.

The Ypres battlefield was a low stretch of ground reclaimed from the sea by dykes. After heavy rain and bombardments, the terrain became nothing but mud. For weeks British, Australian, and New Zealand troops fought the enemy with limited gains. In a final and frenzied effort to achieve victory, Haig ordered the Canadians to finish the job.

Currie didn't agree. He warned Haig it would cost three-quarters of his men, but the supreme commander wouldn't listen. "We ought to have only one thought now in our minds, namely to attack," he said.

After horrific fighting, the Canadians miraculously broke through. Yet some 16,000 men died in the attempt and countless more were wounded. Overall, Haig's victory claimed nearly 250,000 casualties on the British side. Obstinate as always, he never visited the carnage, though one of his senior army officers did. He wept as his boots sank deep into the muck. "My God," he said. "Did we really send men to fight in this?"[22]

Trivia: *In 1924, Field Marshal Earl Haig, commander-in-chief of British and Empire forces, unveiled the National War Memorial to Newfoundland's war dead in St. John's.*

Turn and retrace your steps down Whitehall to Richmond Terrace. Down the street is the Cenotaph. The simple stone monument (cenotaph means empty grave in Greek) was erected in 1920 to commemorate those who died in the First World War. It is decorated with flags of the three services as well as the merchant marine. Sir Fabian Ware (1869–1949), founder of the Commonwealth War Graves Commission, once calculated that if the dead of Britain and the Empire in the First World War were to march four abreast down

> **Trivia:** *John McCrae (1872–1918), a Canadian army doctor, influenced the poppy's adoption as a symbol of war remembrance with his poem "In Flanders Fields."*

Whitehall, they would take three and a half days to pass this monument. Over 60,000 of those dead marchers were Canadians.

Across the street at 70 Whitehall is the Cabinet Office, which coordinates government policy. It stands on the site of an old amphitheatre used in Tudor times for fighting cocks. The buildings constructed here afterward were familiarly known as the Cockpit. In March 1711, this was the scene of an assassination attempt with a surprising outcome for Canada.

70 Whitehall: *A Hawk Makes His Move*

Robert Harley (1661–1724), 1st Earl of Oxford, and Henry St. John (1678–1751), 1st Viscount Bolingbroke, were Tory politicians with big egos and cunning to match. Outwardly friends, in reality they were crocodiles and deep political rivals. During the War of the Spanish Succession with France (1702–13), Harley and St. John (pronounced sin-gin) occupied the most important posts in Queen Anne's government: chief minister and war secretary, respectively. Together they faced mounting pressure to end the war with France but just how to do that set them at odds: Harley was a moderate and St. John a war hawk.

One day in 1711 Harley arrested a French émigré and well-known intriguer named Antoine de Guiscard in St. James's Park. Guiscard had been a spy for the English but intercepted letters incriminated him as a double agent now working for the French. Harley had him brought to the Cockpit in Whitehall for questioning. St. John was there too.

As the interrogation ended, Guiscard lunged with a penknife at Harley, wounding him in the chest. Harley might have been more seriously hurt had he not worn several protective layers of clothing to stay warm. Still he bled profusely and sent word bravely to his sister not to keep dinner waiting for him.[23]

With Harley temporarily out of commission, St. John made his move. He swiftly set in motion a daring plan to end the war with France by launching an assault on Quebec with 5,000 of England's best troops. The intent was to capture the French fortress and use it to sue for peace. For the daring mission St. John chose Sir Hovenden Walker and Colonel John Hill, elevating the latter to rank of general. But as we discovered on Walk 1, St. John's plan proved a disaster: the ships foundered in the St. Lawrence and 900 men drowned. When Harley recovered, the queen granted him an earldom for his bravery — but St. John was left empty-handed.[24]

Trivia: *Sir Robert Walpole (1676–1745) was Britain's longest-serving prime minister. He served twenty years and 314 days. Canada's Prime Minister W.L. Mackenzie King (1874–1950) broke Walpole's record — serving twenty-one years in office — and remains the longest-serving PM in the Commonwealth.*

Immediately next is Downing Street. In 1735, King George II (1683–1760; reigned from 1727) granted the house at number 10 to Sir Robert Walpole (1676–1745), who was effectively prime minister. It has been home to British prime ministers ever since.

When Prime Minister Margaret Thatcher (1925–2013) came to power in 1979 on a wave of industrial unrest in Britain, she hardly could have predicted that a former colony like Canada would stall her plans to reform the country. But the patriation of Canada's constitution in 1980–82 threatened to do just that. How Canada's pirouetting prime minister duped the "Iron Lady" is our next discovery in London.

10 Downing Street: *The Downing Street Double-Cross*

On June 25, 1980, Prime Minister Pierre Trudeau arrived at 10 Downing Street to have lunch with Prime Minister Thatcher. Their politics and backgrounds couldn't have been more different: she was a steely conservative grocer's daughter focused on East-West tensions and he was a flamboyant social democrat focused on the North-South divide.

On the luncheon menu that day were Trudeau's plans to amend Canada's constitution — known as the British North America Act of 1867 — and bring it home from Britain. Trudeau needed Thatcher's support because only the British Government could amend an Act of the British Parliament. Although Thatcher expressed concern that this might slow down her own Tory agenda she agreed, convinced by Trudeau it would be a simple matter. He left Downing Street beaming; she would later claim being tricked.

As the constitutional wrangling between Ottawa and the provinces dragged on in 1980–81, it became clear that passing Canada's new constitution in Britain would be anything but straightforward. For one thing, many British MPs, encouraged by the lobbying of Quebec and others, threatened to take up valuable parliamentary time and stall Thatcher's own legislative program. Nor had Trudeau mentioned between the courses that he might act unilaterally without the consent of the provinces. When British MPs expressed concerns about this, Trudeau told them to just hold their noses and pass his bill.

But what really upset the Iron Lady was Canada's revolutionary Charter of Rights and Freedoms. Trudeau had not mentioned this to Thatcher, perhaps knowing it might spell trouble for her government, which opposed anything remotely *French*. The thought of Trudeau's double-cross made her fume. "Do you have any idea what your prime minister told me?" she told an unnerved Albertan official. "He wanted my assurance it would go through quickly but he never mentioned a bill of rights!" She asked two of Trudeau's ministers who were visiting the same thing: How could she support a charter of rights when British Tories were fundamentally against one?[25]

In the end, Trudeau's constitution did get passed and Maggie carried on with her handbagging of British unions. On a rainy April 17, 1982, Queen Elizabeth II signed Canada's new constitution and, as queen of Canada, acquired legal protection she lacked in Britain: Canada's Charter of Rights and Freedoms.

If you peer through the security gates to the end of Downing Street you will see a wall, beyond which is St. James's Park. Long ago, a rundown and obscure row house stood here that was, from Canada's perspective, perhaps more important than the celebrated "Number 10." It was 14 Downing Street — the old Colonial Office — where a clutch of Dickensian scribes administered Canada and the rest of the British Empire until the building was torn down in 1876. No place was more maligned by those demanding self-government in Canada than this damp and dreary little office that once ruled from the heart of Whitehall.

14 Downing Street: *The Old Colonial Office*

A Canadian visitor to London in the early 1800s would have been surprised to discover that they and the rest of the people in the British Empire were ruled mostly out of a shabby little building at the end of a cul-de-sac. The old Colonial Office was the main link between Canada and Britain. "Only in England," an amazed official wrote, "could an important government department be housed in nothing more than a decent lodging house."[26]

If its outward appearance left much to be desired, so did its interior. The building was a cramped, unkempt space that was so damp stoves had to burn year-round just to keep the heaps of papers dry. On the upper floors, dozens of well-meaning but indifferent bachelor scribes waited for dispatches to arrive from far-flung colonies. They would then set about registering, copying, annotating, and — in the fullness of time — maybe even answering them.

Yet the daily, unhurried routines of these faceless civil servants ran a quarter of the world's population. They appointed governors and bishops, approved local laws and managed commerce and shipping. Colonial Reformers in Canada railed against this centralized control by Britain and demanded more autonomy. Workhouses for the poor were better administered, they claimed. After the rebellions in Canada in 1837–38, change did come about slowly, first in Canada, then in the rest of the British Empire.

Even after Confederation in 1867, the Colonial Office still exerted influence over Canada but it was increasingly more distant and out of touch. This was certainly the case when the Liberal politician Edward Blake (1833–1912) paid a courtesy call. Blake was a bitter political rival of Sir John A. Macdonald's who had forced the prime minister's resignation three years earlier over influence peddling. Sitting in the waiting room at the Colonial Office, Blake was met by a badly briefed official who greeted him cheerily with: "Well, I hope our friend Sir John Macdonald is getting along all right!"[27]

Continuing down Whitehall, the next building on our right is the Foreign and Commonwealth Office (or "FCO"), an Italianate palace built in 1861–68 to house the country's diplomatic service. It was designed by the architect Sir George Gilbert Scott (1811–78). He would have preferred to build something in the Gothic style but in this part of town, even architecture is political. Gothicism was associated with the Tories and they were swept from power just before the FCO was built. So Scott revised his plans along more classical lines for the new kids in town.

The next building on our right between King Charles Street and Parliament Square is H.M. Treasury. At the back are the Cabinet War Rooms, built in 1936 to provide secure offices in the event of war. This warren of small, windowless rooms beneath thick concrete is much the same as when Prime Minister Sir Winston Churchill (1874–1965), his War Cabinet and others used these rooms during the Second World War. It's a fascinating place to visit with an excellent display on Churchill himself. It's well worth a few hours to explore now or at the end of our walk.

At the end of Whitehall, we come to the Houses of Parliament. Cross over Westminster Bridge Road and into Parliament Square. The first memorial we come to depicts

> **Trivia:** *Sir George Gilbert Scott designed the Anglican Cathedral of St. John the Baptist in St. John's, Newfoundland, in his much preferred Gothic style.*[28]

the incomparable Churchill himself. The son of an English aristocrat and American heiress, Churchill was a soldier, war correspondent, writer, and member of Parliament before becoming prime minister in the dark days of 1940. The 1973 bronze statue by Ivor Roberts-Jones depicts the wartime leader in a long military coat walking toward Westminster Bridge. His stern look of determination both inspired and embodied Britain's bulldog spirit in the face of German Nazism.

Although Canadians universally admired Churchill, Prime Minister William Lyon Mackenzie King (1874–1950) was much less enthusiastic. In terms of character, upbringing, and political style, the two leaders were such complete opposites that they could have been nicknamed Oscar and Felix, or the Second World War's Odd Couple.

Churchill Monument: *Oscar and Felix Say Goodbye*

On his last visit to London in 1948, an ailing Mackenzie King took to his bed at the Dorchester Hotel in Mayfair. A steady stream of dignitaries came to see him there, including the king, the prime ministers of Britain and India, and two London clairvoyants.

Churchill was the last to arrive, smoking a large cigar as usual. "I assume Mr. King will not object if I smoke while we are together?" he asked a Canadian diplomat at the hotel room door. Churchill had known King for nearly fifty years and likely knew his intolerance to such vices. The request terrified the diplomat. "I am afraid, Mr. Churchill, that Mr. King's doctors have said smoke might have an injurious effect on his heart condition," he lied. Churchill scowled his famous scowl. "Watch it," he said placing his cigar in an ashtray, and went in to see King for the last time.[30]

Although the same age, the two old warriors were oceans apart in character: Churchill was a gregarious titan who dreamed big, took risks, and drank famously — starting with a half a bottle of champagne every day. By contrast, the only spirits King tolerated were summoned at séances. He was a superstitious and cautious incrementalist who didn't do anything by halves that he could do by quarters.

British prime minister Winston Churchill's statue in front of Parliament. He and Canadian prime minister W.L. Mackenzie King were such an odd pair they could have been cast in a Neil Simon play.

Indeed, their differences were probably at the root of King's first suspicions about the British politician. "It is a serious business having matters in the hand of a man like Churchill," he said early in their acquaintance. On the night Churchill became prime minister, King confided to his trusty diary: "I think Winston Churchill is one of [the] most dangerous men I have ever known."[31]

Churchill never recorded his own views about King, but likely thought him timid and cowardly, especially after Canada signed up to a mutual defence pact with the United States during Britain's bleakest hour in the Second World War. But if politics makes strange bedfellows, war makes even odder friends. Near the end of his life, King ultimately confided to his diary: "I felt that perhaps in more respects than one, he was the greatest man of our times."[32]

Now let's move to the leafy western edge of Parliament Square. Most of the notable statesmen here belong to the nineteenth century but a few hail from more recent times, including two from South Africa: its leader in the Second World War, Jan Smuts (1870–1950), and its first democratically elected president, Nelson Mandela (1918–2013). Canada granted Mandela honorary citizenship in 2001 for his moral leadership and role in bringing about a peaceful end to apartheid in South Africa after serving twenty-seven years in prison.

In a sense this leafy part of London could be called Confederation Corner. That's because in nearby Victoria Street Sir John A. Macdonald (1815–91) and other Fathers of Confederation met to finalize the British North America Act in 1866. And several of the statesmen portrayed here in Parliament Square played varying roles in Canada's long road to Confederation.

Let's start with a statesman who wasn't even British: President Abraham Lincoln (1809–65) just across the street. Lincoln's statue is by the noted American sculptor Augustus Saint-Gaudens and is a copy of one found in Chicago.

Trivia: *Canada's Prime Minister W.L. Mackenzie King often complained Winston Churchill kept him in the dark. On June 6, 1944, an RCMP officer woke King to tell him the invasion of Normandy had begun. The officer had learned about it on the radio.*[33]

Honest Abe may seem the odd man out among this pantheon of Commonwealth parliamentarians. For Canadians, however, he reminds us of a big reason behind Canada's Confederation in 1867: the threat of U.S. invasion. At one-million strong, Lincoln's Union Army emerged from the U.S. Civil War in 1865 as the largest military force in the world. Many believed it might march north right into Canada.

The fear wasn't unjustified. England relied on the South's cotton plantations to feed its industrial cotton mills and many of its merchants backed the South. Some in Canada did too. Although Lincoln had no interest in Canada, his secretary of state William Seward did. He believed annexing Canada would be a "double victory" for the Union. His views were even popularized to the tune of "Yankee Doodle":

> *Secession first he would put down*
> *Wholly and forever*
> *And afterwards from Britain's crown*
> *He Canada would sever.*[34]

It was a threat Canadians remembered only too well from the War of 1812. Many but not all believed Confederation offered the best chance for survival. "I much doubt whether Confederation will save us from Annexation," one Father of Confederation confessed. "Even [Sir John A.] Macdonald is rapidly feeling as I do."[35]

Now let's look at some of the other political grandees here. At one end is Sir Robert Peel (1788–1850), twice British prime minister in the early 1800s. An old-school Tory, he was nicknamed "Orange Peel" for his anti-Catholic views.

Peel did more to change the *economic* nature of Canada's colonial

The figure of British prime minister Robert Peel, who abolished the Corn Laws favouring trade with the colonies. He hastened Canada's economic independence from Britain.

relationship with Britain than any other leader. When he abolished the empire's preferential trading system, it forced the Canadian colonies to compete against others on a level playing field and in turn helped fan the flames for self-government. It all started with corn.

Peel Monument: *Canada and the Price of Corn*

What British legislators called "corn" was, in fact, grain: barley, rye, and wheat. As a largely farming society in the 1700s, Britain had dozens of laws to protect grain supplies for citizens and prices for farmers. These were known as "Corn Laws" and gave price advantages to local grain and colonial imports. Yet at various times, the laws proved disastrous. In 1815, for example, consumers rioted in the streets of London over prices and smashed the windows of leading politicians.

By the mid-1800s, there was so much broken glass around London that politicians finally got the message. Britain was becoming industrialized and free trade was the new mantra. Factory owners reasoned competition made bread cheaper and fed more workers. But another impetus was the worst harvest on record and the Irish potato famine. In 1846, Peel repealed the Corn Laws and opened British markets to cheap foreign grains from every country.

For Canada, the repeal of the Corn Laws came as a shock. That's because Upper Canada and the Maritimes had benefited from the lower duties on their wheat and timber sold to Britain and had invested heavily in canals to transport it there. The repeal of the Corn Laws meant Canada had to compete against the United States and just about everyone else if it wanted to sell its staples in Britain. The result was an economic depression in Canada. When the economy eventually improved, the colonists saw more reason to manage their own affairs.

Next along the row are monuments to Benjamin Disraeli (1804–81), 1st Earl Beaconsfield and Edward Smith-Stanley (1799–1869), 14th Earl of Derby. In 1866–67, the two Conservatives led a precarious

> *Colonies do not cease to be colonies because they are independent.*
>
> — BENJAMIN DISRAELI, 1863

minority government that came to power when the Whigs were unexpectedly defeated. Derby was prime minister and Disraeli finance minister. They forged ahead with a plan by the Whigs to unite the Canadian provinces mainly to avoid paying to defend them.

Of the two men, Disraeli was the more colourful and flamboyant. He was a political showman who shocked Victorian society by wearing ruffled shirts, velvet trousers, and flashy waistcoats. He was known as a "Big Englander" for his love of empire, but like all politicians could be contradictory at times. He told Lord Derby: "It can never be our pretence or our policy to defend the Canadian frontier against the U.S. ... What is the use of these colonial dead weights *which we do not govern?*"[36]

Lord Derby settled on the name Dominion of Canada. "It is so like Derby," said his colleague Disraeli. "He lives in a region of perpetual funk."

Disraeli's 1883 statue is by the Italian-born sculptor Mario Raggi and depicts the pale leader in his flashy Garter robes and his trademark ringlet hair.

The Earl of Derby, on the other hand, was a dull, Lancashire aristocrat who became Britain's longest-serving leader of the Conservative Party — twenty-two years — and three times prime minister. He made the reluctant Disraeli Chancellor of the Exchequer or finance minister despite his lack of numerical acumen. "Relax. They give you the figures," he reassured Disraeli.

The dull Derby influenced Canada in two ways. First, he was the father of Sir Frederick Arthur Stanley (1841–1908), 16th Earl of Derby, who became governor general of Canada and donated a famous trophy to its national game. Second, he gave his blessing to the original if odd name of the new country.

45

Derby Monument: *Call It Derby, Err Dominion Day*

After putting the final touches on the British North America Act, the only decision that remained for the Canadian delegates to the London Conference in 1866 was what to call their new country.

The name Canada was pretty much a no brainer, especially compared to the alternatives being proposed like Borealia and Albionoria. The harder part was to get across the idea that Canada would a big player in the world, self-governing but not entirely independent from Britain. Sir John A. Macdonald and some of the other delegates had proposed calling it the "Kingdom of Canada" but this idea ran into problems down the street at the Colonial Office. Officials there said the term was pretentious and premature for such a young nation. Besides, they added, it would "open a monarchical blister on the side of the Americans" who didn't want a European monarchy on their border.[37] They instructed Macdonald and his gang to go back to the proverbial drawing board.

It was Sir Samuel Leonard Tilley (1818–96), a devout and teetotal member of Parliament from New Brunswick, who suggested the term "Dominion." He is said to have encountered it while reading his bible: "He shall have dominion also from sea to sea and from the river unto the ends of the earth ..." (Psalm 72:8).[38] It was vague, slightly religious, and potentially as unpopular as Tilley's one-time bid to ban liquor in his province. But the Canadians could agree on nothing better and so settled on the name Dominion of Canada.

"I see no harm in the concession to them of the term 'Dominion,'" a British official conceded magnanimously, although others thought the term odd — Queen Victoria among them. But Macdonald claimed later that Derby had insisted upon it. "I was not aware of the circumstances but it is so like Derby," Disraeli later told Macdonald, "a very good fellow, but who lives in a region of perpetual funk."[39]

At the end of the row is Henry Temple (1784–1865), 3rd Viscount Palmerston. He was an early fitness buff who liked to flex his muscles in more ways than one. As Britain's secretary of war for twenty years and foreign minister just as long, he was known for strong-arm tactics in defending the British Empire. While not everyone liked his brinkmanship, he did help ensure Canada's survival during the U.S. Civil War. His statue by Thomas Woolner was erected in 1876.

Parliament Square offers a good vantage point to view the British Houses of Parliament, also known as the Palace of Westminster. So it is here where we will consider the last two discoveries on this walk.

Trivia: *In 1842, Charles Dickens attended the state opening of the Assembly in Halifax. The Governor read the Speech from the Throne, the military band played "God Save the Queen," and the politicians shouted yeas and nays in the debates. "It was like looking at Westminster from the wrong end of a telescope," he said.[40]*

As its name implies, the building began life as a royal residence. The first palace to occupy this site was built in the time of Edward the Confessor (ca.1003–66), a spiritual king closely linked to the foundation of Westminster Abbey. It was a royal residence until King Henry VIII moved his court to the Palace of Whitehall in 1530. Shortly afterward an early form of parliament began to convene here. Like many Commonwealth countries, Canada adopted the "Westminster model" of government. Understanding how this model developed helps explain some of our own odd parliamentary traditions.

Westminster Palace: *The Mother of All Parliaments*

Chapels like great halls were common features of medieval palaces. Following the dissolution of the monasteries and the eviction of monks by King Henry VIII, his son Edward VI (1537–53; reigned from 1547) turned the empty St. Stephen's Chapel in the Palace of Westminster into a makeshift council chamber. Although parliaments had existed as early as the 1200s, they never really had a permanent home until 1547.

The chapel was the ideal place for such meetings. Members sat in the choir stalls opposite each other, close enough to hear but far enough apart not to brawl. Just to make sure, an impartial Speaker sat at the altar to impose order. In time, the stalls on the Speaker's right were occupied by the Government; those on the left the Opposition.

When they were not debating in the chapel, medieval parliamentarians gathered behind the old choir screen where much of Parliament's real work occurred. This became known as the lobby. After St. Stephen's chapel was destroyed by fire, a purpose-built debating chamber was completed in 1857 along the same model. Today St. Stephen's Entrance Hall occupies the old site where Parliament met for centuries.

Maces date back to when heavy clubs were the only way to enforce obedience and eventually became the symbol of royal authority in Parliament. Before every session, a gold mace is placed in front of the Speaker with its crown (or hitting end) facing the government. Even today, no government business can be conducted without it. During the War of 1812, American invaders stole Upper Canada's first mace, which had to be hastily replaced before the legislature could reconvene. The original mace was only returned in 1934.

Another parliamentary tradition was created in 1642, when King Charles I entered Parliament and demanded the capture of five treasonous MPs. The Speaker refused to cooperate, saying only Parliament could command him to speak. This established the Speaker not only as Parliament's referee but its official spokesperson, a role that was sometimes hazardous to the occupant's health. No fewer than nine Speakers met violent deaths in their role, which is why newly elected Speakers in Canada pretend feebly to resist the job despite good pay and lavish perks, including a lakeside estate in Gatineau Park, Quebec.

Like so many historical buildings in London, the Palace of Westminster was badly damaged during the Second World War. It was rebuilt in 1945–50 but not before Prime Minister William Lyon Mackenzie King had Canadian diplomats ship back some of the rubble to build the gothic ruins on his Ottawa estate.[41]

Trivia: *The passage in 1982 of the amended British North America Act (now styled the Canadian Constitution) severed Canada's last tie to Britain's parliament.*

To finish our walk through Whitehall, let's briefly consider Canada's single most important piece of legislation to pass Britain's parliament: the British North America Act of 1867. Although it was a landmark bill to create the first self-governing colony in the British Empire, nobody seemed to notice much.

The House of Commons: *A Parish Is Born*

On March 8, 1867, a young John A. Macdonald and a handful of Fathers-to-be of Confederation waited expectantly in the visitors' gallery of the British House of Commons. Below on the floor, the British North America Act reached its third and final reading. Three years of Macdonald's life had been spent labouring over the terms of Canadian union and now the moment approached. But the birth was unusual. Not because the newborn country wasn't strong and healthy, but that it came into this world without so much as a whelp.

The passage of Canada's defining piece of legislation had been lowkey from the start. It was introduced into Parliament by the Colonial Secretary, Henry Herbert (1831–90), 4th Earl of Carnarvon, who was suffering such a bad head cold no one could hear what he had to say. After passing the House of Lords, the bill was given to an unreliable junior minister to navigate through the Commons where it attracted equally little attention. Indeed at one reading, three-quarters of MPs were absent doing other things.

To Macdonald and the other Canadians it was clear British MPs were indifferent to the creation of their new country. It was as if the BNA Act was a private members bill, Macdonald complained, "uniting two or three English parishes."[42] The moody Alexander Galt (1817–93), another Father of Confederation, expressed even graver concerns. "I am more than ever disappointed at the tone of feeling here as to the colonies," he told his wife. "I cannot shut my eyes to the fact that they want to get rid of us."[43]

Turn now and head back to Westminster Bridge Road where our walk ends at the Westminster Tube Station.

WALK 4:
WESTMINSTER AND LAMBETH

Addresses say a lot about Londoners. Those who live in swanky Mayfair, for example, are either rich as Texans or just diplomats pretending to be. Islington is populated by latte liberals, while privileged conservatives wait for socialist Armageddon near World's End, Chelsea. Living south of the river was once avoided by people of every stripe. Its rough, working-class reputation goes back to when the area was popular for bear baiting, theatres, and music halls. Yet today crossing the river can be as surprising as crossing Montreal's cultural divide of Boulevard Saint-Laurent and discovering a fascinating parallel city.

This walk begins at St. James's Park Tube Station and ends at Westminster Tube Station. Walking distance is about 1.5 miles (2.4 km).

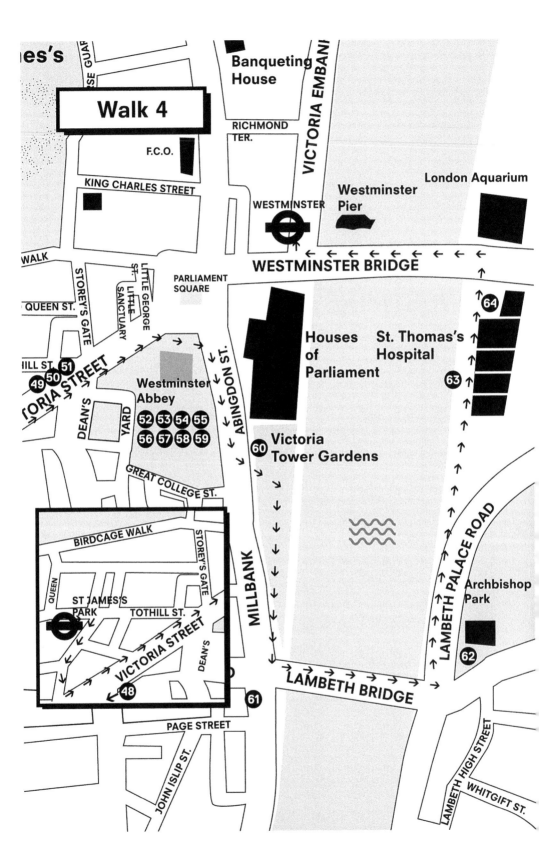

DISCOVERIES

A SHORT HISTORY OF THE AREA

Westminster was once a marshy island west of the medieval city of London. Although it was home to a church dedicated to St. Peter as far back as the 600s, it was the pious Saxon king Edward the Confessor (ca.1003–66; reigned from 1042) who built the first abbey here in 1065 known as the "Minister in the West." Competition for wealthy benefactors was fierce in those days and Edward's abbey struggled against its great rival St. Paul's Cathedral to the east. The expression "robbing Peter to pay Paul" may stem from these early ecclesiastical squabbles.

Over the next centuries, Westminster like the City of London grew in prominence and importance. When King Henry VIII (1491–1547; reigned from 1509) moved his court to Whitehall from Westminster, the old palace became home to Parliament. It's been associated with political mudslinging ever since. Centuries later, tenements in the area were razed to create an imposing array of stores, hotels, and offices for the politically powerful. New arrivals included the Army & Navy Store, which catered to the smart military man, as well as his wife or lady friend — and occasionally all three.

Across the river, Lambeth was no stranger to mud either. Its name may actually derive from the Saxon word for muddy harbour. This area flooded so often it was popularly known as Lambeth Marsh. While it never prospered quite like its neighbour to the north, it was home to a number of medieval manor houses such as Lambeth Manor (later Lambeth Palace), the origins of which date back to 1197. Other great manor houses endure in name only. Henry VIII, for example, demolished Kennington Manor to renovate Whitehall Palace. He may have done this for the convenience of building materials or simply out of spite: the first of his six wives, the Spanish Catherine of Aragon (1485–1536) once lived there.

With the arrival of the Archbishop of Canterbury to Lambeth Palace in the thirteenth century, a number of charitable institutions sprang up south of the river. These included almshouses, schools, and early hospitals like St. Thomas's. A late addition in 1815 was the new Bethlehem Hospital, the oldest charitable institution for the insane in England. Buying a ticket to view the inmates had once been a popular pastime in London and the hospital became familiarly known as "Bedlam." Today, it houses a museum to another type of insanity: war.

THE WALK

At St. James's Park Tube Station, exit nearest Broadway and turn right toward Victoria Street. On our left is the headquarters of the London Metropolitan Police Force, more commonly known as New Scotland Yard, with its familiar revolving triangular sign. The Yard was the world's first civilian police force and derives its name from the precincts of its first headquarters in Whitehall. It moved to this location in 1967. On the ground floor is a crime museum showcasing mementos from its most notorious cases. Unfortunately, it is open to only those in the trade. That is, in *law enforcement*.

Victoria Street ahead of us is a busy commercial thoroughfare which runs west from Parliament Square to Victoria Railway Station. Across Victoria Street is Strutton Ground, a midday marketplace full of T-shirt and vegetable vendors. Just beyond this market is Grey Coat Hospital School, founded in 1698. Today a preparatory school for young girls, it began life as a charity orphanage for Westminster's poor. Above the entrance you will find figures of a girl and boy in traditional Grey Coat uniforms.

> *Hudson's Bay is certainly a country that Sinbad the Sailor never saw, as he makes no mention of mosquitoes.*
> — DAVID THOMPSON

One of the school's famous sons was the adventurer and geographer David Thompson (1770–1857) who journeyed across 55,000 miles (88,500 kilometres) of Western Canada mapping more wilderness than any other explorer. Never without his sextant, Thompson was called *Koo Koo Sint*, the man who looks at stars, by the Indians.

Grey Coat School: *The Man Who Looked at Stars*

David Thompson entered this world as a pauper and left it scarcely any richer: despite a lifetime trapping and exploring Canada, he died penniless, broken in spirit, and badly in debt. What he left behind, however, was a priceless piece of Canadian history: a manuscript of his incredible journeys across Western Canada published only after his death.

Thompson was born in nearby Marsham Street to Welsh parents who came to London in search of work. After his father died, Thompson entered Grey Coat Hospital School where he excelled in mathematics and navigation. At fourteen, he apprenticed to the Hudson's Bay Company as a fur trader and left London for the wilds of Canada, never to return.

As luck would have it, the young Thompson was sent to work under the explorer and fur trader Samuel Hearne (1745–92), in Churchill, Manitoba. Life was dull and uneventful in Churchill, but Thompson helped Hearne write his memoirs, which probably whet the young man's appetite for both adventure and storytelling. At the end of his apprenticeship, he set off on his own with a sextant and nautical almanacs.

Thompson devoted the next years of his life to fur trading, exploring, and map-making throughout western Canada — first for the HBC and then for the North West Company. He charted a route between Hudson Bay and Lake Athabasca across northern Manitoba and Saskatchewan, the future border between Canada and the United States, and made a perilous journey in winter over the Rocky Mountains to the Pacific Ocean in 1811. That he did this half blind and with a lame foot was a testament to his amazing fortitude and determination.

Yet after retiring to Montreal in 1812, Thompson proved less a businessman than an explorer and suffered repeated financial failures. He had to make ends meet by mapping Montreal's streets and pawning his instruments. In 1857, he died in obscurity in Longueuil, Quebec, leaving behind his journal and notebooks under a mountain of debt. These extraordinary tales would be published in 1914 and confirm posthumously his right to the title of Canada's greatest geographer, map-maker, and surveyor.

Now let's turn left on Victoria Street and head toward Parliament Square. Today, this part of the street is a bit modern and soulless, with little to interest us. In the late 1800s, however, 17–19 Victoria Street was the gloomy headquarters of Canada's first "ambassador" to Britain. His appointment was a clear signal that Canada was growing up and ready to take on the Mother Country; if not quite as equals then at least a little more so. Yet he didn't have an easy time of it.

Trivia: *A plaque in honour of David Thompson's explorations and surveying in early Canada can be found on the wall of Grey Coat Hospital School in Westminster. It was unveiled in 2007.*

Grey Coat Hospital School for paupers near Victoria Street. David Thompson, Canada's greatest map-maker, left here to join the Hudson's Bay Company, never to return.

17–19 Victoria Street: *Canada's First Diplomat*

Although Prime Minister Sir John A. Macdonald would campaign later on the theme: "A British subject I was born — a British subject I will die," by 1879, he had come to realize that Britain and Canada didn't always see eye to eye. He decided an official Canadian minister resident in London would be the best way to represent the young country on matters of finance, defence, immigration, and trade. But British officials balked at the idea. Canada was just a *colony*, after all, and not the Hapsburg Empire.

When Macdonald persisted, the British reluctantly agreed to a low-ranking official or a "special commissioner." But that still wasn't good enough for Macdonald, who argued his man in London would serve a general purpose and not a *special* one. He should at least have the rank of *high* commissioner. As at Yorktown, the British threw in the towel. Privately, however, Macdonald fumed over the wordplay. "It was a matter of no importance to the Imperial Government what title we may give our agent," he complained to the governor general. "We might call him *Nuncio* or *Legate* or *legate a latere gubernatoris* if we pleased."[1]

Into this exalted if ill-defined job first stepped Sir Alexander Tilloch Galt (1817–93). A Father of Confederation and Conservative MP, Galt was impatient, unpredictable, and prickly — hardly a smooth, gin-sipping role model for Canada's future cadre of diplomats. To make matters worse, British Tories were voted out of office in 1880 and were replaced by Prime Minister William Gladstone (1809–98) and his unfriendly Liberals. "It could not be worse," Galt fretted to his boss. "The members of the Ministry unmistakably ignore me, from Gladstone downward I have never seen inside of one of their houses."[2]

But it was on the home front that the new High Commissioner battled the most. Horse races, canapés, and club memberships were expensive in London but Galt believed they were the cost of doing business. No sooner was he in the job than he felt obliged to ask for more money. Old Tomorrow flatly refused. In the all-too-familiar refrain of diplomats ever since, Galt told Macdonald huffily: "This cannot be done by staying at home."[3] Rebuked and disillusioned, he tendered his resignation eventually and came home. Perhaps he *was* the quintessential diplomat after all.

Let's continue our walk along Victoria Street. At the corner of Tothill and Victoria streets (2–8 Victoria Street) we come to the site of the old Westminster Palace Hotel (now offices). In 1866, delegates from Ontario, Quebec, Nova Scotia, and New Brunswick assembled here to put the finishing touches on the principles behind Canada's first constitution, the British North America Act. Along this dark desert highway of Victoria Street, you could say we've come to the Hotel Confederation.

Trivia: *After thirty years, Canada vacated its first offices on Victoria Street. "One had to engage a guide and an interpreter in order to find it," one High Commissioner complained. "Oh my, but it was a depressing place."*[4]

The virgin birth wasn't the only miracle worth celebrating on Christmas Eve 1866. Colonial delegates in London also finalized Canada's constitution.

2–8 Victoria Street: *The Hotel Confederation*

The Westminster Palace Hotel may not have served pink champagne on ice like the hotel imagined by the Eagles, but it was billed as the epitome of luxury for its day. British nineteenth-century luxury, that is. Built in 1859 in the French Renaissance style, the 400-room hotel was the first equipped with elevators in London and boasted every modern convenience, except ensuite bathrooms (in fact, there were only fourteen bathrooms). It's probably the reason Canada's cranky newspaperman George Brown (1818–80) deemed it only moderately comfortable.

On the ground floor beyond the front desk was a long conference room decorated in white and gold. It was normally used for lectures and music. But in December 1866 it was here that a small group of colonial politicians, with Macdonald as chairman, finally gathered to hammer out the last details of their union.

The delegates were up against the clock. In New Brunswick, an election loomed that might overturn the colony's vote in favour of union. In Britain, the wobbly Conservative government needed to pass the bill could fall any day. "We must obtain action during the present session of the Imperial Parliament," warned the excitable Charles Tupper (1821–1915) of Nova Scotia, "or all may be lost."[5]

But if old habits die hard, old political habits die harder, and the sixteen delegates soon got bogged down over the same old issues that had blocked earlier negotiations. Frustration was evident among them. "Our friends from the Maritime provinces are excessively fond of talking," one complained.[6]

But Christmas brought another miracle besides the virgin birth. As December 25 drew near, the delegates finally agreed on a set of resolutions. On Christmas Eve, they handed them over to British officials to create a legal document that would eventually become Canada's constitution — and broke just in time to enjoy the holidays.

Trivia: *A commemorative tablet from the conference room where the British North America Act was finalized was presented to Canada after the Westminster Palace Hotel was demolished in 1974. It's now mounted outside the doors to the Library of Parliament in Ottawa.*

Before we move on, let's briefly consider another episode at the Westminster Palace Hotel that occurred during the London Conference. This one left a young Macdonald spending a miserable Christmas in bed — perhaps like Scrooge dreaming of ghosts past, present, and future.

2–8 Victoria Street: *Macdonald's Humbug Christmas*

One night in December 1866, during the London Conference, John A. Macdonald returned late to his room at the Westminster Palace Hotel tired, cold, and maybe even a little drunk. It had been an eventful day. On his way back to London from a visit to the British colonial secretary's country retreat near Newbury, Macdonald had narrowly escaped injury when the train on which he had been travelling jumped the tracks and landed in a ditch. Now safely ensconced in his hotel, Old Tomorrow lit a candle and climbed into bed with his newspapers, pulling the bed curtains around him to ward off the damp winter chill.

The Westminster Palace Hotel where the Fathers of Confederation finalized Canada's 1867 constitution. Advertising to the contrary, some thought the hotel only moderately comfortable.

Perhaps he also poured himself a night cap as he drew a candle near to read.

A few minutes later, Macdonald awoke to find the sheets and bed curtains ablaze. Without time to lose, he leapt out of bed, pulled everything to the floor, and tried to extinguish the flames with water and a bolster pillow. He then ran to George-Étienne Cartier (1814–73) and Alexander Galt in the adjoining rooms to fetch help. Only once the fire was out did Macdonald notice his own wounds. His hair, forehead, and hands were scorched and his shoulder burnt. Yet with a view to his important mission he kept calm and carried on. "I got it dressed and thought no more of it," he said in a letter to his sister.[7]

But Macdonald's injuries grew worse by the day. By the time the delegates had inked their deal, he was running a high fever. His condition was so acute a doctor ordered him to bed over Christmas. As the other delegates set off merrily to visit friends and family for the holidays and to celebrate their accomplishment, Macdonald remained alone in his hotel room, dining only on tea and toast, and more than a little humbug. For Canada's future chieftain, it was far from a merry Christmas.

Across from us is Westminster Abbey. This is Britain's national cathedral, coronation chamber, and royal mausoleum all rolled into one. It is also Britain's most popular visitor attraction.

We'll start our tour by admiring the West Front of the church. Despite the facade's medieval appearance, it is more modern than that. It was designed by the English architects Christopher Wren (1632–1723) and his disciple Nicholas Hawksmoor (ca.1661–1736) and completed in 1745. If visitors from Montreal have a sense of *déjà vu*, there's good reason. Westminster Abbey not only inspired faithful pilgrims but architects too.

Trivia: *During the London Conference, Sir John A. Macdonald visited Highclere Castle, the country home of the colonial secretary Henry Herbert, Lord Carnarvon. It became the informal drafting room of Canada's constitution. Highclere later became famous in the TV series* Downton Abbey.

Westminster Abbey: *Notre-Dame de Westminster*

In the early 1800s, it seemed the *Maudits anglais* (damned English) were everywhere in Montreal. If the establishment of English-speaking McGill University wasn't bad enough, they had raised a monument to Admiral Horatio Nelson in Place Jacques Cartier. So when it came time to build the city's Roman Catholic cathedral, many French-Canadian leaders wanted something brash, showy, and, well, a bit more French in style. What they got didn't exactly answer their prayers.

The problem began with the architect. James O'Donnell (1774–1830) was a Protestant Irishman who specialized in Gothic Revival architecture, then in vogue in England and the United States. He won the commission for Montreal's Notre-Dame with his Irish charm and eloquence and set about designing a Gothic masterpiece to loosely recall Notre-Dame Cathedral in Paris — even down to its dimensions.[8] Yet O'Donnell had never been to Paris to see the original. But he had visited London.

With its neat grid of vertical and horizontal lines, the towers of Montreal's Notre-Dame bear a striking resemblance to those of Westminster Abbey. The narrow pointed arches, finials, buttresses, and other details are also similar. Inside O'Donnell took his inspiration from another London church: St. Martin-in-the-Fields. The result, observers said, was a veritable potpourri of architectural fumbling which "resembles nothing so much as a collection of Gothic shapes cut out of cardboard and pasted together."[9] Jérôme Demers (1774–1853), superior of the Seminary of Quebec, had even graver ecclesiastical concerns. He complained the new basilica looked simply far too *Protestant*.[10]

Now let's go around to the North Porch of the Abbey and head inside. As your eyes adjust, it's easy to mistake the place for a cluttered antique shop with old statuary packed to the rafters. Over 3,000 very important corpses are buried here with over 600 monuments for us to peruse.

Trivia: *The towers of Montreal's Notre-Dame Basilica are known as Temperance and Perseverance. Perseverance looks westward to the English part of the city; Temperance looks eastward to the old Molson brewery.*

One could probably spend the better part of a day here — and at the price of admission why wouldn't you? — but that wouldn't leave us time for the rest of our walk.

Let's begin our tour here in the North Transept. This area is called Statesmen's Aisle. Many of the British worthies we've encountered on earlier walks are memorialized here. Among them is William Pitt (1708–78), 1st Earl of Chatham, and the mastermind behind the British victories at Louisbourg and Quebec in the Seven Years' War. In the same grave is his son, Britain's youngest prime minister, William Pitt (1759–1806), known as Pitt the Younger. He was only twenty-four when he took office.

In ancient Roman togas are Tory Prime Minister Sir Robert Peel (1788–1850), alongside four-time Liberal Prime Minister William Ewart Gladstone (1809–98). Gladstone, known as the Old Grand Man, was anti-slavery as well as anti-imperialist and favoured independence for Canada to avoid further drain on Britain's public purse. With this in mind, he confided that the appointment of Canada's first diplomat was a step in the right direction.[11]

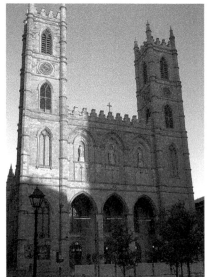

Déjà vu: Montreal's Notre Dame Basilica (right) borrows a detail or two from London's Westminster Abbey, much to the chagrin of some French Canadian churchgoers.

Also in the west aisle is a memorial to George Montagu-Dunk (1716–71), 2nd Earl Halifax, by the sculptor John Bacon. As president of Britain's Board of Trade, in 1749 Halifax ordered an English town to be built in Nova Scotia to counter French settlement in the area, which he immodestly named after himself. The enterprise was criticized as wasteful. Edmund Burke (1729–97), a conservative Whig, threw up his hands over the cost of Halifax, complaining to Parliament: "Good God! What sum the nursing of that ill-thriven, hard-visaged, and ill-favoured brat, has cost to this wittol [cuckold] nation!"[12] Ironically, the two cherubs on Halifax's memorial hold up a mirror of prudence and tread on hypocrisy. Many of Halifax's detractors thought it should have been the other way around.

On this western side of the Transept is a memorial to Jonas Hanway (1712–86). Hanway was an eccentric philanthropist who helped rebuild Montreal after a devastating fire in 1765. As a result of his fundraising, London sent two shiny fire trucks to the stricken city, as well as the controversial bust of King George III that we encountered on Walk 2. Hanway is also thought to be the first Londoner to use an umbrella in the mid-1750s, which ultimately spelled the end of the fur trade. Until then, fur hats made of beaver pelts had kept Londoners dry.

In the Statesmen's Aisle we find a memorial to Robert Stewart (1769–1822), Viscount Castlereagh, an Anglo-Irish statesman renowned for his diplomatic skills in Europe. Yet when it came to the affairs of North America, his talents were a little less obvious.

> *England would be better off without Canada; it keeps her in a prepared state for war at a great expense and constant irritation.*
>
> — NAPOLEON BONAPARTE

Castlereagh Memorial: *A Millstone Around His Neck*

Castlereagh was a tall, painfully thin man who always looked bored and was fond of dressing in black. In January 1812, he became Britain's foreign minister and immediately faced off against a man half his height but many times his ambition: the French military dictator Napoleon Bonaparte (1769–1821).

Focused on Britain's war against Napoleon, Castlereagh miscalculated the anger of Americans over his country's heavy-handed control of the seas to blockade France. Raids on U.S. ships and impressment of their British-born sailors into the Royal Navy angered Americans and confirmed to them Britain "ruled the waves, and waived the rules." So they declared war and invaded Canada.

The result was our War of 1812, a war within a war. The fact that Canada fended off a U.S. invasion owed much to the loyalty of French Canadians, a small but superior British land force, and, not insignificantly, timid American military men.[13] But no thanks was owed to Castlereagh, who described the conflict in North America as a millstone and wanted to end it quickly.[14] When the Americans sent a high-level delegation to Ghent to negotiate a peace, he sent second-rate officials who abandoned Britain's First Nation allies and gave back territory Britain had won. Some were left wondering whose side Castlereagh was really on.

In later years, Castlereagh became increasingly neurotic, to the point where the Duke of Wellington told him "you cannot be in your right mind."[15] To prevent suicide, he was stripped of all knives, razors, and pistols. To no effect. One morning Castlereagh found a small pocket knife and cut his own throat. Immortality in Westminster Abbey wasn't kind either. The poet George Lord Byron (1788–1824) suggested the epitaph:

Posterity will ne'er survey
A nobler grave than this:
Here lie the bones of Castlereagh:
Stop, traveller, and piss.

Let's turn now and head into the north ambulatory with the high altar on our right. In the St. John the Evangelist Chapel on our left is a memorial to Sir John Franklin (1786–1847), who disappeared trying to discover Canada's Northwest Passage. Like his statue in Waterloo Place, this white marble bust was created by the sculptor Matthew Noble and placed here by Lady Jane, Franklin's admiring and determined widow.

His epitaph, by the poet Alfred Tennyson (1809–92), is a great deal kinder than the one proposed for Castlereagh. It reads:

> *Not here: The white north has thy bones; and thou, heroic sail-or-soul, art passing on thine happier voyage now toward no earthly pole.*

Also commemorated in the same chapel is Sir Francis Leopold McClintock (1819–1907), an Irish-born explorer known as the Arctic Fox. McClintock established Franklin's fate in 1859, after discovering some of Franklin's frozen belongings on King William Island. He was also one of the more successful explorers of the Arctic owing to his adoption of Inuit technology.

McClintock Memorial: *An Explorer's Best Friend*

Having joined the Royal Navy when he was only twelve, Francis Leopold McClintock's early career was neither exciting nor extraordinary. All that changed in 1848, however, when he was thirty and sailed to the Canadian Arctic in search of Sir John Franklin's lost expedition.

With their ship stuck in the ice off Somerset Island, McClintock and Sir James Clark Ross (1800–62) used Inuit sleds pulled by dogs to journey across the island. By imitating the Inuit, McClintock and Ross were able to travel great distances and explore new areas previously unseen by Europeans. Back in England, McClintock adapted the sledding technique to take advantage of the manpower available on navy ships. Using teams of men instead of dogs, McClintock covered over 745 miles (1,200 kilometres) on his next trip in the search for Franklin and, in 1855, discovered incontrovertible proof that Franklin and his men had perished. The discovery earned McClintock fame and a knighthood.[16]

But McClintock's sleds would ultimately prove less effective than the Inuit originals. In the 1911 race to the South Pole, Norway's Roald Amundsen (1872–1928) used the Inuit method of sledding to beat Britain's Robert Falcon Scott (1868–1912) to the pole. Scott, who adopted McClintock's method using men rather than dogs, perished on the journey.

In the Islip chapel, next on our right, is a modern floor marker to Admiral Sir Charles Saunders (1715–75), a forgotten but key player in the British conquest of Quebec. With thirty-two years service in the navy, this capable but quiet man skilfully manoeuvred Wolfe's fleet down the St. Lawrence River and landed his troops. Along with Brigadier-General George Townshend (1724–1807), he signed the document of Quebec's surrender.[17]

We now come to the unmistakable monument to the man himself: Major-General James Wolfe (1727–59). At the base is a bronze relief of the assault on Quebec. Above it is a neoclassical sarcophagus supported by two British lions, which is empty (Wolfe is buried in Greenwich), and simply bears his epitaph. But the real showstopper is what's above. It's a Pieta-like composition of Wolfe dying in the arms of two soldiers while an angel of Victory descends with a laurel wreath and palm branch. A lanky, muscular Wolfe is draped modestly only in a cloth.

In a wave of patriotism after Wolfe's death, British members of Parliament voted to erect this monument to the newfound hero of Quebec at public expense. The winner of a national design competition was a relative newcomer to the scene named Joseph Wilton (1722–1803), whose only leg up over more experienced sculptors was that he had already carved a bust of Wolfe.[18] But if MPs believed Wilton actually knew what the man looked like, they were sadly mistaken.

55 | ### Wolfe Memorial: *The Face of a Hero*

Unlike other military heroes, Major-General James Wolfe only became famous in death. Although there are many portraits of him, few if any were painted while he lived. From written descriptions and caricatures by his men, we have some basic facts. Wolfe was six feet tall and scrawny, with flaming red hair and pale, freckled skin. He also had a long beak-like nose and a forehead that sloped back distinctively when viewed from the side. Hardly the muscular man on the Westminster memorial. In fact, some even thought him downright ugly.[19]

For the sculptor Wilton, Wolfe's facial features posed a particular challenge. When Wolfe's body arrived back in England, Wilton went down to Portsmouth to make a death mask. But after weeks at sea the General's corpse was too badly decayed to be of much use. The resourceful Wilton did the only thing he could, given the circumstances. He asked people who knew Wolfe and modelled the hero after a nobleman's servant who some believed resembled him.

Working from this servant's face, Wilton smoothed out Wolfe's bird-like features and gave him a muscular body, like a Photoshop artist might do today. This is the image of Wolfe that endures in stone.

Continue along the ambulatory, which forms a semi-circle around the tomb of Edward the Confessor. At the far eastern end is the Chapel of Henry VII, a fine example of English medieval architecture and the most magnificent part of the abbey. Note in particular its fan vault ceiling.

Henry VII (1457–1509; reigned from 1485) and his wife Elizabeth of York established the Tudor dynasty and are buried in a black marble tomb at the far end of the chapel. Henry is of interest to us because he played an important, if largely unrecognized, role in the discovery of Canada. In 1497, he sponsored an explorer named Giovanni Cabota, better known as John Cabot (ca.1450–99), "to seeke out, discover, and finde whatsoever isles, countreys, regions or provinces of the heathen and infidels whatsoever they be, and in what part of the world soever they be which before this times have been unknowen to all Christians." Henry got less than he bargained for.

Henry VII Tomb: *His Majesty's New Found Fish*

Henry Tudor was a cautious, penny-pinching king whose rule straddled the brutality of the Middle Ages and the dazzle of the Renaissance. Having violently snatched the crown from a previous king at the Battle of Bosworth Field in 1485, Henry discovered his newly acquired treasury was nearly empty and spent the rest of his reign finding ways to fill it.[20] So he wasn't really in a position to be extravagant a few years later when he was offered the chance to finance an amazing voyage across the ocean by a Genoa explorer named Christopher Columbus. Instead Columbus went to Henry's rival, Spain's rich King Ferdinand (1452–1516) and the rest, as they say, is genocide.

Columbus's discovery of the New World in 1492 may have irked Henry a little, particularly since his own fishermen from Bristol had probably known about North America for some time. So when a second Genoan named John Cabot pitched the idea of a northerly route to Asia a few years later, backed by Bristol merchants, Henry wouldn't miss the chance twice. He gave Cabot a monopoly to all trade his voyage generated, less than one-fifth to his depleted treasury, of course.

Alas for Henry, Cabot's adventure yielded nothing but more fish. Cabot's first voyage in 1496 was a failure. On his second, a year later, he planted the English flag in Newfoundland or possibly Nova Scotia, believing it to be Asia. When he returned without riches, Henry grudgingly granted him £10 and a pension "to hym that founde the new isle." The king remained ever hopeful, however, and sent Cabot back a third time, laden with goods to trade with the Chinese for gold and spices. But Cabot vanished never to be seen again. When Henry died so did his country's desire to explore the New World until many years later.

The magnificent Chapel of Henry VII also serves as chapel to the Order of the Bath, the oldest British order of chivalry. Sir John A. Macdonald was made a Knight Commander of the Bath for bringing about Confederation in 1867 and later elevated to the higher rank of Knight Grand Cross.[21] In addition, he became an Imperial Privy Councillor in 1879. He might have received the title right honourable a few years earlier if the Pacific Scandal involving political kickbacks hadn't tarnished his name. As it was, Queen Victoria invited him to her home on the Isle of Wight to receive the honour but didn't offer him any supper. His nameplate can be seen in one of the stalls.[22]

A number of other royals are buried in the Chapel. In the north aisle are Henry VII's granddaughters, the Catholic Queen Mary (1516–58) and her half sister the Protestant Queen Elizabeth I (1533–1603). Across the chapel is a monument to the beheaded Mary, Queen of Scots (1542–87). Henry VII's mother, Lady Margaret Beaufort, is also found here.

In an unmarked grave under the chapel floor is George II (1683–1760), the last king to be buried in the Abbey. He was king for most of the Seven Years' War and approved Pitt's choice of the young Wolfe to lead the expedition against Quebec.

Now exit the chapel and continue around the Ambulatory toward the South Transept and Poet's Corner.

To our left, near the ornate wood Choir Screen, are the graves of a number of well-known scientists. In the nave is a memorial to the New Zealand-born Ernest Rutherford (1871–1937), 1st Baron Rutherford of Nelson, who was chair of physics at McGill University from 1898 to 1907. His work on radiation led to the award of a Nobel Prize in Chemistry in 1908 and ultimately to the development of the atomic bomb.

A spot in Poet's Corner on our left is probably the highest recognition that can befall an English-speaking poet, though it hardly makes up for the lifetime of penury most endure. The tradition of burying poets here began with Geoffrey Chaucer (ca.1340–1400), though this honour apparently wasn't so much for his *Canterbury Tales* as it was for his long association with the Abbey. The other names here read like the bookshelf of a university English major. We'll focus briefly on two.

The first poet on our tour is Henry Wadsworth Longfellow (1807–82), whose marble bust was placed here by British admirers in 1884. Ironically, it was this American poet who helped draw the world's attention to the most shameful act by the British in the history of Canada: the expulsion of the Acadians from Nova Scotia in 1755. This tragedy of the Seven Years' War might have been an historical footnote had it not been for Longfellow's skill in turning a tragedy into a powerful love story that captured the hearts of millions of readers and in the process helped awaken Acadian nationalism and pride.

Trivia: Evangeline *was the subject of Canada's first feature-length dramatic film. It was produced in 1913 and filmed in Nova Scotia.*

Longfellow Memorial: *Evangeline and the Acadians*

The Acadians were French-speaking Catholics caught in a no-man's land in the conflict between New France and New England. Their expulsion from Grand-Pré, Nova Scotia, by British and New England troops was the first time in modern history that a group of civilians was forcibly removed as a threat.[23] Loaded onto ships, they were dispersed across the continent; many settling in Louisiana. Their only crime was to refuse allegiance to one power over another.

Longfellow heard the story of a man and woman separated by the expulsion from a pastor in Boston, and decided to make it the subject of an epic verse in *dactylic hexameter*, the challenging meter of Homer and Virgil. "*Evangeline* is so easy for you to read," he once said, "because it was so hard for me to write."[24] The poem tells the story of a faithful and persistent maiden named Evangeline Bellefontaine who spends her life searching for her lover, Gabriel Lajeunesse, after the expulsion, only to find him years later in a poor house in Philadelphia, where he dies in her arms. The story proved so wildly popular after it was published in 1847 that it was translated into 130 languages.

Longfellow's most famous work had unforeseen consequences. While his intent was merely to portray the faithfulness of women, the poem came to symbolize the plight of the Acadian people who rallied around its story of suffering. They adopted Evangeline as their own Joan of Arc and searched in vain for evidence she was real. But Longfellow's poem was only a work of popular fiction, and he was not one to let facts get in the way of a good story. He neatly omitted, for example, the role his own countrymen had played in the expulsion. Moreover, he had never been to the Acadian people's peaceful and bucolic land. The evocative "forest primeval" of his Acadia was based solely on the forests of Maine.

The second poet we'll consider briefly in Poet's Corner is the Englishman Thomas Gray (1716–71). He was a poor poet who lived above a milliner's shop on Jermyn Street, which we discovered on Walk 2. Gray seemed to like writing melancholy poetry, whether about humans or cats. His masterpiece was "Elegy Written in a Country

Churchyard." It was published in 1751 to great acclaim and had one significant admirer in Canada: Major-General James Wolfe.

Gray Memorial: *The Curfew Tolls for General Wolfe*

For a poet who didn't write a great deal, Thomas Gray certainly had a way with the words. "Elegy Written in a Country Churchyard" contains lines that are probably familiar to those who have never read it. Perhaps the best known is the warning against those who would seek fame and fortune: "The paths of glory lead but to the grave."

Major-General James Wolfe is traditionally believed to have read the poem to his men before launching his famous assault on Quebec. Perhaps he imagined the carnage to come or was contemplating his own fate as he succumbed slowly to the ravages of tuberculosis. "Gentlemen," he said, staring up at the steep, dark cliffs from the river basin, "I would rather have written those lines than take Quebec."

Is the romantic story true? Most likely, say historians, though when exactly Wolfe had time to read the poem before the assault is less certain.[25] What is clear is that Wolfe's leather-bound and annotated copy of "Elegy Written in a Country Churchyard" is now preserved in the Thomas Fisher Rare Book Library at the University of Toronto. It is inscribed to Wolfe by Katherine Lowther, the woman he planned to marry.

Leaving Poet's Corner, we head into the South Aisle of the nave. Here we find a beautiful monument by Robert Adam to Major John André (1750–80) paid for by King George III. André was a dashing British soldier captured in the American Revolution in a plot involving General Benedict Arnold (ca.1741–1801), a rebel leader who famously switched allegiance to the British, and Lieutenant-Colonel John Graves Simcoe (1752–1806), a British spymaster in New York. André was executed while Arnold escaped to New Brunswick. Simcoe, meanwhile, carried his anti-Americanism to Upper Canada as the province's first lieutenant governor.[26]

In the nave we also find the grave of Sir Freeman Freeman-Thomas (1866–1941), 1st Marquess of Willingdon. He was governor general of

Andrew Bonar Law was a private family man who didn't drink, womanize or gamble. "Well, what do you like?" David Lloyd George once asked. "I like bridge," Law replied.

Canada from 1926 to 1931 and was the first to take his advice from the prime minister in Canada rather than in Britain. Canada was a piece of cake compared to his next job. As viceroy of India, he faced off with the great civil disobedience campaigner Mahatma Ghandi (1869–1948).

Also in the nave is a stained-glass window to Donald Smith (1820–1914), 1st Baron Strathcona and Mount Royal. Smith was a wealthy philanthropist and governor of the Hudson's Bay Company who made his home in London. As one of the directors of the Canadian Pacific Railroad, he drove the last symbolic spike at Craigellachie, British Columbia, in 1885. In the process, he badly bent it. Strathcona is not buried here but in Highgate Cemetery in North London, next to his wife.

At the westernmost end of the nave, we come to the grave of Andrew Bonar Law (1858–1923), a native of New Brunswick. He was the only British prime minister born outside of the United Kingdom and probably the least known. The Liberal Prime Minister Henry Herbert Asquith (1852–1928) once quipped: "It is fitting that we should have buried the Unknown Prime Minister by the side of the Unknown Soldier."

59

Law Memorial: *The Unknown Prime Minister*

At sixty-four, the soft-spoken Andrew Bonar Law may not have been the youngest or most charismatic British politician to move into 10 Downing Street, but he was the *only* New Brunswicker.

Law was the son of a Presbyterian minister who emigrated to the colony in 1845. Raised with three siblings near Rexton, Bonar (rhymes with honour) grew up poor as a proverbial church mouse. When his mother died, Law was sent to Scotland to be raised by childless relatives who happened to be very rich. They adopted the young boy as their own.

Law was a serious and studious young man who is said to have read *The History of the Decline and Fall of the Roman Empire* three times before he could vote. With a head for making money and a sizable inheritance, it wasn't long before Law too was very rich. But he was also scrupulously honest, modest, and private, and never drank anything stronger than ginger ale. A friend once called him "a good deed in a naughty world."

As an adopted Scot, Law took politics with his porridge. He ran for Parliament in 1900 and quickly became a leading figure in the Conservative Party. In the wartime coalition government of Prime Minister David Lloyd George (1863–1945), Law served as deputy prime minister before a stunning upset led to him to becoming prime minister in October 1922.

But his time at number 10 was brief. Tired and in poor health, he was diagnosed with cancer and resigned after only 209 days in office. He died shortly afterward.

One of Law's closest friends was the Canadian newspaper baron and financier Max Aitken (1879–1964), 1st Baron Beaverbrook. Like Law, Beaverbrook was a wealthy and political Presbyterian who hailed from New Brunswick. He was with Law right to the last. A satirical poet wrote:

> *Round Pembroke Lodge in Edwardes Square*
> *Like rooks the claimants caw*
> *While Aitken keeps with gargoyle stare*
> *His vigil over Law.*[27]

In the northwest tower chapel of the nave is a patriotic marble tablet with a figure mourning George Augustus Howe (ca.1725–59), 3rd Viscount Howe. He was one of William Pitt's energetic young generals who was carelessly killed on his way to dislodge Louis-Joseph de Montcalm (1712–59) and his French forces from Fort Carillon at Ticonderoga, New York. Wolfe called him the very best officer in the king's service whose loss was "one of the greatest that could befall a nation."

Now let's exit Westminster Abbey from the west door and continue east toward the river. Turn right and head toward Abingdon Street.

Trivia: *The old manse in Rexton, New Brunswick, where Andrew Bonar Law was born is today a national historic site. A cairn notes he was a man of "noble character and sterling integrity who served his king and country faithfully."*[28]

Near the Peers entrance to the House of Lords is a bronze equestrian statue of King Richard I (1157–99; reigned from 1189), by the Victorian sculptor Carlo Marochetti. After a bomb exploded nearby during the Second World War, Richard's raised sword was badly bent. Vincent Massey (1887–1967), Canada's high commissioner to Britain at the time, campaigned to keep it that way as a lasting symbol of the war but city officials thought otherwise and had it straightened. The same couldn't be said for Richard's reputation after having reputedly slept with the king of France.

A little farther on we come to a statue to King George V (1865–1936; reigned from 1910) followed by Abingdon Park, where the medieval Jewel Tower stands. It was built around 1365 and is one of the only remaining parts of the original Palace of Westminster — the other being Westminster Hall. For a small entrance fee, you can learn about the history of Parliament and see where Edward III (1312–1377; reigned from 1327) kept his loot. Otherwise, cross Abingdon Street and enter Victoria Tower Gardens, a quiet riverside park next to Parliament. Here we encounter our next Canadian discovery.

Near the entrance to Victoria Tower Gardens is a 1930 statue by A.G. Walker of Emmeline Pankhurst (1858–1928), a militant suffragette from Manchester who won the right for British women to vote in 1918 after leading a long and sometimes violent struggle. Pankhurst and members of her Women's Social and Political Union were frequently arrested for civil disobedience, illegal marches, and destruction of property. Pankhurst herself was clapped in irons seven times. In 1916, Pankhurst toured Canada and inspired many women seeking the vote there, including Nellie McClung (1873–1951) and Emily Murphy (1868–1933), members of the Famous Five who challenged Canada's definition of "person." Ironically, Manitoba was the first province to give the vote to women in 1916, which only hardened Pankhurst's resolve to win the vote back home in Britain. Many in the suffragette movement contributed to this memorial.

After winning the vote, Pankhurst became a Canadian citizen in 1923. "There seems to be more equality between men and women [here] than in any other country I know," she said about her adopted country.[30] But the militant wasn't about to rest on her petticoat in Canada. She was a natural-born agitator who was soon raising placards and marching against another thorny issue: one that wasn't fit to be mentioned in polite company.

> **Trivia:** *In 1917, Canada produced the world's first sex-education film.* Whatsoever a Man Soweth *depicts a Canadian soldier named Dick meeting a prostitute in Trafalgar Square. An older soldier warns him: "Do you realize young man, the risks you run in association with such women?"*

Pankhurst Monument: *Mrs. P and the French Disease*

Demobilized Canadian soldiers returning from the First World War brought home more than just medals and tales of heroism. They brought back venereal disease. During the war there were over 60,000 cases of sexually transmitted disease among Canadian soldiers, the most widespread being syphilis, or the French Disease.[31] Soon half a million people in Canada were infected. The epidemic galvanized governments, doctors, and reform groups to take action. What was crucially needed to halt the spread of the disease was a popular orator who could lead a moral and public health crusade.[32]

Pankhurst was just what the doctors ordered. After winning the crusade for women's votes in Britain she had briefly fought against Bolshevism in North America, but now needed a steady job that paid well. She moved to Toronto, joined the Canadian National Council for Combating Venereal Disease, and became a well-known spokeswoman for social hygiene. She called this "her greatest crusade."

Like the seasoned agitator she was, Pankhurst whipped up crowds in Canada using her old suffragette hat tricks. She handed out lapel pins, called her talks public health demonstrations, and shamelessly used the media to advance her cause. Visiting colleges, churches, and factories she described venereal disease as the enemy in our midst that attacked families and drove women into prostitution. "Men and women now have votes," she proclaimed. "What they have to do is to forget old grievances and work together in a spirit of co-operation for the new future that lies in front of them."[33]

Right: Mrs. Emmeline Pankhurst's memorial stands in Victoria Tower Gardens next to Parliament.
Below: Pankhurst (left) with Nellie McClung, one of Canada's Famous Five, in Edmonton, Alberta, in 1916.

But even diehard agitators know when to call it quits. Pankhurst's health declined and she eventually grew tired of her Canadian crusade — and Canadian winters. The great crusader packed her bags one last time and returned to Britain, where she died in 1928.

Admire the view of the river and the Lambeth shore as you walk through the park. This promenade offers a fine view of the old Victorian wards of Guy's and St. Thomas's Hospital across the river which we will learn more about shortly. One of London's most dramatic statues is also found in the park: the Burghers of Calais (1915) by the French sculptor Auguste Rodin (1840–1917). The colourful Buxton Memorial and drinking fountain nearby commemorates the leaders of the Anti-Slavery Movement and the 1833 Act of Parliament that emancipated slaves in the British Empire. Upper Canada was the first British colony to ban slavery, but its Act of 1793 didn't apply to current slaves in deference to the local merchants, magistrates, and legislators who owned them. [34]

> **Trivia:** *Venereal disease was so rampant in the First World War that Canadian soldiers often had to drop their trousers for weekly inspections. The ritual was known as the "short arm parade."*

Exit Victoria Tower Gardens at Lambeth Bridge. Just beyond Horse Ferry Road is Thames House. This is home to the secretive British Security Service, more popularly known as the spy agency MI5, which stands for Military Intelligence-Section Five.

If there was a single event that set off the Cold War and its legacy of spying between East and West, it was likely the defection of a Soviet Embassy cipher clerk in Ottawa named Igor Gouzenko (1919–82). His flight in 1945 with 109 classified documents stuffed under his shirt revealed that a Soviet spy network was working in the West to obtain nuclear secrets. One of Gouzenko's allegations was the existence of an important agent in Britain named "Elli." Some believed this was head of MI5 himself, Sir Roger Hollis (1905–73).

The fact that spies might penetrate such lofty places in the British establishment was not inconceivable. One of the most famous spy cases MI5 uncovered was the Cambridge spy ring in the 1950s. This was a group of upper-class young men who were recruited by the Soviets while at university. All of them subsequently obtained key government jobs and passed along secrets. One of these, the so-called "Fourth Man," was a respected art historian named Anthony Blunt (1907–83). Blunt confessed his crimes to MI5 in 1964 but was not identified publicly until 1979. When his treachery was unmasked, the public learned it wasn't just the Soviets Blunt worked for. He was on Canada's payroll, too.

61

MI5 Headquarters: *The Spy Who Loved Art*

Anthony Blunt was a tall, spidery man, with long arms and legs and a drawn face that seemed to many cold and indifferent. Yet his weary detachment masked a brilliant mind when it came to Renaissance art — as well as a gnawing lifelong secret.

As a young man in the 1930s, Blunt viewed the Soviet Union as a bulwark against Fascism. He became a student Marxist, passed secrets to the Soviets during the Second World War, and then embarked on a distinguished career as Keeper of the Queen's Pictures and director of London's Courtauld Institute of Art.

When Blunt was exposed in 1979, his world collapsed like a flimsy shed under the weight of Siberian snow. He was stripped of his knighthood, pursued by the tabloid press, and vilified mercilessly. It also came to light that he was responsible for buying some of Canada's most important European works of art that today hang in Toronto's Art Gallery of Ontario (AGO) and the National Gallery of Canada in Ottawa.

Blunt was paid a retainer to scout out acquisitions for the two galleries, which he put toward a scholarship for Canadians at his institute. Using his connections in the art world, he advised Canadian curators on upcoming art sales that might interest them. It was through Blunt that the AGO acquired works by such notable painters as Sir Joshua Reynolds, Henri Matisse, and Edgar Degas. He also assisted in the purchase of the gallery's first Pablo Picasso and sculpture by Henry Moore. But not all of his choices were welcome. When he once recommended a naughty brothel scene by Henri Toulouse-Lautrec, the priggish governors of Canada's National Gallery turned it down.[36]

Spying wasn't the only blemish on Blunt's career. In 1953, he helped the National Gallery of Canada purchase *Augustus and Cleopatra* by the seventeenth-century French painter Nicolas Poussin (1594–1665). It later turned out to be a fake.

Now let's cross the river into Lambeth. In the early 1800s, this area was very different from today. Before the marshes were drained and the Albert Embankment was added in 1868, the area was a jumble of wharves, warehouses, and custom houses frequented by potters and boatmen. Two urban landmarks that survive are immediately in front of us.

The first is Lambeth Palace on the left with its Tudor gatehouse dating to around 1490. The palace has been the London home of the Archbishop of Canterbury, head of the Church of England, for nearly 800 years, and was once described by those living north of the river as the only picturesque site in Lambeth. Beyond the palace doors are the Archbishop's chapel, a Great Hall containing the church's library, and a public park. Anglicanism spread to Canada with British immigration, particularly

Trivia: *The first Thanksgiving service in Canada was performed by Robert Wolfall, an Anglican chaplain on Sir Martin Frobisher's Arctic expedition in 1578. This occurred forty-two years before the New England Pilgrims celebrated their first Thanksgiving.*

with Tory loyalists fleeing from the United States. One loyalist was the Right Reverend Charles Inglis (1734–1816), the rector of Trinity Church on Wall Street in New York City. He fled the U.S. after uttering the words "God Save the King" in front of George Washington (1732–99). Inglis was consecrated bishop of Nova Scotia at Lambeth Palace in 1787 — the first bishop in Canada.

Adjacent to Lambeth Palace is the partially medieval church of St. Mary-at-Lambeth. It is the oldest structure in the area. One of the windows along the western side of the church depicts a local legend known as the Lambeth Pedlar. He is said to have left land to the church as long as his dog could be buried in the churchyard. St. Mary's narrowly escaped demolition in the 1970s after the number of parishioners declined, and is now the Garden Museum. Archbishop John Moore (1730–1805), who consecrated Bishop Inglis, is buried here with a number of other archbishops.

In the churchyard you will find the grave of Vice Admiral William Bligh (1754–1817), a name that is forever associated with the mutiny on HMS *Bounty*. On his grave is a breadfruit, the food staple that attracted his ill-fated crew to the South Pacific. He lived at 100 Lambeth Road and was a parishioner here.

Before the infamous mutiny, however, Bligh was Master of HMS *Resolution* that sailed on the third voyage of Captain James Cook (1728–79) along the coast of British Columbia. Bligh Island in Nootka Sound bears his name. A cairn there marks the spot where he landed in 1778. Nearby Resolution Cove is named after Cook's ship.

St. Mary's was also the parish church of the family of Lieutenant-Colonel John By (1779–1836), the builder of Canada's Rideau Canal.

The Bys were customs clerks in the area going back several generations. As a child, By had likely watched the teeming commerce of the River Thames pass by his front door and been awed by the river's ability to transport all manner of things. He was born, baptized, and raised all within a stone's throw of here. Although he didn't become a customs clerk on the river like his forebears, water in a way still influenced his life's work. As an army engineer, he built a small canal near Pointe-des-Cascades, Quebec, and designed a factory complex near Enfield Lock in London. His greatest accomplishment, however, would be his downfall.

The grave of the much-maligned William Bligh behind the church of St. Mary, Lambeth. He sailed with Captain James Cook to British Columbia in 1778 where Bligh Island is named after him.

St. Mary-at-Lambeth: *Bye, Bye John By*

The costs for building the Rideau Canal were grossly underestimated from the start. Based on a quick assessment by a civilian commission, the winding canal through the swampy forest between Lake Ontario and the Ottawa River was projected to cost a meagre £169,000. That was good enough for Field Marshal Arthur Wellesley (1769–1852), 1st Duke of Wellington, who was impatient to see his pet project for the defence of Canada get underway. He seized on the figure, pushed the plan through Parliament, and instructed Lieutenant-Colonel John By, a Royal Engineer in the military, "to proceed with all despatch consistent with economy" and not to wait for parliamentary grants.

In 1826, By arrived back in Canada and did what was he was told, hiring 2,000 men and building forty-seven locks and fifty-two dams over five years. He also doubled the canal's width to accommodate steamboats and military barges. Not surprisingly, it wasn't long before costs began to balloon and draw attention back in Britain. The final bill was more than four times the estimate. Had the duke remained in government, he might have defended the cost overruns as necessary. But history didn't work out that way. In 1831, his Tory party was defeated at the polls and the Whigs came to power. Like all new governments, they wanted to show they were more fiscally prudent than the previous guys — especially overseas. Caught in a political bunfight, By became a scapegoat for the expensive canal in the remote Canadian wilderness.

In 1832, By was ordered home where he faced an inquiry on overspending and improper contracts. Fortunately, he kept meticulous records — most importantly, the duke's original orders — and was exonerated from any wrongdoing. But friends were few and far between, and the controversy took a deep personal toll. Instead of being honoured for his feat of incredible engineering, By retired to the countryside and faded from sight. He died a broken man at fifty-six.[37]

Now return to the pathway along the Albert Embankment. As the dates on the ornate lampposts confirm, the Embankment was completed in 1870. The wall was subsequently raised more than half a metre to prevent flooding, which is why the benches along here had to be raised as well.

First along the pathway is a memorial to the secret agents of the Second World War. Known as the Special Operations Executive (SOE), this was a small and clandestine group of men and women who operated behind enemy lines "to set Europe ablaze," in the words of Winston Churchill. They were trained in guerrilla warfare such as propaganda, subversion, and sabotage. The figure on the memorial is that of Violette Szabo (1921–ca.1945), a British spy of French descent who was captured and killed on her second mission in Occupied France. Some of these secret agents trained at the famous "Camp X" near Oshawa, Ontario. This was a covert training ground for Canadian, British, and American agents masterminded by Sir William Stephenson (1897–1989), a Manitoba-born spymaster known as the "Man Called Intrepid."

Further along the Embankment we come to a plaque on the wall placed by the Ottawa Historical Society. It commemorates the birthplace of Lieutenant-Colonel By. He was born in a small brick house that once stood here.

Guy's and St. Thomas's, a university hospital, rises behind the wall beside us. Its origins go back to medieval times when a hospital was built here by monks in honour of Thomas Becket (1118–70), the meddlesome Archbishop of Canterbury who was murdered on orders of the king. Central Hall, which contains an interesting display about the hospital's history, and the red-brick wards facing the river are the only parts of the immense complex that date from the nineteenth century. Queen Victoria opened these buildings in 1871 as a teaching hospital. It attracted medical students from around the world, including one of Canada's most notorious murderers.

At 103 Lambeth Palace Road (now demolished and part of Archbishop's Park) lived Dr. Thomas Neill Cream (1850–92), a medical student at St. Thomas's. Cream was a smartly dressed, broad-shouldered man with a badly crossed eye. If other walking tours of London paint the city's East End as the den of Victorian vice and murder, we are about to learn differently. The arrival of the railroad into Lambeth turned it into a dangerous warren of dark alleys and archways. Cream was convicted of administering deadly strychnine to four prostitutes who lived or worked in the area in 1891–92. His victims were Nellie Donworth of 8 Duke Street, Matilda Clover of 27 Lambeth Road, and Alice Marsh and Emma Shrivell of 118 Stamford Street.

As detectives from Scotland Yard pieced together Cream's murderous habits, they discovered a macabre trail that wound its way back to Canada and the United States, and included up to seven murders. His life would end on the gallows in London with an even-stranger twist.

Guy's and St. Thomas's Hospital: *The Strange Case of Dr. Cream*

Thomas Neill Cream was born in Glasgow and moved to Canada as a child in 1854. In 1872, his parents sent him to McGill University to study medicine. If he had a nasty reputation at the time, it wasn't recorded. One of his professors only recalled he was fond of fancy clothing and could be rather wild.[38]

Soon after graduating, however, things began to turn sour for Cream. It began when he allegedly botched an abortion on his new wife and fled the marriage to study at St. Thomas's Hospital. After she died — possibly from taking medicine he had mailed her — Cream returned to Canada to set up a medical practice with her money. In short order, another woman was dead. Cream dodged a murder charge but his professional reputation was in tatters. He wasn't so lucky the next time. Turning up in Chicago, he was convicted of administering strychnine to a prostitute and sent to the Illinois State Penitentiary in 1881 for life.

Incredibly, the story doesn't end there. Released from prison early for good behaviour, Cream returned to his old stomping ground of Lambeth — and his old ways. Following a series of local murders involving strychnine, Cream was arrested after bragging about his crimes to a retired police officer. After deliberating ten minutes, a jury convicted him of murder and a judge sentenced him to hang.

But it was on the gallows that the strange case of Dr. Cream became even stranger. Before the noose snapped, the hangman reported Cream confessed: "I am Jack" sparking rumours he might be Jack the Ripper. Although the parallels between the two are intriguing, a link is fanciful. While the dapper Canadian may have been capable of such horrific crimes, the methods of the two murderers were very different. More importantly, Cream was in a Chicago prison during the five principal murders attributed to the Ripper. Yet if the story has any truth, he remains the only person to this day to have confessed to the Ripper's crimes.

The Reverend John Smithurst, a missionary in Manitoba's Red River settlement. A lifelong bachelor, he cultivated a tidy garden and the memory of Florence Nightingale.

The construction of St. Thomas's Hospital in 1856 coincided with the return from the Crimean War of nursing pioneer Florence Nightingale (1820–1910). Nightingale gained renown as the Lady with the Lamp for her compassionate care of wounded soldiers in the war. As a leading advocate of better health care, she advised on the creation of separate wards at St. Thomas's to prevent the spread of disease that still exist today. She also insisted that her nurses — sometimes called Nightingales — be clean, quiet, and *sober*. The Florence Nightingale Museum is at 2 Lambeth Palace Road in Guy's and St. Thomas's Hospital.

That Nightingale was wed to nursing is well-known. What is less well-known is that she may almost have wed a man who became a Manitoba missionary.

64

Florence Nightingale Museum: *Manitoba Is for Lovers*

In St. John's Anglican Church in Elora, Ontario, west of Toronto, are stained-glass windows dedicated to the memories of two people: one, the famous nurse of the Crimean War, Florence Nightingale, and the other a largely unknown country rector named John Smithurst (1807–67). Before joining the parish in Elora, Smithurst was a missionary for the Hudson's Bay Company in Manitoba's Red River district. Some say none other than Florence Nightingale herself sent him there.

In an age when women were often little more than property, Nightingale took charge of her own life and never married. But she did have suitors. One of these may have been her cousin William Shore who in an oddly similar tale moved to the United States after failing to woo her.[39]

Smithurst was eighteen years her senior and lived close to Nightingale's family in Derbyshire. Some believe the pair were cousins too and may have been engaged. The story goes the families objected to the marriage and Nightingale encouraged a distraught Smithurst to perform church work instead. "John, I want you to go and be a missionary to the Indians of North America," she reputedly told him. What Smithurst lacked in marriage appeal he made up for in religious zeal. After joining the Church Missionary Society, he moved to Canada's Red River area in 1839 where he baptized over 300 people and started writing the first Cree-English Dictionary. Folks there said their conscientious priest had the best-arranged house and garden in the settlement. [40]

In 1852, Smithurst settled in Elora to become rector. He seems to have perpetuated the Nightingale myth by naming his house Lea Hurst after his and Nightingale's birthplace. A communion service given on behalf of a mysterious admirer and addressed to Smithurst as "a dear friend" similarly fanned the flames of the Nightingale legend and their romantic if uncertain story of unrequited love.[41]

A few steps beyond and we find ourselves at Westminster Bridge. Opened in 1862, the wide bridge is guarded at opposite ends by a bronze statue of Boudicca, a Celtic warrior queen who led a revolt against the Romans in A.D. 60, and a stone lion that used to adorn a brewery in Lambeth. Turn left and cross back over to Westminster Tube station. Alternatively, take the river walkway under the bridge to visit the Southbank attractions such as the London Eye, London Aquarium, Royal Festival Hall, and National Theatre.

WALK 5:

FLEET STREET TO ST. PAUL'S

The obituary for newspapers, like those for popes, aging celebrities, and rock stars of any age, is probably already written. Yet the ink trade's demise may not be a sure wager. For 300 years, the industry has survived changing times and tastes by adopting everything from movable type and steam presses to crosswords, horoscopes, and style sections for women. It is a business constantly reinventing itself, as the abandoned buildings in Fleet Street remind us only too well. Canadian press barons have played prominent roles here over the years but they are not the only noteworthies in this part of town. On this walk through London's former epicentre of news we will meet many people associated with Canada, both heroes and villains, on and off the printed page.

This walk begins at High Holborn Tube Station and ends at St. Paul's Tube Station. Walking distance is about 1.2 miles (2 kilometres). Note: Lincoln's Inn is closed on weekends.

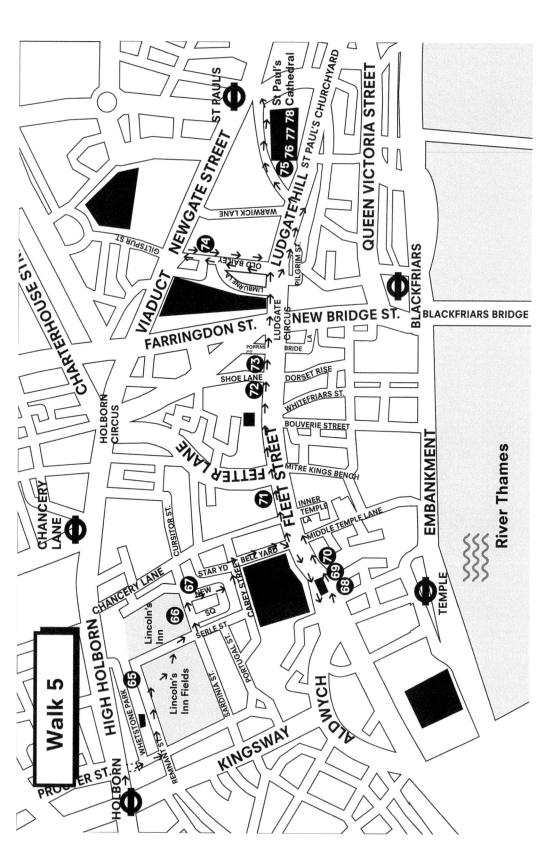

DISCOVERIES

A SHORT HISTORY OF THE AREA

Holborn (pronounced Ho-burn) takes its name from Old Bourne, a vanished and forgotten river. The area's main road, or "high street," runs between Bloomsbury in the west and the City of London in the east. This was once a busy commercial route for country wool traders whose daily passage prompted the rise of pubs, whore houses, and other vices to fleece them of their profits. Today, High Holborn is more likely to be frequented by students from the nearby London School of Economics or two of the four medieval Inns of Court: Gray's Inn to the north and Lincoln's Inn to the south.

The Inns of Court were founded in medieval times as hostels for law students and practising lawyers. Within these early gated communities — one never knows if the walls were to keep lawyers in or angry citizens out — students studied law, ate meals together, and enjoyed pleasant garden walks until they were called to the bar, the traditional courtroom divide where qualified lawyers could plead their cases.

Like High Holborn, the name Fleet Street owes its origins to an ancient river. Fleet is the Anglo-Saxon term for tidal inlet and the river that emptied into the Thames was once an important north-south waterway carrying first manufactured goods and then human waste. Too much of the latter, in fact. The stench became so bad the river was bricked over in the 1700s and officially made a sewer in 1860.

Mind you, the awful odours didn't seem to bother the printers and booksellers who settled in the area, starting in the 1500s. The first was the aptly named Wynkyn de Worde (unknown–1534) who set up one of London's first printing presses in Fleet Street opposite Shoe Lane. He produced relatively inexpensive religious books for local churchmen but also more commercially appealing romantic works for the small but growing number of literate city dwellers. Other publishers followed and soon the street was the established home for the print trade.

To sustain the presses, however, publishers needed more than just ink: they needed news. Information was money after all, and said to have made the Rothschilds rich. The first newspaper, *The Daily Courant*, arrived in 1702 and so many others followed that Fleet Street became widely known for gossip and scandal. Shouted out and sold on every street corner, news fed an insatiable hunger in this city that has never been quenched. The novelist Ford Madox Ford (1873–1939) rightly advised visitors: "You must know the news, in order to be a fit companion for your fellow Londoner."[1]

THE WALK

At Holborn Tube Station, turn right and follow High Holborn eastward about 55 yards (50 metres). Look for the second narrow passage on the right called Little Turnstile and follow it by twists and turns past a pub called The Ship and emerge into Lincoln's Inn Fields. This part of our walk reminds us how quickly the city can become small and claustrophobic. Navigating it makes us feel like old London hands — which by now we are.

Lincoln's Inn Fields is one of the largest and earliest public squares in the city. While it has been a favourite stomping ground for students since the 1300s, it also has some more gruesome associations that we'll leave to other guidebooks.

Just beyond the western side of the Fields, hidden from view, is the London School of Economics, founded in 1895. Numerous Canadian politicians have studied here, including Pierre Trudeau (1919–2000), who never took a degree, and separatist Quebec Premier Jacques Parizeau (b. 1930), who did a Ph.D. in economics.

Walk into the fields and keep to the gravel path on the north side. This is called Canada Walk for a reason that will become clear in a moment.

Just north of us at 12–14 Lincoln's Inn Fields is the one-time residence and now museum of Sir John Soanes (1753–1837), one of Britain's leading architects in the Regency period and an incorrigible packrat. The amazing museum is one of London's most eccentric treasures and worth a visit if time permits. Never has so much been stuffed into so little space.

Soanes is best known for designing buildings like the Bank of England but in 1818 he was approached to design the residence for Upper Canada's new lieutenant governor, Sir Peregrine Maitland (1777–1854), in Toronto. Maitland may have needed convincing to move to Toronto, since he preferred Newark (Niagara) for the capital.

Drawings show Soane envisioned a monumental building for Maitland with a domed entrance but it was never built.[2]

A little farther along the pathway we come to a Canadian maple tree planted by Prime Minister Jean Chrétien (b. 1934) in 1998. It stands across from 20–23 Lincoln's Inn Fields, which was the overseas headquarters of the Royal Canadian Air Force in the Second World War (1939–1945).

When aviation was in its infancy during the First World War (1914–18), Canada had little interest in having its own air force. Consequently, over 20,000 Canadians joined the British Royal Flying Corps (later the Royal Air Force) during the war. After the amazing exploits of a few notable Canadian airmen, however, Ottawa slowly began to change its mind and created the Royal Canadian Air Force (RCAF) on April 1, 1924.

Naturally enough, the RCAF was modelled after its British forebear. It even incorporated the RAF's flag, ranks, uniform, and motto ("Through adversity to the stars"). The services were so similar, in fact, that by the time the Second World War broke out some believed it would be more efficient if Canadian and British air crews served together in one air force. But not everyone shared this view — notably Canada's prime minister.

65

20–23 Lincoln's Inn Fields: *Putting the "C" in RCAF*

Just how Canadian should the overseas Royal Canadian Air Force be? That was a question posed at the start of the Second World War when there were only three RCAF squadrons stationed in Britain. With German raiders bombing London every night, Canada's top air man in Britain, Air Commodore Leigh Stevenson (1895–1989), believed his crews could defend the country more quickly under British control. He saw the RCAF overseas headquarters as a liaison office with no role in directing the Battle of Britain.[4]

His views at first were shared by Charles "Chubby" Power (1888–1968), Canada's affable if boozy minister of defence for air. Power ordered Stevenson to integrate the RCAF overseas into the RAF as quickly as possible to defend Britain. But Power's decision irked his own commander-in-chief, Prime Minister William Lyon Mackenzie King (1874–1950). When the PM learned what his junior minister had done, he nearly fell off his levitating office chair. He told Powers he wanted Canadian boys to fly in all-Canadian squadrons, be served by Canadian ground crews and be ruled by Canadian air chiefs.

Power sobered to the error of his ways and marched off to London in 1941 to fix the problem. When he told his British counterparts that he wanted the Canadian crews back under Canadian command, they reluctantly agreed.

Powers then replaced Stevenson with a new Canadian gunslinger, Air Vice-Marshal Harold "Gus" Edwards (1892–1952), and ordered him "to put the RCAF on the map." Over the next few years, Edwards turned the Overseas Headquarters of the RCAF in Lincoln's Inn Fields into a real command centre. But fighting the enemy as well as the British bureaucracy was tough on poor Edwards. "I find myself in the state that I want to get at somebody's liver, fry it and jam it down his neck, but for the moment I cannot get my hands on the proper person," he once complained.[5]

Follow the path around the square to the southeast corner and cross over Newman's Row into Lincoln's Inn via its ornate gate.

Lincoln's Inn is the prettiest and most authentic of the four Inns of Court in London. By gentlemen's agreement, none of the inns lays claim to being the oldest — though this one probably is. It was founded in the late 1300s on land once owned by Henry de Lacy (ca.1251–1311), 3rd Earl of Lincoln.

The gateway we pass through was built in 1843 at the same time as the Library and New Hall, immediately to our left. The library's collection of law books goes back as far as 1497 and is one of London's oldest. A plaque on the Old Hall directly ahead of us in Old Square dates the building from 1490, the fifth year of the reign of Henry VII (1457–1509; reigned from 1485).

Americans like to point out that William Penn (1644–1718), the founder of Pennsylvania, was a member of Lincoln's Inn. But Canada too can lay claim to some colourful legal characters who studied here. Among them are John Galt (1779–1839), a Scottish novelist and businessman. After studying at the Inn he created the Canada Company to purchase one million hectares (2.5 million acres) of cheap land in Ontario to sell to immigrants. Sadly, Bookkeeping 101 was not on the Lincoln's Inn syllabus and Galt went to jail for running up bad debts. Another noteworthy member of the Inn was Sir Richard Graves MacDonnell (1814–81), a lieutenant governor of Nova Scotia. During the Confederation debates, MacDonnell became alarmed by John A. Macdonald's proposals to reduce the power of lieutenant governors. He warned the future prime minister "you shall not make a mayor of me." Macdonald did exactly that and MacDonnell moved to Hong Kong — happy to leave what he called "the unlucky cul-de-sac" that was Canada.[6]

Others associated with Lincoln's Inn include Charles Ogden (1791–1866), the chief prosecutor of the 1837 rebels in Lower Canada, William Osgoode (1754–1824), first chief justice of Upper Canada for whom Osgoode Hall in Toronto is named, and John Simcoe Saunders (1795–1878), the last unelected provincial secretary in New Brunswick.

But two other members of the Inn deserve our more fulsome attention. One had a knack for disturbing the peace. The other helped restore it.

66

Lincoln's Inn: *B.C.'s Brawling Barrister*

George Hunter Cary (1832–66) was a promising young barrister of Lincoln's Inn. In 1859, he accepted the post of attorney general of British Columbia after James Douglas (1803–77), the first governor of the colony, appealed for "gentlemen of the best education and ability" to help him run the place. Douglas and the good people of B.C. got more than they bargained for.

From the moment Cary arrived in Victoria, controversy followed him like a winter shadow. Irascible and short-fused, he was renowned for throwing tantrums and cursing his superiors. *Outside* the courtroom, his behaviour was even worse. Cary once attacked a defendant with a horse whip and became such a public nuisance he was put in jail for disturbing the peace. His behaviour grew even more erratic after he was nearly ruined financially by building an elaborate country estate called Cary Castle. Even Governor Douglas began to doubt the mental balance of his attorney general.

The final straw came when a relative saw Cary out in the garden with a candle at night sowing peas amongst the potatoes. A week later he was certified insane. To lure him back to London for treatment, his family concocted a fake telegram announcing Cary's appointment as lord chancellor of England (head of its courts). He returned to London with high expectations of donning silk robes of state but died here soon afterward of "paralysis of the brain." He was only thirty-four years old.[7]

Walk ahead toward the chapel and into Old Square. The most famous phrase in Canadian politics may have been coined here: "Peace, Order, and Good Government," found in our 1867 constitution. Whereas independent-minded Americans enshrined "life, liberty and the pursuit of happiness" in their constitution, Canadians enshrined collective harmony and order in ours. Or did we? As we are about to discover, this wasn't exactly how the Fathers of Confederation set out to define Canada, but rather how a Lincoln's Inn barrister did.

22 Old Buildings: *Peace, Order, and Good Government*

The Fathers of Confederation may have agreed on the terms for union back in 1866–67 but the man who actually drafted the text was a little-known barrister of Lincoln's Inn.

Sir Francis Savage Reilly (1825–83) was born in Dublin and graduated from Trinity College in 1847. He was called to the bar in 1851 and joined Lincoln's Inn, where he specialized in arbitration, insurance cases, and train wrecks. His legal chambers were located at 22 Old Buildings.

In 1866, Britain's Colonial Office approached Reilly to draft the legal text of the British North America Act. He agreed but may have soon regretted it. What was supposed to be a simple three-day job stretched out over many weeks when he couldn't get hold of the Canadian delegation to bring legal clarity to their ideas. "I can't make bricks without clay, to say nothing of straw," he complained in frustration.[8]

Eventually Reilly did manage to sit down with Sir John A. Macdonald and the British colonial secretary, Henry Herbert (1831–90), 4th Earl of Carnarvon, to turn their ideas into a legal document. But Reilly was clearly more than just a scribe. In one of his drafts he proposed a name for the new colony: the United Province of Canada, though this was rejected by the Canadians. His more enduring addition, however, was perhaps the word "order."

In earlier drafts of their agreement, the Fathers of Confederation had always used the phrase "peace, *welfare*, and good government." For stiff empire men like Reilly and his Tory boss Carnarvon, not only was the choice less eloquent, but welfare probably seemed a bit too coddling, nannyish, and Liberal. They preferred a good old-fashioned Victorian sense of order and capitalized it just for good measure. In doing so, Reilly and Carnarvon helped define the attributes of Canadian society. For his services to Britain and the empire, he was knighted in 1882.[9]

Now head back to New Square and exit through the south gate into Carey Street. As the bankruptcy courts are just across the road, it's wise not to tell people exactly where you are. To be "on Carey Street" is a local euphemism for being broke. Here and on Searle Street we find stores where barristers can purchase horsehair wigs — court dress for British lawyers for hundreds of years. (Canadian courts dispensed with the practice in the nineteenth century.) Walk to Bell Yard, turn right, and head to the Strand.

The impressive jumble of Gothic Revival turrets and spires on our right are the Royal Courts of Justice (or Law Courts). Conveniently for Fleet Street, this is where civil cases, including libel, are tried. They were opened by Queen Victoria in 1882 and are said to contain a thousand rooms and over 3.4 miles (5.5 kilometres) of corridors. Above the judge's entrance on the north side are statues of a cat and dog representing litigants in court.

Trivia: *Peace, order, and good government appeared in the first constitutions of several Commonwealth countries including New Zealand and South Africa.*

On a treed island in the middle of the street is St. Clement Danes church. How this church became associated with Danes is a bit of a mystery, though some believe a king of Danish descent is buried beneath it. Despite escaping the Great Fire in 1666 unscathed, the church was rebuilt by the architect Sir Christopher Wren (1632–1723) in 1681. His protégé James Gibbs (1682–1754) added the steeple in 1719.

In front of the church stands a 1905 bronze memorial to four-time British prime minister William Ewart Gladstone (1809–98) dressed grandly in his ceremonial robes of Chancellor of the Exchequer (or finance minister). At the base of the statue are four female figures representing education, aspiration, courage, and (somewhat oddly) brotherhood. Noticeably absent is parsimony.

68. Gladstone Monument: *Mr. G Says No*

William Gladstone was a tight-fisted Liberal politician and anti-imperialist who opposed spending money and taking risks, no matter how small. This was certainly true when it came to supporting a colony like Canada.

In appearance, Gladstone was the polar opposite of his Conservative rival, Benjamin Disraeli (1804–81). Whereas Disraeli was dark, sensuous, and cloaked in Romanticism, Gladstone was pale, rough, and charmless with wispy chin hairs and unruly sideburns. Unlike Disraeli, Gladstone was relatively unskilled in oratory and more importantly, the art of flattery. The one who noticed the most was Queen Victoria. She complained Gladstone addressed her as if she were a public meeting and much preferred the smoother Disraeli.

Gladstone feared money spent in Canada was money lost forever: the colony would inevitably desert Britain like the United States had and leave the British Treasury to pay the bills. So he argued against financing defences and the Intercolonial Railway and withdrew British soldiers from Canada in 1871, leaving behind only a handful of soldiers at Halifax and Esquimalt. The attitude of "Gladstone & Co." frustrated Sir John A. Macdonald and his pals, who felt abandoned by the British Government. "It is very grievous to see half a continent slipping away from the grasp of England with scarcely an effort to hold it," Macdonald's then-finance minister, Alexander Galt (1817-93), once complained about Gladstone's parsimonious ways.[10]

Like many of the churches in the area, St. Clement Danes was badly damaged in the Second World War. It was rebuilt with contributions from British, Commonwealth, and Allied air forces and designated the Central Church of Royal Air Force in 1958. Plaques in the floor, made of Welsh slate, commemorate British and Allied air squadrons that fought in the war, twenty-nine of which are Canadian.

On the left wall near the altar is a Roll of Honour that lists of the winners of the Victoria Cross. This is the highest military honour for gallantry in the British and Commonwealth forces. Three of the early winners of the "VC" listed here were Canadian flying aces: William "Billy" Avery Bishop (1894–1956), William George Barker (1894–1930), and Alan Arnett MacLeod (1899–1918). Sadly, the last two of these men died soon after the war. Barker won his VC for a dramatic dogfight over Canadian lines in France, but was killed in a plane crash near Ottawa in 1930. His raid was recalled in *The Snows of Kilimanjaro*, a short story by Ernest Hemingway (1899–1961). MacLeod, on the other hand, won his VC for rescuing his comrade from a fiery plane wreck and carrying him to safety under fire — only to die himself during the great flu epidemic of 1918. That leaves us with one flying ace to consider in more detail: the most charismatic and controversial of the three.

69

St. Clement Danes: *Billy Bishop's Other War*

Born in Owen Sound, Ontario, Billy Bishop was a gregarious young man who attended Canada's Royal Military College in Kingston, Ontario, before shipping out to France with the Canadian cavalry in 1915. Just before the deadly battle of the Somme, he transferred to Britain's Royal Flying Corps to become a pilot. In the course of 184 sorties, he claimed an astonishing forty-seven victories. His record would eventually climb to seventy-two — the highest of any air ace. But it was his audacious, single-handed dawn raid on a German airfield in 1917 that earned him the distinguished VC. As the first Canadian flyer to win the award, Bishop was hailed a national hero.

But after Bishop's death, you could say his real battle began. In 1977, the play *Billy Bishop Goes to War* cast the hero in a less positive light and was followed by a National Film Board docudrama called *The Kid Who Couldn't Miss.* It raised questions about the airman's seventy-two victories and sparked so much outrage that the Senate established a commission to investigate. (Not surprisingly, it couldn't reach a conclusion.) Even an official historian of the RCAF weighed in, saying Bishop was a liar and a cheat who didn't deserve his VC.[11]

Yet the evidence for and against Bishop may never be definitive. As a fighter who often flew solo behind enemy lines, Bishop had few witnesses to his triumphs. Moreover, tracking air victories at the time was more art than science. If Bishop was guilty of embellishing the truth, so were many others. In their eagerness to identify rivals to the Red Baron, the Allies desperately needed heroes and Bishop was a good as any out there. Truth, as the saying goes, is the first casualty of war.

Two other Canadian airmen listed here won their VCs in the Second World War. Their awards were never controversial. The airmen were Flight Lieutenant David Ernest Hornell (1910–44) and Pilot Officer Andrew Charles Mynarski (1916–44).

> **Trivia:** *Canadian flying aces Billy Bishop and William Barker created Bishop-Barker Aeroplane Lines in 1919. They flew flying boats out of Toronto until the company went broke three years later.*

St. Clement Danes: *Two Heroes of the Sky*

David Hornell was born on Toronto Island and joined the Royal Canadian Air Force in 1941. One night in June 1944, while he was flying his twin-engine amphibian aircraft off the coast of Scotland, Hornell and his crew engaged a German U-boat patrolling in the North Sea. In the melee that followed, Hornell's plane was badly damaged and lost an engine. Ignoring more gunfire from the U-boat, Hornell managed to sink it and then miraculously land the blazing plane in heavy sea swells. With only one lifeboat, he and his crew took turns in the freezing water where Hornell kept up everyone's spirits with his cheerful manner. After twenty-one hours at sea, Hornell succumbed to exposure and died shortly after being rescued. He was buried in Scotland.

Andrew Mynarski was born and raised in Winnipeg, the son of Polish immigrants. In 1941, he enlisted in the Royal Canadian Air Force and trained in Edmonton and Calgary before coming to England in 1943. On the night of June 12, 1944, Mynarski was a mid-upper gunner on a Lancaster bomber involved in a sortie over France. When his aircraft was hit, a fire broke out between the mid and rear gunner turrets. As Mynarski prepared to abandon the aircraft, he saw that the rear gunner was trapped. Without hesitating, he fought through flames to rescue his comrade but the rear gunner couldn't be freed. He told Mynarski to save himself and Mynarski reluctantly went back to the escape hatch. Before leaping to safety, he turned and saluted his trapped comrade.

Incredibly, however, the rear gunner survived the plane crash while Mynarski died from burns after his parachute caught fire. He was buried in France and is commemorated at the Valiants Memorial near the National Cenotaph in Ottawa.

Outside the entrance to the church are statues of Air Chief Marshal Hugh "Stuffy" Dowding (1882–1970), head of RAF Fighter Command during the Battle of Britain, and Sir Arthur "Bomber" Harris (1892–1984), head of RAF Bomber Command. Both are works by the British sculptor Faith Winter. Protests marked the unveiling of Harris's statue in 1992, as he was responsible for the firebombing of Germany. Thousands of Canadian airmen died in pursuit of Harris's controversial strategy.

Let's now head down historic Fleet Street, sometimes called the "street of shame" for the unscrupulous scribes and ambitious press barons associated with it. In doing so, we pass a statue of Samuel Johnson (1709–84), London's great man of letters, author of the first English dictionary, and the man most associated with Fleet Street. We'll encounter Johnson a few more times on our walk.

Trivia: A ferry to the Toronto Island Airport is named in honour of Victoria Cross winner David Ernest Hornell. The airport is named after Billy Bishop.

Immediately in front of us is a bronze gryphon used to mark a significant urban boundary. This is the site of Temple Bar where we pass from the City of Westminster into the City of London (known colloquially as "the City"). In more gruesome times, the heads of traitors were displayed here. The original Temple Bar was a gateway that was removed to facilitate traffic. We will see it at the end of our walk in Paternoster Square.

Immediately on our left is Twinings Tea Shop and Museum (216 Strand) which took over Tom's Coffee House in 1706. Next is Messrs. Hoare Bankers (37 Fleet Street), a private bank established in 1672. On the wall beside the bank is a plaque that marks the site of the Mitre Tavern, demolished in 1829. It is here that Samuel Johnson often dined with his celebrated biographer, James Boswell (1740–95). On one occasion in July 1763, Johnson compared news about Canada to his Christian faith. There were many reasons to doubt news about the British victory at Quebec, he told Boswell, "Yet, sir, notwithstanding all these plausible objections we have no doubt that Canada is really ours. Such is the weight of common testimony. How much stronger are the evidences of the Christian religion."[12]

Directly across from Hoare's Bank is St. Dunstan-in-the-West church (at 186a Fleet Street).

Outside the church is a memorial to Alfred Harmsworth (1865–1922), 1st Viscount Northcliffe. He was Britain's first press baron. In 1896, he and his brother Harold founded the populist *Daily Mail.* It sold over a million copies by 1902 and once had the largest circulation in the world.

In 1905, the Harmsworths ventured into Newfoundland in search of paper to supply their newspaper empire. In exchange for building a mill in Grand Falls-Windsor, the brothers were given extensive timber and water rights in the region. When the subsequent owner of the mill closed it in 2009, Newfoundland seized the company's assets saying the closure violated the 1905 agreement with the Harmsworths.[13] The case was settled after Canada agreed to pay compensation to the mill owners.

Above the vestry door set back behind a mobile coffee stall is another statue of interest: an effigy of Queen Elizabeth I (1533–1603; reigned from 1558). It's notable because it dates from the queen's lifetime and may be an authentic likeness.

Beset with treasonous plots, Spanish Armadas, and suitors by the dozen, Good Queen Bess probably didn't think much about Canada. Royal interest in the New World had waned since the disastrous voyages of John Cabot (ca.1450–99) in the time of her grandfather. But saddled with debts, stagnant trade, and the growing might of Spain, Elizabeth was interested in reaching the riches of Asia. With southern routes blocked by other powers, she needed a route to get there.

St. Dunstan-in-the-West: *Queen Elizabeth's Dreams of Gold*

The wars of King Henry VIII (1491–1547; reigned from 1509) and subsequent mismanagement by his daughter Queen Mary (1516–58; reigned from 1553) had left England weakened and badly lacking money. What the country didn't lack were swashbuckling pirates ready to fill the queen's treasury with gold. One of these was Sir Martin Frobisher (ca.1539–94) a tough and courageous mariner raised in London. He believed that the way to Asia lay through Canada's Northwest Passage. After fruitless attempts to find a backer, Frobisher took his plan to the queen who cajoled a group of courtiers to pay for it.

In 1576, Queen Elizabeth waved off the explorer and his two ships bound for Canada. The first land he found he named wisely for his sovereign (Queen Elizabeth Foreland near Baffin Island) and the next immodestly for himself (Frobisher Bay). There he dug up some rocks with metallic shine and brought them back to London in high expectation. Three assayers rejected the rocks as Fool's Gold (actually marcasite) but a fourth believed he could turn them into gold by the mysterious art of alchemy. It was enough to spark a mini gold rush in Canada and a second voyage for Frobisher. This time his backers told him to forget about Asia and just bring back more rocks. In her excitement, the queen awarded Frobisher a royal charter, invested her own money, and locked up his rocks with the crown jewels.

Two voyages later, the gold rush and the queen's excitement were over. Ten times more rock only proved ten times more worthless. Frobisher's backers went belly up and the queen lost her investment. To escape the axe, Frobisher wisely teamed up with the pirate Sir Francis Drake (1540–96) and went after easier loot that didn't involve alchemy: Spanish ships laden with gold. These raids proved so profitable that Elizabeth's treasury was soon full and her Arctic enterprise soon forgotten.[14]

Just past Fetter Lane, we come to signs for Dr. Johnson's House (17 Gough Square). This is a whimsical detour if the fancy takes you. The house was built around 1700 and is one of the last-remaining residences of its type. Take note of the security features above the door. The world's first English dictionary was compiled here and published in 1755. It was unrivalled for a hundred years, until the publication of the *Oxford English Dictionary*. Among Johnson's timeless definitions are:

> Oats: *"a grain, which in England is generally given to horses, but in Scotland supports the people;"* and
> Lexicographer: *"a writer of dictionaries; a harmless drudge."*

Fool's rush in: Martin Frobisher sparked a mini gold rush in Canada in 1576 when he returned from his voyage with a ton of useless rocks.

Continue along Fleet Street eastward. On the north side is the former *Daily Telegraph* Building (135–141 Fleet Street) built in 1928–31, with six stately Greek columns across its front. It was once the jewel in the crown of a media empire headed by Conrad Black (b. 1944), Baron Black of Crossharbour, the last of three Canadian press barons to own a bit of the sidewalk here. At one time Black owned newspapers in Australia, Britain, Canada, Israel, and the U.S.

72

135–141 Fleet Street: *Black and White and Read All Over*

Founded in 1855, the *Daily Telegraph* was one of Britain's most successful newspapers and so politically right wing that journalists nicknamed it the *Torygraph*. But by the mid-1980s, the iron lady of print was haemorrhaging money. The owners knew what to do — like other newspapers, adopt new printing methods and move out of expensive Fleet Street — but they lacked the cash to do it. What they needed was a white knight who could help save the paper.

Conrad Black bought his first newspaper in his twenties and kept on buying them until he had acquired a chain. Later he won control of Argus Corporation, a Canadian company that owned Dominion Stores and Massey-Ferguson. His personal fortune grew to $100 million. But what he really wanted to be was an international press baron and began to scout around for acquisitions. In 1985, he quietly offered the owners of the *Telegraph* $17 million for a 14 percent stake in the company. "All I have to worry about is which pocket the money comes from," he told them.[16]

But the Canadian knight's chivalrous offer came with a hitch: the right of first refusal if the owners needed more dosh. And inevitably they did. A few months later Black advanced $34 million to the owners in return for 50.1 percent of the company's shares — enough to win control of it. "I've hit the jackpot," he told a friend. Robert Maxwell, another British press baron, was duly impressed. He congratulated the Canadian on "landing history's largest fish with history's smallest hook."[17]

Black's purchase of the *Telegraph* made him an international press baron and gave him a coveted entrée into British society. Yet when it came time to join the House of Lords like other press barons before him, Black ran into a little snag with Canada's Prime Minister Chrétien, who blocked the move. In order to don his ermine robes, Black was obliged to renounce his Canadian citizenship.

His reign as chairman of the newspaper would last fifteen years until he sold the *Telegraph* under his own financial duress in 2004.

A few doors down at 120–129 Fleet Street, we come to a truly fascinating piece of modern 1930s showmanship. This was once the headquarters of the *Daily Express*, which overtook Northcliffe's *Daily Mail* as the most widely read newspaper in the world.

> **Trivia:** *The novelist Evelyn Waugh is believed to have parodied the former* Daily Express Building *and its owner,* Lord Beaverbrook, in his 1938 novel Scoop *about life at a fictional newspaper,* The Daily Beast.

Although the *Express* vacated the building in 1989, it has been restored and is now used by an investment bank. Inside the sleek chrome and marble lobby, silver maple leaves adorn the newspaper's name behind the reception desk. Encased overall in gleaming black glass called Vitrolite, it has been described as "quietly elegant in a tight-fitting black dress."[18] It's an image that probably would have pleased the man who commissioned it: Fleet Street's first Canadian-born press baron: William Maxwell Aitken (1879–1964), 1st Baron Beaverbrook. When it opened in 1932, the gleaming headquarters stood in

The lady of Fleet Street: Lord Beaverbrook's modern Daily Express *building. It has been described as "quietly elegant in a tight-fitting black dress."*

stark contrast to the staid *Telegraph* down the street. The newspaper hailed its premises as "Britain's most modern building for Britain's most modern newspaper."

120–129 Fleet Street: *Lord Beenacrook*

William Aitken was a strange gnome-like man born in Ontario but raised in New Brunswick. Small and intensely energetic, he had a large head, impish grin, and penetrating stare. After early attempts at journalism, selling insurance, and managing a bowling alley, Aitken settled on a profession far more lucrative than all of them combined — bonds and company mergers — and became a millionaire before he was thirty. In 1910, he moved to London just in time to dodge a securities scandal that might have sent him to jail.

Once in Britain, Aitken wasted no time sitting around on his laurels and got himself elected a Conservative MP before he was even entitled to vote. In 1917, he went to the House of Lords and adopted the name Beaverbrook, after a stream where he reputedly fished as a boy. Recalling the securities scandal back in Canada, some nicknamed him Lord Beavercrook or Beenacrook.[20]

Newspapers were high among Beaverbrook's passions — after politics, women, and money. In 1916, he quietly purchased Britain's *Daily Express* and introduced new features to boost its sagging circulation. These included sports and leisure coverage, lively headlines, and a popular new American invention: the crossword puzzle. The changes worked. The newspaper's circulation rose to 1.6 million in 1929 from 277,000 in 1916. By the mid 1930s it was the best-selling newspaper in the world.[21]

As one of the most powerful men in Britain, Beaverbrook naturally had friends in high places. Among them was Sir Winston Churchill (1874–1965). He said Beaverbrook was "at his very best when things are at their very worst." Another friend was Andrew Bonar Law (1858–1923), a fellow New Brunswicker who was prime minister for a short time, with Beaverbrook's help. Law's last words to Beaverbrook were: "You are a curious fellow."[22]

Max Aitken, the impish Lord Beaverbrook, was Canada's first press baron of Fleet Street. He was a newspaper man, politician, and notorious philanderer — and one of the most powerful men in Britain.

Continue across Ludgate Circus toward St. Paul's Cathedral. The street Old Bailey on our left follows the line of London's old Roman Wall. The Central Criminal Court (15 Old Bailey) with its large dome and depiction of Lady Justice on top stands beyond on the site of the infamous Newgate Prison, which was demolished in 1904. Dr. Thomas Neill Cream (1850–92), the Lambeth Poisoner from Canada whom we discovered on Walk 4, was hanged and buried within the prison grounds. As "the Old Bailey" courthouse, the building has witnessed a number of sensational criminal trials including that of Dr. Harvey Crippen (1862–1910), the "cellar murderer," who was arrested in Canada along with his mistress, Ethel Le Neve (1883–1967).

Trivia: *The deep well courtroom at Victoria Hall in Cobourg, Ontario, is the only one of its kind in Canada. It is modelled after the original courtroom in London's Old Bailey.*

74

Old Bailey Criminal Court: *Ms. Le Neve Escapes the Noose*

Harvey Crippen was a homeopathic doctor from Michigan — small, polite, and balding — who sold fake medicines to the sick and the gullible. He did it so convincingly that he expanded his company first in Toronto and then in London. In 1892, he met and married a lusty music-hall singer named "Belle Elmore" (her real name was Cora Turner). Their marriage proved a disaster: she ordered him about, spent all his money, and apparently cheated on him too.

In June 1910, Belle disappeared. Suspicions grew when Crippen was seen frequently in the company of his secretary, a petite and quiet English typist named Ethel Le Neve. Police were called in and a grue-some discovery was soon made: human remains in Crippen's cellar.

Crippen and Le Neve (disguised as a boy) had meanwhile fled the country on the SS *Montrose* to Canada, but the captain alerted police by wireless, who gave chase on a faster ship. They boarded the *Montrose* and arrested the astonished couple while their ship was still steaming up the St. Lawrence River.

The 1910 murder trial of Crippen and Le Neve at the Old Bailey took London, and the world, by storm. The prosecution painted Crippen as a henpecked husband who poisoned the domineering Belle rather than divorce her. He was found guilty and sentenced to hang. Le Neve was acquitted. She left London for Toronto and resumed a quiet typing career under a new name. What the jury never heard, however, was testimony that Le Neve had been seen researching poisons in a library. It seems Le Neve may have been an escape artist as well as a typist.[23]

We now find ourselves near the end of our walk at St. Paul's Cathedral, the architectural masterpiece of Sir Christopher Wren (1632–1723). It is the fourth cathedral since 604 to stand on this site. The previous cathedral, in the gothic style, burned down in the Great Fire of 1666. One of the only surviving artifacts from the old cathedral is the shrouded effigy of the poet and preacher John Donne (1572–1631). It miraculously fell through the burning floor into the safety of the crypt below.

Queen Anne's statue in front of St. Paul's Cathedral. She feted four Indian kings in London to win their support for a campaign against the French, but they took their own counsel. Annapolis Royal, Nova Scotia, is named after her.

Before we go inside, let's pause a moment at the statue of Queen Anne (1665–1714; reigned from 1702). At the time the statue was placed here in 1712, the real Anne was gouty, bloated, and so large she had to be hauled up stairs by ropes and pulleys. None of her seventeen pregnancies resulted in a royal heir.

"Queen Anne's War" (1702–13) was the name given to a series of clashes between the English and French in Newfoundland, Nova Scotia, and New England. Two botched attempts to capture Quebec also occurred during her reign, in 1709 and 1711. When her namesake war ended, France gave up its territorial rights to Nova Scotia and Newfoundland for good.

> **Trivia:** *After the murder trial of Dr. Crippen, the captain of the SS* Montrose *went on to command the* Empress of Ireland, *which sank in May 1914 near the exact spot in the St. Lawrence River where the couple were arrested.*

The female figures at Anne's feet symbolize her realms: Britannia (England) holding her trident, Hibernia (Scotland) with her harp, and Gallia (France) with her crown. America is depicted as an Indian warrior. A severed human head under the warrior's foot suggests the uneasy alliance Britain forged with North America's first peoples for over a century.

In fact, the Iroquois deliberately tried to keep the skirmishes between the English and the French in North America from escalating to all-out war. They occupied a strategic position sandwiched between French Canada and the Anglo-American colonies and, until 1754, maintained a delicate balance of power by shifting their support from one side to the other.[24] Naturally, both European powers tried to win their loyalty with gifts to tilt the balance in their favour. Britain even offered some Iroquois leaders an all-expense-paid holiday to London.

75

Queen Anne Monument: *Four Iroquois Kings*

London's West End theatres have attracted visitors of all kinds for hundreds of years but perhaps none so unusual or as sensational as four Iroquois kings who sat down to a performance of *Macbeth* in 1710. Tall, muscular, and covered head to toe in tattoos, they were so popular with the audience that they upstaged the actors. What, if anything, the warriors thought or understood of the Scottish play of kingly murder they diplomatically kept to themselves.

The four kings (three Mohawks and one Mohican) were invited to London by Queen Anne. (They originally numbered five but one didn't survive the voyage.) It was a month-long state visit and the city rolled out the red carpet for them. Besides attending the theatre, they paraded around in royal carriages, toured sites like St. Paul's Cathedral, and met with the queen at St. James's Palace. She was so impressed that she asked them to sit for portraits by her court painter John Verelst (ca.1675–1734). She also presented them with a silver communion set still in use today at her Majesty's Royal Chapel of Christ Church in Deseronto, Ontario.

As always the red carpet had a purpose. The British wanted to win the Iroquois's support for an attack on the French stronghold at Quebec the following year. But the Iroquois were no fools. They knew their survival depended on maintaining a balance of power among the superpowers. As long as England and France were fighting each other, they wouldn't be fighting them.

After being feted in London, the warriors agreed to help the British. Once home, however, they quietly sent word to the French what was afoot.[25]

Now let's head up the long flight of steps into St. Paul's Cathedral. These steps were far too difficult for the frail Queen Victoria to climb in 1897 when she celebrated her Diamond Jubilee, so her service of Thanksgiving was conducted outside. During the Second World War, the iconic image of St. Paul's rising above the plumes of smoke helped rally the spirit of Londoners. In fact, the cathedral's survival owes a nod of gratitude in part to Lieutenant Robert Davies (1900–75), a Canadian soldier. He defused a bomb in front of St. Paul's and won the George Cross for his bravery.

Trivia: *When the British conquered Port-Royal in Nova Scotia for the last time in 1710, its name was changed to Annapolis Royal after Queen Anne.*

The most popular memorials inside are those to Christopher Wren, Vice Admiral Horatio Nelson (1758–1805), 1st Viscount Nelson, and Field Marshal Arthur Wellesley (1769–1852), 1st Duke of Wellington. Our attention, however, will focus on some others.

Before descending into the crypt, walk to the Dome and then turn right into the south transept. Here, on the western wall, we find a memorial tablet to Major-General Sir Isaac Brock (1769–1812), commander of troops in Upper Canada during the War of 1812. He died at the Battle of Queenston Heights near Niagara Falls and became so legendary that towns, streets, and a university were named after him. The memorial here, by Sir Richard Westmacott, shows Brock dead in the arms of a fellow soldier as an Indian ally — the real secret of his military success — looks on.

76

Brock Memorial: *The General's Secret Weapon*

Sir Isaac Brock was born in Guernsey and joined the British Army when he was fifteen. After uneventful military service in the Caribbean and Europe, he went to Canada in 1802 with his regiment, the 49th Foot.

Life in Upper Canada was sleepy and dull for the tall, energetic military officer. For ten years he did little but train militiamen and chase army deserters. He complained of being "buried in this inactive, remote corner" of the world away from the Napoleonic wars in Europe that promoted soldiers they didn't kill. Just when he was about to take his leave, the United States declared war on Britain.

With a U.S. invasion imminent, Brock's first task was to rouse his fellow countrymen to defend their homeland. With only a small fighting force of 1,600 regular troops, he needed civilian volunteers desperately. But many in Upper Canada had recently moved from the U.S. and others didn't want to be on the losing side in a war that seemed so lopsided. So Brock had to "speak loud and look big" to prove he could beat the Americans. He did this with the help of his Indian allies.

Knowing Americans had deep-rooted fears about Indians, Brock falsified a note about their numbers in his army and let it fall into American hands at Fort Detroit before attacking it. Terrified for their safety, the U.S. forces there surrendered — without so much as a single gun being fired.

Brock faced his second test shortly afterward, when an American force crossed the Niagara River and took command of a British battery on Queenston Heights. Unfortunately, Brock's earlier success in Detroit may have made him too confident. He led his forces hastily up the slope and was felled quickly by an American sharpshooter. The sight of his corpse demoralized his patchwork army of British regulars, militia, and Indian warriors but eventually they rallied and attacked the Americans with even greater ferocity. "I thought hell had broken loose and let her dogs of war upon us," said one U.S. soldier.[26] Once again, it was the terrible war whoops of the Indians more than European firepower that brought the enemy to heel. Ironically, in a war that had no victors, it was the Indians who lost the most.

Now let's descend into the crypt where two more memorials await us. As we descend, take note of the bust of Sir John A. Macdonald.

The first memorial we'll consider honours our last Canadian-born press baron on this walk: Roy Herbert Thomson (1894–1976), 1st Baron Thomson of Fleet. His memorial reads: "He gave a new direction to the British newspaper industry. A stranger and adventurous man from nowhere, ennobled by the great virtues of courage and integrity and faithfulness."

> In 1963, U.S.S.R. President Nikita Khrushchev told the wealthy Roy Thomson: you can't take it with you. "Then I am not going," Thomson replied.

Thomson Memorial: *Lord of the Press and Penny*

Roy Thomson never spent a nickel he didn't have to. As the head of a media empire and self-made millionaire, he counted pens and pencils and watched costs scrupulously. He also carried his own luggage, ate at McDonald's, and took public transit to work every day. "I'd rather read a balance sheet than a book," he once confessed.

Unlike other press barons on Fleet Street who wanted to influence politics, Thomson never did. For him, editorial content simply went around advertising. Newspapers were a *licence to print money*, he said.

The son of a Toronto barber, Thomson was a high school dropout and a latecomer to the world of success. He failed as a farmer and tried selling auto parts just when the Great Depression hit and gas stations closed. In 1930, he obtained a franchise to sell radios in North Bay, Ontario, and soon realized that his poor sales had much to do with the fact there was no radio station to listen to. So he started his own, and then went on to buy other stations in Kirkland Lake and Timmins. One of the radio stations shared office space with the local newspaper, so he bought that too. With a pushy aptitude for sales and a keen eye for the bottom line (despite notoriously poor vision), Thomson's empire grew. At fifty-five, he became a millionaire when a million dollars was still a lot of money.

In the U.K., Thomson went on acquiring and picked up the *Scotsman* newspaper and a local Scottish television station. In 1964 his media holdings were so enormous he was elevated to the peerage as Baron Thomson of Fleet. But the biggest feather in his cap was yet to come. At seventy-three, he purchased *The Times* — Britain's most important quality newspaper — and truly became the lord of Fleet Street.

Our last memorial of note marks the final resting place of someone we have encountered before: the "very model of a modern major-general," Sir Garnet Wolseley (1833–1913), 1st Viscount Wolseley. On Walk 3, we learned about this can-do Victorian's attempted rescue in 1884 of Major-General Charles Gordon (1833–85) in Sudan with the help of Canadian raftsmen. Years earlier, however, Wolseley successfully led one of the most logistically challenging expeditions ever undertaken in the British Empire: one across 620 miles (1,000 kilometres) of rugged Canadian wilderness to find another man, the controversial Métis rebellion leader Louis Riel (1844–85).

> **Trivia:** *After Lord Thomson's death, his son Ken sold off most of his father's newspapers to focus on digital news. In 1989, his company merged to become Thomson Reuters.*

78

Wolseley Memorial: *The Red River Challenge*

The transfer of Rupert's Land to the Government of Canada in 1869–70 led to the inevitable clash of cultures between the people who occupied the land and white *parvenu* settlers arriving mostly from Ontario. Louis Riel may have led an arguably justified rebellion, but it was his foolhardy execution of an English settler that set the prairie grass ablaze. The flames spread eastward to Ontario, where there were indignant calls for his head.

The military expedition to Fort Garry (now Winnipeg) to capture Riel was Wolseley's first independent command, and a huge logistical test of his abilities. Since the U.S. wouldn't allow him to go through Minnesota, Wolseley had to go the longer and more treacherous way by Thunder Bay, Lake Winnipeg, and the Red River. His force consisted of 400 British troops and over 700 Canadian militia, along with voyageurs to guide and paddle the maze of lakes and rivers. Between the rebel and Wolseley lay forty-seven portages, some five miles (nine kilometres) of rapids, and millions of mosquitoes. In May 1870, he and his men set off with the cry "For Fort Garry!" In all history, Wolseley liked to say, never had such an operation been attempted.

The keys to Wolseley's success were good men and good boats. The latter not only had to carry up to twelve people each, but tents, ammunition, weaponry, and food and supplies for sixty days — though the journey took ninety-six. Spirits along the difficult route remained high with plentiful songs, campfires, and pipe smoking. But when the force finally arrived at Fort Garry in late August, they found the doors open and Riel gone. "Personally I am glad that Riel did not come out and surrender," wrote Wolseley afterward. "For I could not then have hanged him as I might have done had I taken him prisoner while in arms against his sovereign."[27]

As we take our leave of St. Paul's Cathedral, we pass the Chapel of the Order of St. Michael and St. George in the south aisle. This order was established in 1818 and its chapel contains the nameplates of all those who have received the award since 1906. Among them is Sir Arthur Currie (1875–1933), head of the Canadian army in the First World War, and later principal and vice-chancellor of McGill University.

Exit St. Paul's Cathedral and walk around to the redeveloped Paternoster Square (Latin for Our Father) where the old Temple Bar archway now stands. It was placed here in 2004 after an extensive refurbishment. St. Paul's Tube is found on the east side of the cathedral where our walk ends.

Trivia: *Britain's Order of St. Michael and St. George has three classes: Companion (CMG), Knight and Dame Commander (KCMG), and Knight Grand Cross (GCMG). Some people joke the initials stand for "Call Me God," "Kindly Call Me God," and "God Calls Me God." Sir George Perley, a Canadian politician, told voters his KCMG stood for "Keep Calling Me George."*

WALK 6:
MAYFAIR

When a young Princess Victoria ascended the throne in 1837, the fun and frolics of the preceding years under her cavorting uncles came to an end. The queen set a standard for the age by upholding fidelity and domesticity as the new moral code. White wedding dresses like the queen's became popular expressions of this. A happy home life was important for men, too, if only to escape the avarice of the industrial revolution and a miserly bachelorhood like Ebenezer Scrooge's. Yet the strict rules and conventions on marriage created hardships for some of Queen Victoria's subjects by locking them into loveless marriages or encouraging public shame. These included a few with links to Canada as this walk through London's first suburb reveals.

This walk begins at Green Park Tube Station and ends at Piccadilly Circus Tube Station. Walking distance is about 1.9 miles (3 kilometres).

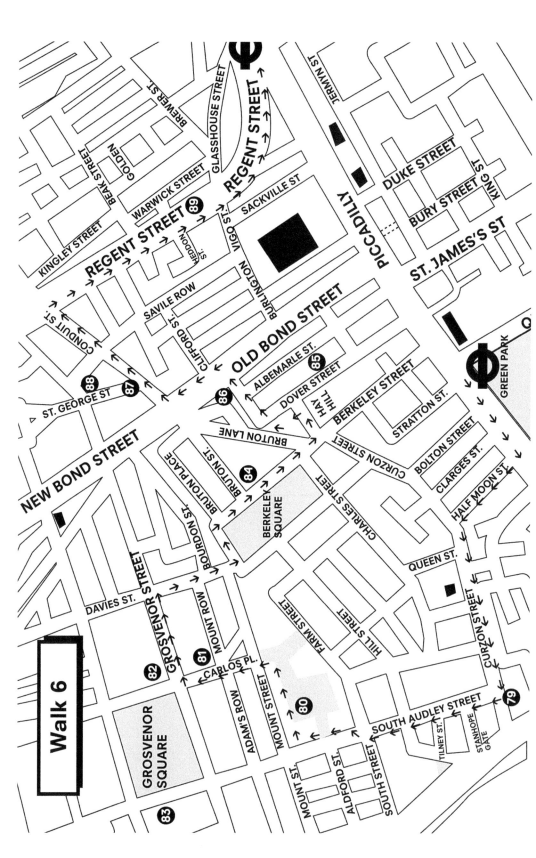

DISCOVERIES

79 19 Curzon Street: Dizzy's Double

80 Mount Street Gardens: Colonel Nicholson Waits

81 9 Carlos Place: Canada's First Green?

82 1 Grosvenor Square: Princess Louise Stays Home

83 28 Grosvenor Square: Lord Strathcona's Shame

84 17 Bruton Street: The Last Queen of Canada?

85 Brown's Hotel: AC-DC Slept Here

86 Allies Statue: Two's Company, Three's a Crowd

87 Conduit Street: Captain Vancouver Gets Caned

88 St. George's Hanover Square: The Second Mrs. Mac

89 130 Regent Street: Lord Stanley's Mug

A SHORT HISTORY OF THE AREA

Mayfair is a posh residential and commercial enclave with high-end shops and price tags to match. It is bound by Piccadilly and Oxford Street to the north and south and by Regent Street and Park Lane east and west. It owes its name to an annual spring fair that arrived here around 1686 from nearby Haymarket Street.

What was more or less a respectable rural fête soon acquired a dubious reputation. As early as 1708, officials complained it was a magnet for those who "meet to game and commit lewd and disorderly practices." The fair persisted until the area's developers and wealthy suburbanites put a halt to it in what may have been the world's first — but certainly not last — case of NIMBYism.

Given the area's location on the edge of town, it was inevitable that rural and urban lifestyles would clash here. Nowhere was London growing more rapidly in the 1700s than in the suburbs. As fairgoers enjoyed their last dances around the maypole, neighbouring fields were being ploughed up for six grand housing estates centred around large garden squares.

Sir Thomas Grosvenor (1655–1700), an aristocrat from Cheshire, controlled the largest of the developments that became known as the Grosvenor Estate. He obtained the property from his marriage to a girl who was only twelve. The rents from tenants on this land would eventually make Grosvenor's descendents the richest family in Britain and ultimately dukes of Westminster in 1874.

The centrepiece of this new estate was Grosvenor Square, developed in 1725–31. It was here that London's leading aristocrats lived in an exclusive enclave of style and privilege. In the early 1800s, the average household contained fourteen people, most of them servants. But by the close of the century professional parvenus began moving in, starting with a doctor. It was the beginning of the end for Mayfair's grand homes and the wealthy families that occupied them.[1] During the Second World War, U.S. general Dwight Eisenhower (1890–1969) set up his army headquarters here and the area has been known ever since as Little America.

To be fair, the area wasn't all about money and might. When the new parish of St. George's Hanover Square was created in 1711, the churchwardens did give a thought to the less fortunate. They built the Mount Street workhouse in 1735, a proud if somewhat awkward addition to the gentrified neighbourhood of Mayfair.

THE WALK

At Green Park Tube Station, walk westward along the north side of Piccadilly. This wealthy stretch of sidewalk was once known as Rothschild Row, owing to the number of wealthy descendants of Nathan Mayer Rothschild (1777–1836) who occupied mansions here overlooking Green Park. Rothschild was a phe-nomenally successful bond trader

> One cannot understand the Conservatism of Canada without thinking of Disraeli.
> — CANADIAN PHILOSOPHER GEORGE GRANT

during the Napoleonic Wars and became founder of the London branch of the world's one-time largest bank. The imposing mansions of his family members stretched down the street to the home of Field Marshal Arthur Wellesley (1769–1852), 1st Duke of Wellington, at Hyde Park Corner. Some say it was Rothschild's gold, rather than Wellington's army, that really defeated Napoleon Bonaparte at Waterloo.

At Half Moon Street turn right into Mayfair. At number 40 lived Robert Baldwin Ross (1869–1918), the devoted friend of Oscar Wilde (1854–1900) whom we met on Walk 2.

Turn left and continue along Curzon Street to Tribeck Street. Just across from us, behind a fence and treed garden, is Crew House (1730), one of the original neighbourhood mansions now occupied by an embassy. Parallel to us on our left through an archway is Shepherd

British prime minister Benjamin Disraeli loved to dress up and had an ugly charm about him. In this he had something in common with Canada's Sir John A. Macdonald.

Market where the annual May Fairs took place. This charming little area of sidewalk cafés and restaurants retains a cramped village atmosphere and reputedly is still home to the "madams of Mayfair." Take a minute to discover the area — and by that I mean *the shops and restaurants* — and then continue along Curzon to South Audley Street.

At the juncture of South Audley Street is 19 Curzon Street. This was the home of the cultured and dandyish British prime minister Benjamin "Dizzy" Disraeli (1804–81), 1st Earl of Beaconsfield. He was Conservative leader in the British House of Commons during the passage of the British North America Act in 1867. He was also Queen Victoria's favourite statesman after giving her the title of "Empress of India" in 1876. On his deathbed, mind you, he refused her a final visit. "She would only ask me to take a message to Albert," he quipped about her dead husband.

As a "Big Englander" and pro-Empire, Dizzy was always cordial with visiting Canadian officials. With one in particular, he even shared a few things in common.

79

19 Curzon Street: *Dizzy's Double*

When Sir John A. Macdonald (1815–91) stepped from his train at Euston Station in 1881, his startled British host thought he had seen a ghost. Six weeks earlier, the legendary Prime Minister Benjamin Disraeli had died at his home in Mayfair and now it seemed he had returned on the 13:56 train from Liverpool in the ultimate political comeback. Though separated by about ten years in age, the similarities between Macdonald and Disraeli were indeed uncanny.

Like Macdonald, Disraeli had an "ugly charm" about his face. They shared prominent noses, frizzy dark hair, and piercing eyes surrounded by pale-white skin. Both men were also charming and witty, and shared a fondness for wearing colourful, even theatrical clothes, to catch people's attention. Moreover, each was married in the same high-society church.

Yet their similarities went beyond just appearances. Macdonald and Disraeli shared a conservative ideology that proved popular with rich and poor voters alike, and won big majorities by adopting political reforms. They also each had despised political rivals: for Disraeli it was William

Gladstone and for Macdonald it was George Brown. When the Canadian prime minister frequently accused his adversaries of "veiled treason," he was actually borrowing a term coined by his doppelganger Dizzy.[2]

On an earlier visit to London in 1879, Macdonald lodged with Disraeli at his country house near High Wycombe. He had came to London in August to obtain financing for another railroad scheme, this time to the Pacific, but most parliamentarians were off hunting grouse and couldn't meet him. Although Disraeli loved to wear tweed hunting gear, he wasn't much of a sportsman — "I prefer peacocks to pheasants," he once joked — so invited Macdonald to his country house where they dined and talked about politics in his Tudor library instead. While Disraeli didn't agree to fund the Canadian railroad, he certainly took to the younger politician. Maybe it was because he saw a little of himself in Macdonald. He described him as "gentlemanlike, agreeable, and very intelligent: a considerable man with no Yankeeisms except a little sing-song occasionally at the end of a sentence."

Let's now turn and walk up South Audley Street. As we pass Tilney Street, look down on our left. This is the art deco Dorchester Hotel built in 1928–31. During the Second World War, the Canadian diplomat Charles Ritchie described it as a luxury liner with the remnants of London society on board. Canada's wartime prime minister, William Lyon Mackenzie King (1874–1950), often stayed here when in town. During his last visit in 1948, he held séances or "sittings" in his suite with local clairvoyants, despite his poor health. During one session, he received messages from his mother and Franklin Delano Roosevelt (1882–1945), both dead at the time. According to King, the U.S. president warned him to *watch Asia*. "In every way, the best of all the sittings I have had," he noted in his diary.[3]

Continue along South Audley Street toward the green spire. This is the Grosvenor Chapel, a simple brick church opened in 1731 for the wealthy Grosvenor family. Through the gates alongside it we come to Mount Street Gardens. Here we find a quiet oasis in the heart of Mayfair with a forgotten link to Canada.

As park-like as Mount Street Gardens are today, they were formerly the burial grounds for the local parish church of St. George's Hanover

Square. In 1854, Mount Street and many other burial grounds in central London were closed for health fears and eventually became residential gardens.

One person of note who was buried in this former parish burial ground was Colonel Francis Nicholson (1655–1728), a soldier and governor of so many North American colonies he was known as the "governor of governors." Much to his chagrin, the one governorship that eluded him was that of Quebec. In the early 1700s, he led two land assaults against the French citadel to capture it for the English. Each time he was unsuccessful.

Mount Street Gardens: *Colonel Nicholson Waits*

Francis Nicholson was a soldier from Yorkshire with oodles of energy and a hot temper to boot. In 1687, he sailed to New England and began a career governing an impressive string of Anglo-American colonies, including Nova Scotia and Placentia (Newfoundland).

But when it came to governing French Canada, life had a way of making Nicholson sit and wait. Not once but twice. The first occasion was in 1709, after England agreed to a two-pronged attack on Quebec. One prong would be led by the Royal Navy via the St. Lawrence River and the other would be a diversionary attack on Montreal led by Nicholson up Lake Champlain from New York. But when the ships never arrived, Nicholson was left stranded in the American wilderness with 1,500 colonial soldiers for months. Dysentery broke out, men dropped like flies, and the ragtag army was forced to limp home.

The second time occurred two years later. In 1711, Queen Anne's new Tory government was emboldened to try once more for the big prize. Nicholson rallied some sceptical colonists and marched to his position on Lake Champlain in support of a massive naval effort led by Sir Hovenden Walker (ca.1656–1728) and General John Hill (ca.1680–1735). This time Nicholson's land force was even larger.

But as we discovered on Walk 2, the attack never came. Walker's ships foundered on a shoal in the St. Lawrence and the remaining ships and crew turned tail. In Quebec, French Canadians celebrated their survival by naming their old church in the centre of town *Notre-Dame-des-Victoires* (Our Lady of Victories). Still waiting to attack in the woods, Nicholson lost his temper when he learned of the second failed attempt. "Roguery! Treachery!" he cried out in a rage. He threw his wig to the ground and stamped on it.[4]

Exit Mount Street Gardens at the far end across from the Church of the Immaculate Conception, opened in 1849. It has a colourful altar and interior by the architect of Gothic Revival Augustus Pugin (1812–52) that is worth a peek.

Head up Carlos Place toward Grosvenor Square. The beautiful Connaught Hotel, built in 1894–96, is at the corner with a lovely reflecting pool in front. The hotel was known once as the Prince of Saxe-Coburg Hotel but was, like the German name of the present Royal family (Saxe-Coburg), discreetly changed to something more English (in the case of the royals: Windsor) during the First World War.

On the third floor of 9 Carlos Place on Mount Row lived someone we've encountered before: the unconventional *fin-de-siècle* Anglo-Irish writer Oscar Wilde (1854–1900). He moved here in 1881 as a struggling but ambitious young poet. He had previously shared a home in Chelsea with an Oxford socialite, but his unorthodox

> It is hoped that Wilde will now be dropped into obscurity. We do not imagine that even silly people will care any longer to take lessons from him in aestheticism.
>
> — HALIFAX MORNING CHRONICLE, AFTER WILDE'S CONVICTION[5]

poetry had put an end to that arrangement. But buoyed by the success in New York of Gilbert and Sullivan's operetta *Patience*, which parodied the aesthetic movement and the likes of Wilde, he decided to set off on a speaking tour of North America to earn some money from his newfound notoriety.

9 Carlos Place: *Canada's First Green?*

In 1882, a twenty-eight-year-old Oscar Wilde embarked on a lecture tour to over one hundred cities across the United States and Canada. In the age before radio and TV this was the popular way to get noticed. His legendary witticisms started at the customs hall. "I have nothing to declare but my genius," he told the press. He went on to call Niagara Falls, the honeymoon capital of North America, the first disappointment of marriage.

In Canada, Wilde journeyed a 1,000 miles (1,600 kilometres) by first-class rail and drew small but curious crowds in Montreal, Ottawa, Toronto, Quebec City, and throughout the Maritimes. His aesthetic message amused some but not all. While he dined with Sir John A. Macdonald in Ottawa, he was snubbed by the governor general, John Campbell (1845–1914), Marquis of Lorne, and a patron of the arts himself. Lorne may have found the poet's manner shameful or perhaps a little too close to home.

Although Wilde spoke mostly on the decorative arts, he regularly ended his talks with an attack on pollution. To Wilde's aesthetic point of view, a delicate silk embroidery and a pristine Canadian forest were equally beautiful. Like a David Suzuki in velvet knee breeches, he spoke out against industrial destruction sweeping across Canada. In Ottawa, for example, he denounced sawmills disfiguring the Ottawa River, killing fish, and destroying habitat. "This is an outrage," he said. "No one has the right to pollute the air and water which are the common inheritance of all; we should leave them to our children as we have received them."[6]

Some took umbrage with Wilde and his pioneering green ideas. But his views about beauty did spark discussions about industrial ugliness disfiguring the Canadian landscape — in particular the telephone poles and overhead wires springing up around the country, which have never gone away.[7]

Continue up Carlos Place into Grosvenor Square. This large development once rivalled St. James's Square that we discovered on Walk 2 as the most fashionable address in London. It is now mostly offices, embassies and swanky restaurants. Its central garden is the largest in

London after Lincoln's Inn Fields.

Along the west side of the square is the old American Embassy designed by the Michigan architect Eero Saarinen (1910–61), best known for tulip chairs and his archway in St. Louis, Missouri. When the

> *What a lovely sight Grosvenor Square is on a day like this, particularly when one has at one's back the hideous American Embassy.*
>
> — CANADIAN HIGH COMMISSIONER PAUL MARTIN SR., MAY 1978[9]

embassy opened in 1959, it was widely criticized for destroying the grand houses that once stood there (including one with a Canadian connection, but we'll come to that shortly). Over the years, tastes have evidently changed. Now the former embassy is a listed building requiring any future development to respect its modernist design.

Directly in front of us is 1 Grosvenor Square, once the chancery of the Canadian High Commission in London until it was sold for $530 million in 2013. Previously it was the U.S. embassy from 1938–60. It is to here that the isolationist ambassador Joseph P. Kennedy (1888–1969) was exiled from Washington. He arrived with his family (including his son John, future U.S. president) but eventually resigned in 1940 over differences with his boss Franklin D. Roosevelt. There's a statue of Roosevelt by the Scottish sculptor Sir William Reid Dick in the square gardens, as well as one of General Dwight Eisenhower, who had his military headquarters here.

As our walks don't take us into nearby Belgravia, we'll use this spot to talk about a high-society couple associated with Canada and quite familiar with the aesthetic circle of Wilde and others: John Campbell, Marquis of Lorne, and his bride, Princess Louise Caroline Alberta (1848–1939), sixth child of Queen Victoria.

The artistic Louise (some called her "the rebel princess") had a studio 1.5 miles (2.4 kilometres) east of here at Kensington Palace and often exhibited her work at the *avant-garde* Grosvenor Gallery on Bond Street. (Like Wilde, the gallery was spoofed in *Patience.*) In the 1870s, the young couple, just back from their honeymoon, lodged in Belgravia (coincidentally at 1 Grosvenor Crescent) before Lorne was appointed Canada's governor general and moved to Ottawa with Princess Louise in 1878. But she wasn't to stay long.

82

1 Grosvenor Square: *Princess Louise Stays Home*

Queen Victoria had reason to smile over the marriage of Princess Louise and the Marquis of Lorne. It seemed a suitable match. Her unconventional daughter adored the arts and music, liked to paint and sculpt and was, for the times, a thoroughly modern woman. Her son-in-law, too, enjoyed the arts: tall and sensitive, he preferred poetry to making speeches. Even as an MP, he preferred to listen rather than talk.

But theirs turned out to be a loveless marriage. The couple remained childless and it soon became evident to observers like the queen that the princess went out of her way to avoid her husband. She instead spent a good deal of time with others, including a sculptor with whom she had been intimate. Louise liked the company of other men it seemed, and some said that was Lorne's problem too. Their married lives only diverged further when they were sent to Canada.

The princess didn't take to Ottawa. Some said she clashed with Agnes Macdonald (1836–1920), the severe wife of Sir John, or that Rideau Hall was not to her liking. Then again, maybe the sleepy capital was too dull and unsophisticated for her tastes. For all, or none, of these reasons, she soon went back to England for a long sojourn. She left Ottawa again for two years following a sleigh accident there.

Lorne, on the other hand, flourished in Canada. He travelled across the country, put in place the foundations for academies and a national art gallery, and even proposed a national anthem he had composed with the help of the great Sir Arthur Sullivan (1842–1900). When his term ended, he told Macdonald with genuine regret: "I should like to stay here all my days."

In due course, the Lornes even went their separate ways in death. He was buried in Scotland and Louise at Windsor Castle.

Trivia: *A statue of Queen Victoria by Princess Louise stands near Kensington Palace along the Broad Walk in Hyde Park. Both mother and daughter attended the unveiling in 1893, but not the Marquis of Lorne.*

The marriage of Princess Louise and the Marquis of Lorne illustrates the strict social norms that bound loveless couples in Victoria's England. Divorce was difficult if not out of the question.

The loveless Lornes. Princess Louise liked the company of other men and some said that was her husband's problem too.

If the queen's marriage was a model of fidelity and happiness, she expected her subjects to behave the same way. Yet across the square, where the former U.S. Embassy now stands, another family with Canadian connections struggled with the strict marriage code. For this couple, however, it wasn't so much a question of love as the validity of the marriage act itself that put them at odds with the strict Victorian moral code.

Strathcona House at 28 Grosvenor Square was a large, stately mansion owned by the wealthy businessman and diplomat Donald Smith (1820–1914), 1st Baron Strathcona and Mount Royal. Smith had started out as fur trader with the Hudson's Bay Company and had climbed the corporate ladder to become the company's governor. For him, it was never a question of mixing

> **Trivia:** *In 1900, Donald Smith personally outfitted a Canadian regiment to fight in the Boer War, which he named Lord Strathcona's Horse. Its members were largely cowboys and officers of the Northwest Mounted Police.*

> *I have breakfast at 9 am and dinner at 9 pm and that gives me 11 hours daily for work.*
>
> — DONALD SMITH, 1ST BARON STRATHCONA

business with pleasure; *business was pleasure*. Along the way he helped create the Canadian Pacific Railway and Bank of Montreal. In 1896, the elderly but tireless businessman was appointed Canada's high commissioner to London. Still going strong on his ninety-third birthday, he told a reporter the best way to live to an old age is by not thinking about age but just going on doing your work.[10]

Smith entertained lavishly in Grosvenor Square. Yet for all his wealth and popularity, the Grand Old Man was troubled until the day he died by the whispers and innuendos about his "squaw wife," Bella, and the legitimacy of their only child.

83

28 Grosvenor Square: *Lord Strathcona's Shame*

On a fine day in November 1913, Lady Strathcona collapsed while walking her dog in Grosvenor Square and died. Following her funeral at nearby St. Mark's Church on North Audley Street, she was interred in Highgate Cemetery in North London. After some sixty years of marriage, the elderly Lord Strathcona was distraught. "She was my stay and comforter throughout a long life," he said. Agnes Macdonald called Bella's death "a bleak, black day."

If Smith was a successful and rich businessman who moved in the highest circles, his marriage to Bella had always raised a few well-heeled eyebrows. The circumstances of their marriage had always been a lifelong embarrassment to him. He had met Bella soon after going to Labrador with the HBC in 1848. She was of mixed Scottish and Indian blood, and already had a son from a marriage to another fur trader. Bella and Smith fell in love and Bella gave birth to Smith's daughter, Margaret, in 1854. Because they were not legally wed, Smith solemnized the marriage himself as was customary in remote Canadian areas. Just to make doubly sure, he did it again in front of lawyers before coming to London as high commissioner. But it was never enough to silence whispers and prevent questions about the circumstances of his marriage or his daughter's legitimacy.

As his own end drew near, the Grand Old Man took to his bed in Grosvenor Square and began to disperse his immense fortune to charities throughout Canada, the United States, and Britain. But he also took extraordinary steps to protect his daughter's inheritance from opportunists who he feared would rob his daughter of her fortune. He died still working in bed. Rather than be honoured in Westminster Abbey, he chose to be buried next to his much-loved wife.

Leave the square by Grosvenor Street and take Davies Street into Berkeley Square. This is a former village square named for an aristocratic family whose ancestral home was Berkeley Castle in Gloucestershire. The plane trees in the square are said to be among London's oldest, planted in 1789.

Berkeley Square has long been associated with the rich and famous. Nicky Clarke (130 Mount Street) near the corner of Berkeley Square was and remains hairdresser to London's evolving A-list, including the late Diana (1961–97), Princess of Wales. Annabel's (44 Berkeley Square) is another chic establishment. It's a private dinner club where Lord Black celebrated his marriage to Barbara Amiel with friends in 1992.

After the Blacks' fortunes hit rock bottom, his wife Barbara Amiel told Maclean's: "I am Lady Black of no-fixed address."[11]

Across the square is Jack Barclay Bentley (18 Berkeley Square). This luxury car showroom stands on the site of a townhouse once owned by Lord and Lady Strathmore (17 Bruton Street). Their daughter Elizabeth Bowes-Lyon married Albert, the king's second son, the stammering Duke of York, and later King George VI (1895–1952; reigned from 1936). It was in this house that the duchess gave birth to her daughter the future Queen Elizabeth II (b. 1926; reigned from 1952), Canada's long-reigning monarch and, if republicans one day get their way, maybe its last.

17 Bruton Street: *The Last Queen of Canada?*

Princess Elizabeth was born at 2:43 a.m. on April 21, 1926, after a difficult delivery ending in what royal code termed "a certain line of treatment" — a risky Caesarean section. She was named Elizabeth Alexandra Mary, after her mother and two living queens.

Her grandparents were among the first to visit the baby. "Such a relief and joy," wrote Queen Mary in her diary after the birth. She called Elizabeth a little darling with a lovely complexion and pretty, fair hair.[12] Although the king's first grandchild, no one expected the newborn princess to become queen. She was third in line to the throne after her uncle and father. Only when her uncle abdicated unexpectedly to marry Wallis Simpson in 1936 was the ten-year-old princess from Mayfair thrust into the limelight as the heiress presumptive.

In 1953, following the death of her father, Elizabeth was proclaimed by Canada's parliament queen of Canada. She became the first monarch to read a speech from the throne. A few years later, she made an official visit to the United States on behalf of Canada. In some twenty royal visits, the queen has crisscrossed the country many times over. She has also had to deftly navigate some tense moments. In 1976 she opened the Montreal Olympics, despite death threats from separatists, and was duped by a French-Canadian radio host pretending to be Jean Chrétien in 1995. In both cases she kept her royal cool.

Yet her most significant moment as queen of Canada came on April 17, 1982, when she proclaimed Canada's new constitution and severed Canada's last ties to her own Parliament in Britain.

Should she survive republican calls for her head in Canada and reign on her throne beyond September 9, 2015, Elizabeth will surpass the sixty-three-year-and-two-hundred-seventeen-day reign of her great-great-grandmother, Queen Victoria, and become by the grace of God Canada's — and Britain's — longest-serving monarch.

Trivia: *Since the sixteenth century, some thirty-two British and French kings and queens have reigned over Canada.*

At the bottom of the square, take Hay Street and then Grafton Street to reach Albemarle Street. This is named after Christopher Monk

(1653–88), 2nd Duke of Albemarle and the man behind the country's first official boxing match. Albemarle didn't actually fight himself but, like a typical aristocrat, put

his butler and his butcher into the ring. The butcher won.

Albemarle Street has some interesting associations. For instance, number 13 was once the Albemarle Club, where Oscar Wilde's troubles began in 1895 after the receipt of a badly spelled note addressed "For Oscar Wilde, posing somdomite (*sic*)." This provoked him to sue unsuccessfully for libel and ultimately led to his downfall.

Brown's Hotel is also here. Dating from 1837, it is one of the city's oldest. Overlooking the street on the second floor is the Niagara Room in honour of the International Niagara Commission that met here in 1890. The commission was headed by the world's most famous physicist of the age, William Thomson (1824–1907), Baron Kelvin. He once said: "In science there is only physics. The rest is stamp collecting."

Kelvin's job was to find a way to harness the electrical power of Niagara Falls. Electricity was the way of the future, even for stamp collectors, but how to develop it was the problem. After holding an international competition, Kelvin's commission failed to find anyone who could not only develop electrical power but distribute it across long distances. The answer to Kelvin's dilemma finally emerged following a battle between two American household names: Thomas Edison (1847–1931) and George Westinghouse (1846–1914).

Brown's Hotel: *AC-DC Slept Here*

For American entrepreneurs, Niagara Falls was not so much a wonder of the natural world as it was an untapped opportunity to make money. Although settlers had operated various types of mills at the falls since 1725, large-scale development had proven dangerous and expensive. Added to these difficulties was the problem of how to transmit the power from the falls to urban areas where consumers demanded it.

Thomas Edison and Lord Kelvin were leading proponents of the system called Direct Current (DC) in which electricity flows in one direction. It was a simple system but problematic. Electricity could only travel short distances this way and required thick and expensive copper cables. Westinghouse and a little-known Serbian inventor named Nikola Tesla (1856–1943) favoured a different method called Alternating Current (AC). This system overcame DC's problems by changing the direction of electricity at regular intervals. The two systems battled it out until Kelvin attended the Columbian Exposition in 1893 in Chicago. When the great physicist saw the light powered by Westinghouse's AC generators, he switched his allegiance and the matter was settled. In 1896, the first electric generator at Niagara Falls was put into action and over the next few years grew to ten, providing electric power to places as far away as New York City. Canada was less quick off the mark but at least benefited from the delay. Its first publicly owned generator at the falls was the largest constructed and went into operation in 1921 — well after the great AC-DC debate had been won.[13]

Continuing on we reach Bond Street, a fashionable shopping thoroughfare that takes its name from Sir Thomas Bond, another seventeenth-century property developer.

Where Old Bond Street becomes New Bond Street is a bronze statue of two idle codgers swapping stories on a bench like they're waiting for their wives to finish shopping. But looks can be deceiving. In this expensive part of town, they are *too* relaxed for that.

In fact, the work by Lawrence Holofcener is called "Allies" and depicts wartime leaders U.S. president Franklin Roosevelt and Sir Winston Churchill (1874–1965). Someone who is amusingly absent from the scene is Canada's prime minister William Lyon Mackenzie King (1874–1950). King took delight in being photographed with these wartime giants, since it made him look like the lynchpin that held together the "special relationship" between Britain and the United

Spare me that nonsense. It's dangerous. We're set up for direct current in America. People like it, and it's all I'll ever fool with.

— Thomas Edison on alternating current[14]

States. But it was all political sleight of hand to fool voters. He may have had his photos snapped with them at the Quebec Conferences in 1943

and 1944, but then he quietly disappeared into the background while Roosevelt and Churchill got down to the business of running the war.

Allies Statue: *Two's Company, Three's a Crowd*

Churchill and Roosevelt met for the first time aboard the HMS *Prince of Wales* off the coast of Newfoundland in 1941. Although this was ostensibly in Canadian waters, no one had bothered to invite Canada to the party. Churchill and Roosevelt wouldn't make the same mistake again — at least on the surface. During the war, they held two conferences in Quebec City and Prime Minister King played host. He told Canadians: "It will be looked upon in years to come as one of the great events in our national history." But he still didn't get invited to any important meetings.

Yet as every politician knows, a picture is worth a thousand words — and maybe even a few votes. Whenever Roosevelt and Churchill posed for the press, King was right there beside them chatting like the kingmaker he wasn't.

So effective was his publicity trick that some fifty years later his role at the wartime Quebec Conferences was still a matter of debate. In 1998, a furore erupted when Quebec erected memorial busts to the British and American leaders to mark the conferences but King was left out (again). While historians agreed it was entirely appropriate, Prime Minister Jean Chrétien (b. 1934) was incensed. "To deny the presence of Prime Minister Mackenzie King in a homage to this conference in Quebec City is absolutely unacceptable, in bad taste and should never have been accepted," he said in his own charming way.[15] Hovering somewhere over a Ouija board, King probably grinned.

Just north of us across Oxford Street, Bond Street becomes Vere Street. Here can be found the old Marylebone Chapel, or St. Peter's Vere Street, designed by the architect James Gibbs (1682–1754) and built in

The 1796 cartoon "The caneing in Conduit Street" depicts an unhappy ship hand attacking Captain George Vancouver. With its publication, Vancouver's reputation was bruised as much as his skin.

1724. The oldest protestant church in Canada, St. Paul's Church in Halifax, Nova Scotia, is modelled after this one. St. Paul's, however, has one notable difference. The upper gallery there was known as the slave gallery until the arrival of the Black Loyalists in 1783. After that, it was known as the Negro gallery.

Cross over Bond Street and proceed up Conduit Street. In 1796, this was the scene of a violent altercation between the explorer Captain George Vancouver (1757–98) and an unstable aristocrat with a nasty grudge.

87

Conduit Street: *Captain Vancouver Gets Caned*

In September 1796, George Vancouver and his brother Charles were leisurely walking up Conduit Street when a young man crossed the street and set upon them viciously with a cane. The attacker was Thomas Pitt (1775–1804), 2nd Baron Camelford, a violent and unstable aristocrat who had served as midshipman under Vancouver during his landmark voyage up the coast of British Columbia several years earlier.

As if the attack wasn't injury enough, an embarrassing cartoon of the incident appeared in the press a few weeks later. It depicted a quivering Vancouver shouting "Murder! Murder! Watch! Constable!" as two street urchins laugh nearby. The frail and exhausted Vancouver's reputation was bruised as much as his skin.

Pitt was the troubled member of a wealthy and connected family. When he joined Vancouver's expedition in 1791, his father was only too happy to see him go. But on the long sea voyage, Pitt proved equally hard to manage. He disobeyed Vancouver's orders not to have contact with women in Tahiti and was lashed twenty-four times — harsh discipline for sure but not overly for the period. Nevertheless, a grudge was born. After several more infractions and several more floggings, Vancouver finally abandoned Pitt in Australia and told him to make his own way home.

Word of Vancouver's harsh discipline on the voyage reached London and tarnished his achievements on the west coast of Canada. Things only got worse when Pitt arrived back the following year and continually harangued him. Vancouver retired to the country to finish his journals but died just a few pages short of completing them. The unstable Pitt would go on to be nicknamed "the half-mad lord." He died in a duel, finally abandoned by everyone.[16]

From Conduit Street, look up St. George's Street to Hanover Square. This area was named by an astute property developer who wanted to win the good graces of the unpopular George Ludwig, the Elector of Hanover, who had recently become Britain's King George I (1660–1727; reigned from 1714). On the right is the high society church of St. George's Hanover Square designed by John James (ca.1673–1746), an apprentice to Sir Christopher Wren (1632–1723).

Besides being the church where the composer Frederick Handel (1685–1759) worshipped, guidebooks say St. George's Hanover Square is also notable for having the first covered church portico in London. If not particularly elegant, it at least kept guests dry at weddings, including Canadian ones.

Agnes Bernard met John A. Macdonald while shopping on Bond Street in 1866 and married him in nearby Hanover Square. He broke his marriage vow to stop drinking.

88

St. George's Hanover Square: *The Second Mrs. Mac*

In December 1866, Sir John A. Macdonald took a break from the wrangling of the London Conference to do some retail therapy. Then, as now, Bond Street was a favourite place to stroll up and down, shop, or just peer through store windows at expensive luxury goods. By chance, he came upon Agnes Bernard (1836–1920) doing the same. She was the sister of Macdonald's private secretary, and lived in Mayfair. Macdonald remembered Agnes from years before, in Canada. Having by then been a widower for ten years, he craved a wife and the Victorian respectability that came with one. The two courted briefly in London and Macdonald asked for her hand in marriage.

Agnes was a tall, strong woman with a sharp wit but little charm. At thirty years old, she was much younger than Macdonald's fifty-two. But it was not the difference in age as much as Macdonald's legendary drinking that concerned her family. Macdonald assured them he would mend his ways and they took him at his word. The couple were married in Agnes's parish church of St. George's Hanover Square.

The wedding took place early on the morning of February 16, 1867, and was the social occasion of the London Conference. The church was so full it seemed to Agnes there was an avenue of people from the door to the altar. Francis Fulford (1803–68), a Montreal bishop, officiated, and the daughters of the London delegates served as bridesmaids. After the nuptials, the guests breakfasted at the Westminster Palace Hotel, where Macdonald joked he had come to affect a political union but felt bound to try the idea out himself.

Agnes returned with Macdonald to Canada where married life often proved difficult. Conversation in the house was always political and she wondered sometimes if even the flies in the kitchen were holding parliament. Moreover Macdonald's vow to stop drinking was soon abandoned and Agnes dealt with it by becoming harder and less approachable as the years went by. She outlived her husband by some thirty years and died in 1920 in Hove, East Sussex.[17]

Continue up Conduit Street into Regent's Street on the edge of Mayfair. A broad, gently curving avenue, it extends from Regent's Park in Marylebone to Waterloo Place and was designed by the architect and master urban planner John Nash (1752–1835).

Regent Street has always been a place to buy china and silver. At 130 Regent Street we find a green plaque that commemorates the purchase of one such trinket. It reads: "Lord Stanley of Preston purchased the original Stanley Cup from a silversmith at this site in 1892 for the people of Canada to commemorate amateur and professional hockey. The Cup is now in the Hockey Hall of Fame in Toronto."

Trivia: *In 1889, Lord Stanley was the first governor general of Canada to visit British Columbia. In naming Stanley Park, he dedicated its use and enjoyment to "peoples of all colours, creeds and customs, for all time."*

89

130 Regent Street: *Lord Stanley's Mug*

After an absence of 114 years, professional ice hockey's greatest trophy — the Stanley Cup — returned to London in 2006 with all the hoopla fans in a city indifferent to the sport on ice could give it. And like any excited visitor to the capital, the Cup rode a double-decker bus, visited the Tower of London, and took a turn on the London Eye. It ended its city tour at the unveiling of a plaque to mark where it was purchased in 1892. Little did its vice-regal owner then imagine the bright future it would have.

In 1888, Sir Frederick Arthur Stanley (1841–1908), 16th Earl of Derby, took up his post in Canada as governor general. With his trimmed beard streaked with grey, a stocky frame, and broad forehead, people said he resembled the future King Edward VII, only fitter. He not only liked Canada and impressed everyone with his French, but took to hockey like a schoolboy. His son Arthur took to it even more. He and some players donned red flannel shirts and called themselves the Rideau Hall Rebels. They went on to establish the Ontario Hockey Association.

No doubt Arthur's enthusiasm for the game rubbed off on his father. Stanley instructed an aide-de-camp, Captain Charles Colville, to purchase a suitable trophy for an ice hockey championship for about $50 while he was visiting London. Colville strolled up and down Regent's Street before settling on a silver-plated punchbowl with gold gilt interior measuring 18.5 centimetres high and 29 centimetres wide offered by the silversmiths G.R. Collis & Company. On it he had engraved "Dominion Hockey Challenge Cup From Stanley of Preston." It was presented for the first time to the Montreal Amateur Athletic Association in 1893.[18]

If Stanley was pleased with Colville's purchase, he didn't actually show it. "It looks like any other trophy, I suppose," he once told a reporter who asked about it.

Now follow Regent's Street down to Piccadilly Circus, where our walk concludes.

Mayfair's high-society church: St. George's Hanover Square. Both Macdonald and Disraeli were married here. Macdonald said he had come to London to affect a political union, but felt bound to try it out himself.

WALK 7:
GREENWICH

To call this chapter a walk is not entirely honest. To discover the Canadian connections in the Royal Borough of Greenwich, five miles (eight kilometres) east of the city, we'll need to take a pleasant boat ride on the River Thames. Greenwich is the historic heart of maritime London and a UN world heritage site renowned for its architecture, naval museum, and Prime Meridian — zero degrees longitude, the centre of world time. So relax and enjoy the ride. After a week of walking, we deserve a break.

This walk begins at Westminster Tube Station and ends at Cutty Sark DLR Station for Maritime Greenwich. Walking distance in Greenwich is about 1.8 miles (3 kilometres) and involves a steep climb. The boat ride takes about thirty minutes.

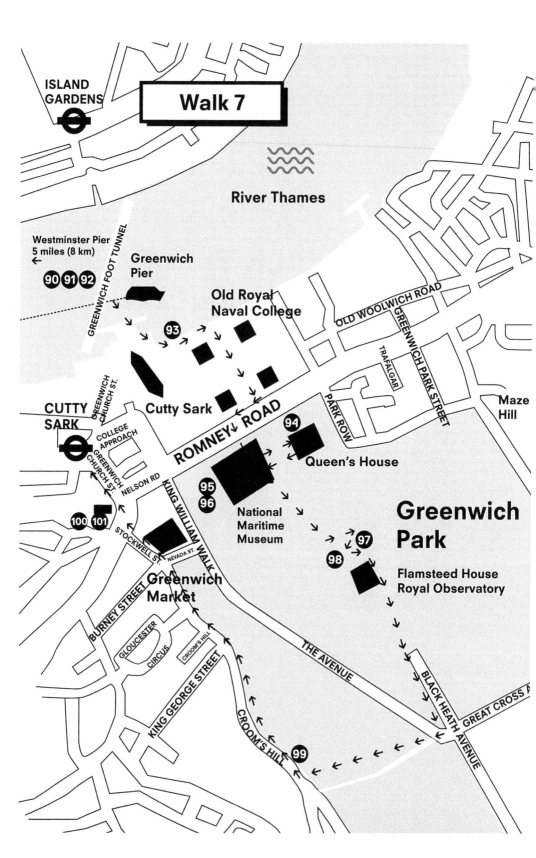

DISCOVERIES

A SHORT HISTORY OF THE AREA

The name Greenwich derives from the Saxon word *Grenevic* for green port or bay. This was once a pleasant fishing village settled briefly by the Romans, who built a temple on the hill. Others liked it too. They were marauding Danes who camped here periodically and launched violent incursions into the countryside in search of loot. In 1011, they kidnapped Alfege (ca.954–1012), the archbishop of Canterbury, and murdered him when they didn't obtain a ransom. Like the Romans, the Danes eventually tired of the wet English weather and returned home.

No strangers to nastiness themselves, the Tudors also took a shine to Greenwich and made the Palace of Placentia ("the pleasant place") their home beside the river many centuries later. This is where King Henry VIII (1491–1547; reigned from 1509) and his daughters Queen Mary I (1516–58; reigned from 1553) and Queen Elizabeth I (1533–1603; reigned from 1558) were born. In 1694, the palace was rebuilt in the Baroque style under the direction of the ubiquitous architect Sir Christopher Wren (1632–1723) and became the Greenwich Hospital for naval seamen. It in turn became the Royal Naval College from 1873 until it was decommissioned in 1998.

Much like St. James's Park, which we discovered on Walk 1, Greenwich Park was a royal hunting ground later redesigned under the Stuarts by the French gardener of Versailles, André Le Nôtre (1613–1700). Its 183 acres (74 hectares) included broad avenues lined with elms and oaks and a Royal Observatory built in 1675 not far from the site of the old Roman temple. Twice a year the park hosted a jolly country fair. Boatloads of revellers would disembark at the pier here to enjoy the rides, games, and menageries and escape the evil miasmas of London. But not everyone was charmed by the pastoral pleasures. The great man of letters Samuel Johnson (1709–84) came here with his biographer and sidekick James Boswell (1740–95) and asked him if he didn't find it very fine. "Yes, sir, but not equal to Fleet Street," his companion said. "You are right, sir," Johnson replied, and the two urbanites quickly returned to the comfort of their city.

While Greenwich has remained largely frozen in time, across the river the same is certainly not true. This marshy area was named the Isle of Dogs after King Henry VIII reputedly kennelled his hunting dogs here. As Britain and its empire grew through trade, the River Thames became a congested jumble of wharves and ships. In 1799, private interests created one massive dock complex here. By 1930, it employed 100,000 people, had 2,000 riverside wharves, and processed some 35 million tons of cargo a year.[1] Little wonder the German *Luftwaffe* set it ablaze during the Second World War. Afterward, the docks went from bad to worse and were eventually shut down only to be reborn with gleaming office towers in a new age of electronic commerce.

THE WALK

At Westminster Tube station, follow the signs to the Westminster Millennium Pier. Boats to Greenwich depart every forty minutes or so. If you have time before your boat departs, visit the Battle of Britain Monument unveiled in 2005 just steps away along the Embankment. It commemorates the first major turning point in the Second World War and those who contributed to it.

> **Trivia:** *One-in-ten of all the Hurricane fighter aircraft that served in the Second World War were made in Canada.*

After the defeat of France in 1940, Germany's leader Adolf Hitler (1889–1945) expected Britain to sue for peace. When the British government refused, the Nazi leader launched relentless air attacks on London, Plymouth, and Coventry. The bombardment, known as the Battle of Britain, endured many months. The German air force or *Luftwaffe*, however, failed to gain the superiority it needed over the smaller Royal Air Force. When the battle was won, Prime Minister Winston Churchill (1874–1965) said in a famous address that never had so much been owed to so few.

RAF Memorial: *The Canadian Few*

As many as a hundred or more of Winston Churchill's "famous few" in the Battle of Britain were Canadian. Many were dispersed across various units in the Royal Air Force but a significant number were concentrated in just two fighter squadrons: the No. 1 Squadron of the Royal Canadian Air Force under its Saskatchewan leader, Ernie McNab (1906–77), and the RAF's No. 242 All-Canadian Squadron under the famed British pilot Douglas Bader (1910–82).

McNab's squadron had its baptism of fire before it even got off the ground. While undergoing training near Croydon in South London, it came under attack by fifteen German Messerschmitt-110s, causing severe damage to its planes and equipment. Despite the chaos left on the field, the squadron was soon airborne with its Hawker Hurricanes, the small but reliable workhorses that were responsible for more than half of all the victories in the Battle of Britain. McNab himself achieved Canada's first score in the air. On August 15, 1940, he shot down a German Dornier bomber over Kent while training with a British crew. On another day, his squadron was involved in three separate air battles against German raiders between breakfast and dinner. Three members of his No. 1 Squadron won Distinguished Flying Crosses for their bravery, including McNab.[2]

Bader's group, the RAF's No. 242 All-Canadian Squadron, became operational earlier than McNab's. In 1940, it saw heavy combat in France during the evacuation of British ground forces at Dunkirk. It was made up of sixteen Canadians, as well as other nationalities badly demoralized from losses in their previous squadrons. At first, the idea of a British squadron leader wasn't popular with the Canadians. But Bader was an inspiring war hero who had lost both his legs in a plane crash and still kept flying. His strong character rallied the men and became the basis of a book and a movie called *Reach for the Sky.*

Now let's board our boat for the pleasant thirty-minute trip to Greenwich along the River Thames, London's oldest highway. Along the way we pass numerous city landmarks such as Shakespeare's reconstructed Globe Theatre, St. Paul's Cathedral, Tate Modern, Tower of London, and Tower Bridge.

Trivia: *In 1607, the explorer Henry Hudson took communion in the church of St. Ethelburga in London. The event was memorialized with a stained glass window. The church survived the Great Fire of 1666 and the Blitz, but not an IRA bomb in 1993.*

The first dock east of Tower Bridge is called St. Katharine Docks. This mixed residential and commercial area was once a complex of wharves and warehouses dating back hundreds of years. On April 17, 1610, the explorer Henry Hudson (ca.1565–1611) sailed from here on the *Discoverie* bound for Canada. He was never to return.

St. Katharine Docks: *The Regrettable Choices of Henry Hudson*

Henry Hudson led three voyages — two in search of a polar route to Asia via Russia for the Muscovy Company and one into the interior of New York State on behalf of the Dutch — before embarking from St. Katharine's Pool on a voyage to find the Northwest Passage to the Pacific. Apart from these cursory facts, not much is known about the mysterious man. As to his last days, we only have the untrustworthy testimonies of his surviving crew. They paint a picture of a zealous seaman but a poor and unprepared leader whose escalating mistakes sealed his fate.

Hudson's first regrettable decision was his crew. They were a quarrelsome lot that included Robert Juet and Henry Greene. Before long these two dissolute ship hands intrigued against Hudson and provoked a mutiny. Hudson's poor handling of the crisis divided the crew further. Hudson's greater mistake, however, was his failure to bring enough provisions for the journey and then refusing to replenish supplies when he had the chance.

After a miserable winter on rationed food in what is now Hudson Bay, the prospect of continuing the quest for the Pacific Ocean was too much for the crew. On the morning of June 24, 1611, Juet and Greene seized Hudson, his son, and some loyal followers and set them adrift in a small boat never to be seen again. The mutineers then steered home, though Juet and Greene conveniently didn't survive.

Back in London, the ragtag crew were tried for murder and blamed Juet and Greene to save their skins. The Admiralty may have bought their story or felt their knowledge of the Arctic was too commercially valuable to lose. Either way, they were acquitted of any crime.

> *This is not a risky project. Doing one building there would be risky; doing a dozen is not.*
>
> — CANARY WHARF DEVELOPER PAUL REICHMANN[3]

As we approach the deep U-bend in the river, we get a close-up view of Canary Wharf on the Isle of Dogs. Today, this behemoth of steel and glass bears no resemblance to the area's origins. Yet the docks of the 1800s and its redevelopment in the 1980s were both staggering financial undertakings for their times. Where ships unloaded at the Canary Wharf One Canada Square now towers, a familiar beacon on the edge of the city and once the tallest skyscraper in London. It is said to be a cross between Big Ben and Brookfield Place, the former World Financial Center in New York. Designed by the Argentine architect César Pelli (b. 1926), it is named not for the former docks on which it stands but for the home and native land of its builder.

Canary Wharf: *Paul Reichmann's Dream*

Paul Reichmann (1930–2013) was born in Vienna and immigrated to Canada from Tangier, Morocco, where black markets and free-for-all capitalism taught him to survive by his wits. In Toronto, he established a tile-importing business with his two brothers and branched out into property development. Polite, hardworking, and devout, lenders trusted him implicitly. Before long his company, Olympia & York, was the largest landlord in New York City.

Canary Wharf was his biggest project. Reichmann dreamed of a second financial centre in London to rival the monopoly of the "the City," which charged high rents and lacked modern, spacious offices. Canary Wharf seemed to fit the bill. In 1987, he acquired the 71-acre (28-hectare) property and set about building a Manhattan-style office complex at a cost of £3–4 billion.

But luring tenants to east London proved more difficult than Reichmann ever imagined. It was not just a case of offering cheaper rents. Build an expressway and they will come, he reckoned. Unfortunately, government infrastructure in the form of the Docklands Light Railway was only scheduled to open three years after Canary Wharf. In addition, opponents dissed the project. "I personally would go mad if I had to work in a building like that," Prince Charles once said.[4]

But what turned Reichmann's dream into a nightmare were not so much events in London but elsewhere. Canary Wharf was financed by commercial rents in North America, which tumbled in the recession of the early 1990s. Olympia & York's investments also took a hit and Reichmann went bust. In 1991, *Forbes* had rated his fortune at $7 billion. After Canary Wharf's collapse in 1992, the magazine recanted. "We seem to have been off by a nice round $9 billion," it said.[5]

On the other side of the river we pass an inlet known as Deptford. This was once home to the Royal Dockyards, first built in 1513 for King Henry VIII. It was a familiar meeting place for royals as well as courtiers, sailors, and pirates licensed by the state. Shakespeare's contemporary Christopher Marlowe (ca.1564–93) is buried in the churchyard named for St. Nicholas, patron saint of sailors. Depending on which story you believe, he either died in a drunken brawl or was murdered by royal agents. Deptford is also where the explorer Sir Francis Drake (ca.1540–96) was knighted and where *Discovery* and *Resolution*, the two ships of Captain James Cook (1728–79), were outfitted for his last voyage. Cook, the greatest maritime explorer and navigator of his age, will figure prominently on our walk when we reach Greenwich.

At Greenwich Pier it's time to do a bit of walking. Disembark and follow

Trivia: *In 1995, Paul Reichmann led a consortium of investors that regained control of Canary Wharf. He held the post of chairman, Canary Wharf Group, until 2004.*

The Greenwich monument to Frenchman Joseph Réné Bellot, Lady Jane Franklin's devoted follower, who died in his second attempt to find her lost husband in Canada's north.

the Thames Path eastward along the river in front of the Old Royal Naval College. This Baroque masterpiece is now run by a charitable trust with the University of Greenwich and Trinity School of Music.

Along the river path we come to a granite obelisk. Strangely enough, this memorial in the heart of maritime London commemorates a French rather than British sailor.

After the disappearance in 1845 of Sir John Franklin (1786–1847) in Canada's Arctic, Joseph René Bellot (1826–53) won the friendship and respect of the British people for joining the search to look for the explorer. Sadly, his quest ended tragically, like so many others in the Arctic. Bellot's admirers erected this monument by Philip Hardwick in 1855.

Bellot Monument: *Lady Jane's Devoted One*

Joseph René Bellot was born in Paris in 1826. A good student of humble means, he entered the École Navale in Brest and eventually rose to the rank of sub-lieutenant in the French navy.

The disappearance of Sir John Franklin in 1845 captivated the young officer. He believed the search for the missing British explorer should be an international one and wrote to Franklin's wife, the indomitable Lady Jane, to volunteer his services. He also wrote to Canadian William Kennedy (1814–90), who was preparing to set off on the second expedition financed by Lady Franklin. Kennedy, like Franklin's wife, was impressed by Bellot's conviction, skill, and evident Gallic charm. "We are really very fond of him," said one of Franklin's nieces after meeting him. Despite its initial misgivings, the British Admiralty was charmed too and agreed to let him go.

Kennedy's expedition never determined Franklin's whereabouts or fate, but Bellot proved a worthy choice for the voyage. When Kennedy became separated from his ship in a bad storm, Bellot daringly sailed it to safety and went back to rescue him. Using the new technique of sledding adopted by earlier explorers, he and the Canadian then covered some 1,100 miles (1,770 kilometres) on ice and reached the northern tip of the continent. On his return, Bellot was hailed a hero and elected a fellow of the Royal Geographical Society.

Despite his fame, Bellot remained devoted to Lady Franklin and her cause. In 1853, he returned to the Arctic to help another expedition, this one led by the Halifax-born Sir Edward Belcher (1799–1877). While attempting to deliver a message to Belcher, Bellot slipped through the ice and was never seen again. Only the Frenchman's walking stick was ever recovered.

Continue on until you reach the water gate, turn and proceed through the college's grand square. Here we find in the centre a marble statue of King George II (1683–1760; reigned from 1727) in Roman toga though the elements have badly erased his features. He was king at the time of Quebec's capture in 1759. When warned that Wolfe was mad, George reportedly replied: "Mad, is he? Then I wish he would bite some of my other generals!"

Head up the stairs between the magnificent buildings topped with twin cupolas and gold weather vanes. The Painted Hall on the right is where sailors ate their meals and has been described as the finest dining hall in Europe. In the chapel on the left there is a marble memorial to Franklin and his lost crews from the *Terror* and *Erebus*.

Many seamen associated with the college served in Canada. In the nearby Greenwich Hospital Burial Grounds (now in Pleasaunce Park in East Greenwich except for a mausoleum) are the resting places of many seafarers with Canadian connections. They include Isaac Townsend (ca.1685–1765), a naval commander who served at Louisbourg in 1746; Nathaniel Portlock (ca.1748–1817), one of Captain Cook's crew members who went on to become a successful fur trader along the Pacific Northwest; and Sir Richard Goodwin Keats (1757–1834), who was a governor of Newfoundland from 1813 to 1816. Keats was perhaps the first politician ever to record how difficult Newfoundlanders were to govern.

Trivia: *The poor work performed at Deptford on Captain Cook's ships in 1776 forced the explorer to seek shelter to make repairs in Nootka Sound, British Columbia, in 1778.*

The weathered and faceless statue of King George II, the first British king of Canada, in the courtyard of the Old Royal Naval College in Greenwich.

At Romney Road walk back westward and cross over to the National Maritime Museum. It houses the largest collection of maritime artifacts in the world, including 200 items linked to Canada. In the interests of time, we won't examine all of them.

Let's first visit the Queen's House just to the east of the museum. It is associated with two queens: Anne of Denmark, wife of King James I (1566–1625; reigned from 1603), who commissioned it from the architect Inigo Jones (1573–1652), and Henrietta Maria, wife of Charles I (1600–49; reigned from 1625), who never really enjoyed it owing to something called the English Civil War.

On the ceiling of the Great Hall used to be a painting depicting Peace reigning over the Arts by the Italian Orazio Gentileschi (1562–1639), Henrietta's favourite court painter. Today the ceiling is blank. Like many royal *objets d'art*, the painting was sold off after her husband, the king, was executed and was eventually purchased by John Churchill (1650–1722), 1st Duke of Marlborough, for his London home. It's likely he purchased it to celebrate the end of the War of the Spanish Succession (1701–14) in which he made his name. Under the war's peace terms, France ceded the Hudson's Bay Company territory, Newfoundland, and Acadia to England but kept Prince Edward Island, Cape Breton, and the fortress of Louisbourg.

On the second floor of the Queen's House there is a rotating selection of 4,500 paintings from the National Maritime Museum's fine-art collection. Among the collection is a painting by Godfrey Kneller of Sir John Leake (1656–1720), one of the greatest admirals of his time. He was another governor of Newfoundland and fought skirmishes with the French there during the War of the Spanish Succession. One who didn't

The monument to the lost crews of Arctic explorer Sir John Franklin in the chapel of the Old Royal Naval College.

fight was Newfoundland governor John Graydon (ca.1666–1726). Fearing that he may be outnumbered by French forces hiding in Placentia Bay, he returned to England without firing a shot against the enemy and was accused of cowardice. A sailor associated with another coast of Canada is Sir Fairfax Moresby (1786–1877), commander-in-chief in the Pacific from 1850–53. He recommended the development of a naval base at Esquimalt, B.C., which Britain's Royal Navy occupied until 1905.

Another portrait in the collection is that of Admiral Sir Charles Saunders (ca.1714–75) by Richard Brompton. We encountered this sailor during Walk 4 in Westminster Abbey. The portrait depicts Saunders in his gold-embroidered uniform wearing the sash of the Order of the Garter. His hand gestures behind him to where French rafts drift ablaze toward the British fleet on the St. Lawrence in 1759. History has largely forgotten Saunders, but he played a critical role in the Battle of Quebec. Without his efforts, Wolfe would never have succeeded on the Plains of Abraham.

94

The Queen's House: *The Quiet Admiral*

Charles Saunders joined the Royal Navy before he was fifteen and rose up the ranks with the help of senior brass. A man of few words, when he did speak people found him too direct and terse. He was wed to the navy and had few personal friends. Apart from briefly guarding the Newfoundland fishery, Saunders only spent one summer in Canadian waters. But it would be a summer that changed the country's destiny.

Britain's plan to capture Quebec in 1759 (like so many previous efforts) called for a coordinated land and sea effort. While the army under Wolfe would be responsible for taking the fortress, the navy had to deliver Wolfe and his men safely up the St. Lawrence and protect their backs from warships that might arrive from France. Prime Minister William Pitt (1708–78) knew what military infighting could be like. He told both men that success depended on an "entire Good Understanding between our Land and Sea Officers."

A veteran with thirty-two years of service, Saunders did everything to support Wolfe. He was given the formidable command of nearly two hundred ships including the *Neptune* of ninety guns, two three-deckers, the *Princess Amelia* and the *Royal William*, and one hundred twenty transports. Having successfully navigated the immense armada up the dangerous St. Lawrence, Saunders positioned the fleet to supply and support the attack. He also had to fend off French fire ships sent to burn his fleet.

After Wolfe's death, Saunders ensured that the British garrison at Quebec was well armed and provisioned, even at the expense of his own supplies for the dangerous journey back. Although he was fêted for his contribution to the victory, Wolfe always overshadowed his role. When Saunders died, he was interred in Westminster Abbey. The writer and politician Horace Walpole (1717–97) said of him, "No man said less, or deserved more."

Now let's make our way back to the National Maritime Museum. Just near the colonnade that connects the Queen's House to the museum once stood a life size bronze statue of Captain James Cook (1728–79) gazing up the hill with legs confidently astride. Museum officials removed the statue in 2003 and have yet to find a spot for it. It's fitting that it should return because no other sailor is more closely associated with Greenwich and maritime history than Cook himself.

As we learned on Walk 1, Cook's early career was spent charting much of the coastline of eastern Canada, the St. Lawrence River and later Newfoundland and Labrador. But that is only half of the story when it comes to Canada. In 1778, Cook returned to the continent on his third and last voyage of discovery, only this time by way of the Pacific Ocean.

Cook wasn't the first European on Canada's Pacific West Coast. The Spanish had already been there and possibly even fellow countryman Sir Francis Drake (ca.1540–96).[6] On this voyage Cook took two sailors whose names are known to us for different reasons: William Bligh (1754–1817), master of HMS *Resolution*, and George Vancouver

> **Trivia:** *Cook's arrival in Nootka Sound, B.C., in 1778 led to a booming trade in sea otter pelts. This caused the animals' near extinction until trade was banned in 1911.*

(1757–98), a midshipman on HMS *Discovery*. Bligh was a gifted and rising naval star whose adoration for Cook was equalled only by his contempt for everyone else. He would later gain notoriety as the protagonist in the mutiny on the HMS *Bounty*. Vancouver, an intelligent if strict young sailor, would return to Canada's western shore in 1792 and survey the coast in great detail.

National Maritime Museum: *Cook and the Nootka Peoples*

After two incredible voyages of discovery, Captain James Cook wasn't quite ready to retire. Although forty-eight and old to be a sea captain by the standards of the time, he still had a taste for salt water. So he agreed to command a third voyage of discovery. This time he would search for the elusive Northwest Passage — not via the Atlantic Ocean as countless explorers in the centuries before him had tried and failed to do — but via the Pacific. Fame and glory enticed him as much as a prize of £20,000 to anyone who would find an Arctic route.

After sixteen months at sea, Cook made landfall in March 1778 near Eugene, Oregon. He was greeted by dreadful storms that battered his ships with sleet and snow. As he inched northward along the coast, he finally took shelter in Nootka Sound, midway up Vancouver Island, to make badly needed repairs. He stayed a month but didn't really take to the place. Maybe it was the Nootka people who visited his ships frequently to trade, sometimes in as many as a hundred canoes. They seemed to fleece his men at every opportunity and even charged him for the right to use the land. "There did not seem to be a single blade of grass that had not a separate owner," Cook complained. When an item was stolen by one of the locals, he said dryly: "This is an American indeed!"[7]

As for the local inhabitants, they were later identified as the Mowachaht bands of the Nuu-chah-nulth nation. Natural traders, they were at first cautious about the white newcomers. But they prized in particular the iron and bronze on Cook's ships, which they described as giant seagulls carrying great bounties. In exchange for these metals they offered beautiful sea otter pelts, oils, and other goods. Among these were said to be trinkets given to them by the Spanish explorer Juan Perez (1725–75) who had visited a few years before. That's fitting perhaps since Nootka means "it goes around."

Eighteenth-century marine explorers like Cook were confounded by the problem of longitude. While *latitude* (one's position north or south of the equator) was determined by observing the sun's

position with a quadrant or astrolabe, *longitude* (one's position east or west) was more difficult to find. It could only be measured using complicated astronomical charts or calculated in terms of time. Since the world rotates 360 degrees in twenty-four hours, every hour time zone corresponds to a distance of 15 degrees longitude. To determine how far east or west navigators had travelled, all they had to do was compare the time at their location by observing the sun with the actual time at their departure point. Sounds simple, right?

Wrong. This "time method" of determining one's longitude at sea required a very special clock. To tell what the time was back home it had to measure time accurately in all sorts of conditions like pitching seas and extreme hot and cold climates. No clocks could do this until 1759, when an English provincial carpenter named John Harrison (1693–1776) produced a chronometer known as H4. Before long, copies of this invention were standard issue for British sea captains, thanks in part to Cook.

National Maritime Museum: *Cook's Pocket Watch*

On his third and final voyage of discovery in 1776, Captain James Cook set sail with an unusual crew and cargo. Besides two Americans, a royal gardener, and a Tahitian tourist taking home a souvenir suit of armour, Cook's ships carried a menagerie of cows, goats, pigs, sheep, and a peacock. All that was missing were women to complete his ark, Cook said in exasperation. The animals were a personal gift of the king, who sent them along to encourage Pacific islanders to adopt farming and stop eating each other.[8]

Cook also carried on board some impressive pocket watches. These were copies of John Harrison's pioneering H4 chronometer known as K1 and K3 after its maker, Larcum Kendall (1721–95). Cook had used K1 on his second voyage and praised its utility over the more complicated method of using star tables to determine longitude. He called the watch his "trusty friend" and "our faithful guide through all the vicissitudes of climates."[9]

On this voyage K1 went with Cook in the *Resolution*; a cheaper version known as K3 went in the *Discovery*.[10]

Waylaid for a month in Nootka Sound, Cook compared the hour at Greenwich to his local hour in Resolution Cove, aided by these timepieces. For the first time in history, he established the longitude of Canada's western shore. He calculated it as 126°, 42' west, which was off by a few degrees. Yet with this and other measurements he took on the coast, the width of Canada from sea to sea was finally established.[11]

On a curious note, K1 continued to perform magnificently for Cook on his third voyage, right up to the moment of his death in Hawaii when it mysteriously stopped. K3 kept on ticking and went on to serve in Newfoundland in the 1780s and on Vancouver's subsequent voyage to Canada's Pacific coast in 1791–95. All the pocket chronometers can be found in the National Maritime Museum's collection.

Now it's time to head to the top of Greenwich Hill via the tree-lined Jubilee Avenue. Rest assured it is worth the climb, as the crest that awaits commands one of the most impressive views of London.

At the top we find the splendid but lonely figure of Major-General James Wolfe (1727–59), the British hero of Quebec and sometime resident of Greenwich. The eight-foot statue depicts him standing quietly with his hand on his hip, dressed in his cloak and three-cornered hat. It was unveiled in 1930 by a descendant of Wolfe's worthy adversary, Louis-Joseph de Montcalm (1712–59), and was sculpted by Robert Tait McKenzie (1867–1938).

Trivia: *While Cook didn't map Canada's west coast, he did determine its shape.*

Wolfe Monument: *Look Up, Look Way Up*

Robert Tait McKenzie was born near Almonte, Ontario, the son of a Scottish Presbyterian minister. From his boyhood, he adored playing sports and became a lifelong friend to another Almonte legend, James Naismith (1861–1939), the inventor of basketball.

After graduating from McGill University in medicine in 1892, McKenzie began a career focused on physical education, first in Montreal and then in Philadelphia. But in his spare time he also started painting and sculpting athletes using his exceptional understanding of anatomy. By 1930, he had given up teaching and devoted his talents exclusively to sculpture.

McKenzie was known to labour prodigiously on his commissions. It was not unusual for him to work until 2 a.m., take a steam bath or plunge into a pool, and then pick up where he left off. At first his constant artistic theme was sports and athleticism but as his reputation grew he began sculpting more general public memorials, especially after the war.

In 1927, McKenzie was asked by Canada to prepare a sculpture of Major-General Wolfe for Greenwich Park. It would take three years to complete as McKenzie had to navigate approvals with three committees, as well as Parliament and the king, who was chief ranger of the park. McKenzie wanted to portray a decisive moment in Wolfe's life and spent six months reading everything he could about him. He found the exact moment in Francis Parkman's *Montcalm and Wolfe* when Wolfe spies with his telescope a hidden path up from the St. Lawrence to the Heights of Abraham. McKenzie captured this moment in bronze: Wolfe has just lowered his telescope and is planning his attack in the pre-dawn hours of September 13, 1759.

When the statue was finally unveiled, McKenzie's feelings were mixed. The site overlooking the Royal Naval Hospital was a fine one but he thought the pedestal far too high, as it put visitors right under Wolfe's most prominent facial feature. "Most people will be looking straight up his nose which was what I wanted to avoid," he said. "That is the trouble of having to deal with three different committees."[12]

The Royal Observatory a few yards away was built by Christopher Wren for the first astronomer royal, the Reverend John Flamsteed (1646–1719). It was Flamsteed's tireless measurements of the stars night after night that led to the creation of a star almanac, which guided sailors until the invention of Harrison's clock.

Should you pay to tour John Flamsteed House and the Royal Observatory, you will also see on display in the Time Galleries another version of Kendall's chronometer (K2) used by William Bligh (1754–1817) on HMS *Bounty*. Like K3 it was a cheaper version and never worked very well. It was taken by the mutineers in 1789 to Pitcairn Island and only returned to Britain in 1840.

You don't actually have to enter the Observatory to make our next Canadian discovery, as the Prime Meridian is marked in the courtyard and on the outer wall next to the footpath.

While Greenwich was used to set longitude by the British from the late 1700s onward, it wasn't until a century later that it was adopted as the Prime Meridian associated with world standard time. Before then cities and towns actually kept their own time. But in the age of steam trains this became a problem, especially across vast areas like the United States. If railroads didn't follow the same clock, how would travellers make their connections? Trains therefore were the spark that ignited the movement to adopt universal standard time. And it was an enterprising Canadian who helped push for this new world order.

Canada's Sanford Fleming was a leading advocate of Universal Standard Time based on a prime meridian. He just didn't want the meridian to be at Greenwich.

The Prime Meridian: *Sandford Misses His Train*

On a sunny July afternoon in 1876, a forty-nine-year-old public servant named Sandford Fleming stood on a railway platform in Ireland waiting for his train. It never arrived. The railway had misprinted "p.m." for "a.m." and Fleming's train had long since gone. Any normal human being might have shrugged off the error without much ado. But not a scientist like Fleming.

The mix-up at the railway station helped Fleming to campaign for the idea of a twenty-four-hour clock. People could count to twenty-four just as easily as twelve, he believed. His thinking went even further and grew into a concept of standardized time around the world based on one-hour time zones for every fifteen degrees of longitude.

The problem was where to start the world clock. While Greenwich's Prime Meridian was a logical place for it, the French had their own meridian in Paris and Fleming didn't want to upset them. He favoured a neutral meridian somewhere in the Pacific Ocean, which won the support of some scientists but predictably not Britain's Astronomer Royal who presumably enjoyed his monopoly selling nautical charts showing zero degrees longitude at Greenwich. He campaigned against the upstart Canadian's idea and the concept of universal standard time stood still for a while, so to speak.[13]

But not for long. Fleming teamed up with a like-minded American named Cleveland Abbe (1838–1916), chief of the United States Weather Service. Together they lobbied for standardizing time across the U.S., where the vast geography made railway schedules hard to synchronize. The railway companies loved the idea and it spread rapidly. Congress eventually called a global conference in 1884 to decide once and for all the location of the Prime Meridian. Fleming still stubbornly opposed Greenwich but two-thirds of all navigational charts in the world were aligned with it already. So the world decided to set its clock here too.

Return now to Wolfe's statue and walk down the broad avenue of Greenwich Park toward Blackheath, gruesomely named for the victims of the bubonic plague said to be buried there. Keep to the right at the end of the parking lot and follow the avenue of trees to the edge of the park. Here we find Macartney House, the Greenwich home of Major-General Wolfe's parents. With its view across the park to the Observatory, it's little wonder Wolfe called it "the prettiest situated house in all of England."

In 1738, the Wolfe family moved to Greenwich from Westerham, Kent. They first lived in town before purchasing this house on the edge of Greenwich Park in 1752. It was next to Lord Chesterfield's summer home and was smaller then, having been enlarged afterward by the

The Greenwich home of Major-General James Wolfe, where he often returned on leave from the army. He called it the prettiest situated house in all of England.

architect Sir John Soanes (1753–1837). Wolfe often came here on leave from the army to recuperate from poor health. There was a touch of sentimentality to his visits. "I lie in your chamber, dress in the General's little parlour, and dine where you did," he wrote to his mother while she was away in Bath for the social season. He added: "The most perceptible difference and change of affairs (exclusive of the bad table I keep) is the number of dogs in the yard...."[14]

It was here too in late 1759 that the fallen hero's body returned to a recently widowed Henrietta Wolfe, and now childless mother.

99 Macartney House: *Henrietta's Sacrifice*

Henrietta Thompson (ca.1700–64) was a pale beauty with dark hair, a high forehead, and proud bearing. Like her famous son, she suffered from a frail constitution and hot temper. Her husband, Edward Wolfe (1685–1759), was a military man fifteen years her senior. The two married in 1724 and had their sons James and Edward in quick succession. With her husband away often, Henrietta kept a watchful eye over her boys. Both were destined to take the king's shilling like their father. At fifteen, James joined the army and left home; Edward followed two years later. Before long, the younger Edward was dead of tuberculosis.

In the years following, Henrietta and James developed an uncommon devotion. He wrote to her continually. She kept all his letters, right up to the last. With her, he could shed his military persona and be philosophical, loving, even sentimental. She was his spiritual guide. Although he disliked cards, he promised to play piquet with her all day long. "The greatest thing that I wish for here is to see you happy," he wrote lovingly. He returned to Greenwich whenever he could.

Seventeen fifty-nine was a bad year for Henrietta. In March, her husband died. Then James went to Quebec. In his last letter to his mother he claimed to be in good health, but nothing was farther from the truth. Like his brother, James likely had TB. If he hadn't been felled by a sniper on the field near Quebec he would have died, probably from coughing up his own blood.

With James gone, Henrietta remained alone in the house with only her family's memory to keep her company. To honour the bequests her son had left in his will, she asked the army for a larger pension but was refused. Only when she died herself five years later was the lonely widow of Greenwich able to fulfil her son's wishes by dispersing her own estate according to his will.

We must walk back into town now. Find the gate to the right of Macartney House, which leads out of the park to Croom's Hill. Descend the gently sloping street as Wolfe himself must have done many times. At 12 Croom's Hill we pass the Fan Museum, a hidden curiosity devoted entirely to fans and fan-making. Follow Stockwell Street to Greenwich High Street.

Designed by the architect Nicholas Hawksmoor (ca.1661–1736), St. Alfege Church rises prominently in front of us. St. Alfege was an archbishop martyred here and a church dedicated to his memory has been associated with this site for a thousand years. This current version was built in 1712–14 to replace a medieval one that collapsed after a storm. It

St. Alfege Church is named after an archbishop of Canterbury martyred on this spot. It is the final resting place of Major-General James Wolfe and his family.

didn't help that its foundations had been weakened by too many burials below it. Even with this more modern church, the habit was hard to kick.

St. Alfege Church: *Wolfe's Tomb*

In the age of sail, news of both Wolfe's victory and death at Quebec on September 13, 1759, only reached London six weeks later. It was, in fact, preceded by Wolfe's own dismal dispatch to his superiors about the poor chances of victory that year, which made the news all the more astonishing when it arrived. As word spread so did jubilation. Church bells pealed, firecrackers were set off, and town feasts were held with beer and sheep roasted whole. Only in Greenwich was the rapture muted out of respect for a mother in mourning.

A month after the victory, the *Royal William* anchored off Portsmouth with the body of Wolfe. The ship had narrowly escaped disaster on a shoal in the St. Lawrence and was lucky to make it back at all. A stone casket taken from a convent in Quebec was lowered onto a barge and rowed to shore, escorted by a flotilla of boats. Cannons fired in tribute. The hearse, accompanied by two of Wolfe's comrades, then set off for Greenwich. Thousands lined the route to watch it go by.

There would be no state funeral for Wolfe, nor burial among the greats in Westminster Abbey. Henrietta Wolfe insisted on a private family ceremony for the last member of her family and most-cherished son. His remains were brought back to the family house where they lay in state briefly, draped in a black pall and covered in laurel leaves. The English hero of Quebec was then quietly interred in the family crypt in St. Alfege, next to his father. Just five mourners witnessed the burial.

Also in St. Alfege is a commemorative plaque to the first European explorer of the Canadian prairies, Henry Kelsey (ca.1667–1724). He journeyed there in 1690–92. Although there is a good deal unknown about him, this early explorer of Canada was likely born and schooled in Greenwich. Church records indicate he certainly later married, baptized his children, and died here.

After one hundred discoveries in London, we've come to our last one.

Kelsey Memorial: *The Poet of the Plains*

Henry Kelsey joined the Hudson's Bay Company in 1684 as a seventeen-year-old apprentice and was sent to York Factory, a fur-trading post on Hudson Bay in northern Manitoba. Described in company reports as an active lad, Kelsey enjoyed the company of the local Indians and soon understood their languages. Somewhere along the way, he also acquired an odd knack for verse: the introduction to his 1693 journal is written entirely in rhyming couplets.

Keen to diversify its trade at York Factory, the HBC sent Kelsey inland. Unlike explorers of the following century, Kelsey was neither a surveyor nor a map-maker. His descriptions of landmarks, like his verse, were rudimentary and have only served to confound historians trying to trace his exact route ever since. His likeliest path was along the Hayes and Saskatchewan rivers to The Pas, Manitoba, and from there across to the Red Deer River in Saskatchewan. Kelsey describes part of this journey:

> *Through Rivers which run strong with falls/thirty three carriages (portages) five lakes in all.*

While his route and much about him may be puzzling, what is certain about Kelsey is that he was the first European to record seeing grizzly bears and herds of bison on the Canadian plains. He also met with the Assiniboine peoples and possibly Sioux and was the first HBC employee to observe and record their religion and way of life. In total, Kelsey would spend nearly forty years with the HBC and make the journey to Canada from England six times. He was eventually promoted governor of all the trading posts on Hudson Bay, a post he held until 1722.

Return now to Greenwich Pier. Our journey ends at the famous tea-clipper *Cutty Sark.* Built in 1869, it set the world speed record by sailing from China to Britain laden with tea in 107 days. It's named after the witch in "Tam o' Shanter," a poem by Scotland's Robbie Burns (1759–96). Her short and revealing garment is known as a cutty sark. The figurehead of the witch on the bow of the ship was carved in 1956 from a block of Douglas fir presented to the Cutty Sark Society by the Canadian Lumberman's Association.

The Cutty Sark DLR line on the left takes us back to town via Canary Wharf.

NOTES

Introduction

1. Charles Lynch, *The Lynch Mob, Stringing Up Our Prime Ministers* (Toronto: Key Porter Books, 1998), 183.

Walk 1: Two Royal Parks

1. Seán Jennett, *The Official Guide to the Royal Parks of London* (London: HMSO, 1979), 12.
2. Frederick A. Pottle (ed.), *Boswell's London Journal* (New York: McGraw-Hill, 1950), 231.
3. James Morris, *Heaven's Command* (London: Penguin Books, 1979), 359; Kenneth Bourne, *Britain and the Balance of Power in North America 1815–1908* (London: Longmans, 1967), 404.
4. Christopher Hibbert, *Wellington: A Personal History* (Reading, MA: Perseus Books, 1979), 173.
5. "Federal Lack of Action on War Memorial 'Scandalous,' Says Black," *CBC News*, August 16, 2007, www.cbc.ca/news/world/federal-lack-of-action-on-war-memorial-scandalous-says-black-1.689969.
6. Issued by St. Stephen's Bank of New Brunswick until 1886.
7. Joseph Schull, *Laurier, the First Canadian* (Toronto: Macmillan, 1965), 355.
8. Norman Hillmer and Jack Granatstein, *Empire to Umpire* (Toronto: Copp Clark Longman, 1994), 17.

9. *Oxford Dictionary of National Biography*; Vincent Massey, *What's Past is Prologue: The Memoirs of the Right Honourable Vincent Massey* (Toronto: Macmillan, 1963), 255; Claude Bissell, *The Imperial Canadian: Vincent Massey in Office* (Toronto: University of Toronto Press, 1986), 40. There is a plaque at 36 St. Mary's Terrace in Hastings, East Sussex, where Archibald Belaney, or Grey Owl, lived.

10. Max Beloff, *Britain's Imperial Sunset, Volume 1: Britain's Liberal Empire 1897–1921* (London: 1969), 20–21, quoted in David Reynolds, *Britannia Overruled* (London and New York: Longman Group, 1991) 10.

11. The approximate value of $146,000 in 1911, www.bankofcanada.ca/en/rates/inflation_calc.html.

12. J. Simpson and G. Martin, *The Canadian Guide to Britain, Volume 1: England* (Toronto: Macmillan, 1985), 7.

13. Simon Schama, *Dead Certainties, Unwarranted Speculations* (New York: Alfred Knopf, 1991), 21–22.

14. Benjamin West was appointed historical painter to the king the following year and would paint four more copies of his famous painting. The 2nd Duke of Westminster presented the original, dated 1770, to Canada in 1918 in recognition of its contribution to the First World War.

15. Tom Bower, *Conrad and Lady Black: Dancing on the Edge* (New York: Harper Press, 2006), 148.

16. Anne Chisolm and Michael Davie, *Beaverbrook, A Life* (London: Pimlico, 1992), 174.

17. Chester W. New, *Lord Durham: A Biography of John George Lambton, First Earl of Durham* (London: Dawsons of Pall Mall, 1968), 564.

18. Arnold Smith with Clyde Sanger, *Stitches in Time* (London: Andre Deutsche, 1981), 285.

19. Ibid., 65.

20. Hillmer and Granatstein, 252. In 1994, with Nelson Mandela as president, South Africa returned to the Commonwealth family.

21. David Adamson, *The Last Empire* (London: I.B. Tauris & Co. Ltd, 1989), 15–16.

22. William Kilbourn, *The Making of the Nation, A Century of Challenge* (Toronto: The Canadian Centennial Publishing Co., 1965), 69.

23. Robert Hardman, "The Most Loathsome Bird in Britain," *Mail Online*, June 4, 2008.

24. Vincent Massey, 276–77.

25. Tom MacDonnell, *Daylight Upon Magic: The Royal Tour of Canada 1939* (Toronto: Macmillan, 1989), 244.

26. Jean Lacouture, *De Gaulle, the Ruler: 1945–1970* (London: HarperCollins Publishers, 1991), 450.

27. Ibid., 456.

28. James Morris, *An Imperial Retreat* (London: Penguin Books, 1979), 337.

29. John H. Plumb, *The First Four Georges* (New York: John Wiley & Sons, 1967), 148.

30. *The Journal de Bougainville*, quoted in C.P. Stacey, *Quebec, 1759, The Siege and the Battle*, revised edition (Toronto: Robin Brass Studio, 2002), 225.

31. The New Chart of the St. Lawrence River was published the following year, 1760.

WALK 2: ST. JAMES'S AND PALL MALL

1. William Bernstein, *A Splendid Exchange: How Trade Shaped the World* (London: Atlantic Books, 2008), 248–49.

2. Richard Grenville, quoted in Brian Tunstall, *William Pitt, Earl of Chatham* (Great Britain: Hodder and Stoughton Limited, 1938), 89.

3. J.M. Scott, *The Book of Pall Mall* (London: Heinemann, 1965), 63.

4. Robert Windeler, *Sweetheart: The Story of Mary Pickford* (New York: Praeger, 1974), 118–19.

5. *American Experience*, "Mary Pickford," www.pbs.org/wgbh/amex/pickford.

6. Charles Foster, *Stardust and Shadows: Canadians in Early Hollywood* (Toronto: Dundurn, 2000), 284.

7. Eileen Whitfield, *Pickford* (Toronto: Macfarlane, Walter & Ross, 1997), 202.

8. G. Graham, *The Walker Expedition to Quebec, 1711* (Toronto: Champlain Society, 1953), 44.

9. Charles Davies, *Bread Men: How the Westons Built an International Empire* (Toronto: Key Porter Books, 1987), 39.

10. And, of course, to keep Jermyn's costs down.

11. Arthur Pound and Richard Day, *Johnson of the Mohawks* (New York: Books for Libraries Press, 1971), 431.

12. Ibid., 430. Guy Johnson's house still stands in Amsterdam, New York, not far from his more-famous relative's home. It is one of many properties loyalists fleeing to Canada abandoned for which they were never compensated. Today the old Erie Canal runs past its front door.

13. James Roy, *Joseph Howe* (Toronto: Macmillan, 1935), 96.

14. Phillip Buckner, "Campbell, Sir Colin," in *Dictionary of Canadian Biography*, vol. 7, (Toronto: University of Toronto/Université Laval, 2003), www.biographi.ca/009004-119.01-e.php?&id_nbr=3290.

15. Charles Ritchie, *The Siren Years 1937–1945* (Toronto: Macmillan of Canada, 1974), 147.

16. And remained so until the Carlton Club, which was even more Conservative, was created in the 1830s.

17. John Keegan, ed., *Churchill's Generals* (London: Weidenfeld and Nicolson, 1991), 108.

18. Ibid., 125. Liddell Hart quoted.

19. Owen Cooke and Norman Hillmer, "Alexander, Harold Rupert Leofric George, 1st Earl Alexander of Tunis," *The Canadian Encyclopaedia* (Edmonton: Hurtig Publishers, 1985).

20. Anthony Lejeune, *The Gentlemen's Clubs of London* (London: Parkgate Books, 1984), 289.

21. Tom Bower, *Conrad and Lady Black, Dancing on the Edge* (New York: Harper Press, 2006), 13. In the 2007 *Canadian Who's Who*, Lord Black lists the Athenaeum and the Beefsteak as his other London clubs.

22. Anthony Lejeune, 67.

23. Burgoyne surrendered his army in October 1777 at Saratoga, New York, and returned to England. The American Revolution continued until General Cornwallis's defeat in 1781 at Yorktown.

24. Roy MacLaren, *Commissions High, Canada in London* (Kingston/Montreal: McGill-Queen's University Press, 2006), 325.

25. Claude Bissell, *Imperial Canadian: Vincent Massey in Office* (Toronto: University of Toronto Press, 1986), 54; Charles Lynch, *The Lynch Mob: Stringing up our Prime Ministers* (Toronto: Key Porter Books, 1988), 178.

26. Vincent Massey, *What's Past is Prologue: The Memoirs of the Right Honourable Vincent Massey* (Toronto: Macmillan, 1963), 241–42.

27. Ibid., 268.

28. Nancy Gelber, *Canada in London: An Unofficial Glimpse of Canada's Sixteen High Commissioners, 1880–1980* (London: Canada House, 1980), 58.

29. Choral Pepper, *Walks in Oscar Wilde's London* (Salt Lake City, UT: Peregrine Smith Books 1992), 33–34; H. Montgomery Hyde, ed., *Trials of Oscar Wilde, Vol. 70: Notable British Trials* (London: W. Hodge and Company, 1948), 206.

30. Carl Bishop, *The Beaver: Exploring Canada's History* (February-March 2006), 34(6), quoting *The St. James Gazette*, September 24, 1890. It should be noted there are other origins of the story.

31. Maureen Borland, *Oscar Wilde's Devoted Friend* (Oxford: Lennard Publishing, 1990), 16.

32. Even Wilde's headstone in Père Lachaise Cemetery by British sculptor Jacob Epstein (1880–1959) proved controversial. It was decorated with a flying figure encumbered with large privates. Parisians covered up the stone in shame until someone came along with a chisel and emasculated it.

33. Richard Ellmann, *Oscar Wilde* (Markham, ON: Viking, 1987), 260.

34. James Noonan, *Canada's Governors General at Play* (Ottawa: Borealis, 2002), 284.

35. Maybe because he didn't completely understand the game, Grey never took part in a ceremonial kick-off. That honour went to his descendant, the 6th Earl Grey, in 1986 (James Noonan, 290).

36. Charles Ritchie, *Storm Signals: More Undiplomatic Diaries* (Toronto: Macmillan of Canada, 1971), 128.

37. Leslie Plommer, *Globe and Mail*, February 16, 1981.

38. Stephen Clarkson and Christina McCall, *Trudeau and Our Times, Volume 1: The Magnificent Obsession* (Toronto: McClelland and Stewart, 1990), 317.

39. Ibid., 385.

40. Paul Martin, *The London Diaries 1975–1979* (Ottawa: University of Ottawa Press, 1988), 313.

41. King James II (1633–1701; reigned 1685–88). Peter C. Newman, *Company of Adventurers*, Volume 1 (Viking, 1985), 102.

42. Ibid., 105.

43. Now located at 69 St. James's Street. The old club in Pall Mall was hit by an incendiary bomb in 1940.

44. Fred Anderson, *Crucible of War* (New York: Alfred Knopf, 2000), 311; John H. Plumb, *Chatham* (London: Collins, 1953), 75.
45. Charles Ritchie, *The Siren Years*, 78.
46. Massey Diary, April 1, 1937 quoted in Claude Bissell, 9.
47. Vincent Massey, 251.
48. Charles Ritchie, *Storm Signals*, 124.
49. Alan Gowans, *Looking at Architecture in Canada* (Toronto: Oxford University Press, 1958), 78.
50. Charles Greville quoted in Adam Shortt, *Lord Sydenham* (Toronto: Morang & Co., 1908), 43–44.
51. David Bercuson et al., *Colonies: Canada to 1867* (Toronto: McGraw-Hill Ryerson, 1992), 332.
52. Paul Martin, *London Diaries*, 202.
53. Vincent Massey, 291.
54. John H. Plumb, *The First Four Georges* (New York: John Wiley & Sons, 1967), 143.
55. John Kalbfleisch, "The First of a Long Line of Royals," *Montreal Gazette*, September 7, 2008.
56. Nancy Gelber, 36.

Walk 3: Trafalgar Square and Whitehall

1. Rodney Mace, *Trafalgar Square Emblem of Empire* (London: Lawrence and Wishart, 2005), 46.
2. J.P. Kenyon, *Stuart England* (London: Penguin, 1983), 75.
3. James Adams, "Faceoff Over Bard a Battle of Wills," *Globe and Mail*, April 13, 2009.
4. Peter and Douglas Richardson, *Canadian Churches: An Architectural History* (Toronto: Firefly Books, 2007), 44.
5. Thomas R. Millman, "Mountain, Jacob," in *Dictionary of Canadian Biography*, Volume 6, (Toronto: University of Toronto/ Université Laval, 2003), www.biographi.ca/009004-119.01-e.php?&id_nbr=3040.
6. Except for the columned portico. Mountain couldn't afford that and chose a flat façade instead. Alan Gowans, *Looking at Architecture in Canada* (Toronto: Oxford University Press, 1958), 70.
7. Peter and Douglas Richardson, 121.

8. Rodney Mace, 200. The ambassador's wife was Lady Emma Hamilton, Nelson's soon-to-be mistress.

9. Scurvy is a painful disease caused by a deficiency in vitamin C. It would eventually be remedied by eating sauerkraut.

10. Tom Pocock, *Nelson's Women* (Andre Deutsch, 2005), 57.

11. Ibid., 72.

12. René Lévesque, *Lévesque Memoirs* (Toronto: McClelland and Stewart, 1986), 130–31.

13. Walter Thornbury, "Whitehall: Historical Remarks," in *Old and New London: Volume 3* (1878), 337–61, www.british-history.ac.uk/report. aspx?compid=45158.

14. Julian Symons, *England's Pride, the Story of the Gordon Relief Expedition* (London: Hamish Hamilton, 1965), 106–07.

15. R.T. Naylor, *Canada in the European Age 1453–1919* (Vancouver: New Star Books, 1987), 491.

16. John Boileau, "The Nile Voyageurs," *Legion Magazine* (January 1, 2004), www.legionmagazine.com/en/index.php/2004/01/voyageurs-on-the-nile.

17. R.T. Naylor, 57.

18. Jack Granatstein, *The Generals, The Canadian Army's Senior Commanders in the Second World War* (Toronto: Stoddart, 1993), 31.

19. C.P. Stacey, *Memoirs of a Canadian Historian: A Date with History* (Ottawa: Deneau Publishers, 1982), 235.

20. Jack Granatstein, 112–13.

21. Ibid., 111, quoting Alanbrooke papers.

22. John Laffin, *British Butchers and Bunglers of World War One* (Gloucester: Sutton Publishing, 2003), 118.

23. Irvin Ehrenpreis, *Swift: The Man, His Works and the Age*, Volume 2 (London: Metheun & Co, 1967), 468–69.

24. Antoine de Guiscard died in London's Newgate Prison. The jailor pickled his body and charged the curious a penny to see it. Peter Jones, "Antoine de Guiscard, Abbé de la Bourlie, Marquis de Guiscard," Electronic British Library Journal, 1982, 111, www. bl.uk/eblj/1982articles/article6.html.

25. Stephen Clarkson and Christina McCall, *Trudeau and Our Times, Volume 1: The Magnificent Obsession* (Toronto: McClelland and Stewart, 1990), 322.

26. Ged Martin, *Britain and the Origins of Canadian Confederation, 1837–67* (Vancouver: UBC Press, 1995), 118.

27. D.M.L. Farr, *The Colonial Office and Canada 1867–1887* (Toronto: University of Toronto Press, 1955), 23.

28. Geoffrey Simmins, ed., *Documents in Canadian Architecture* (Peterborough, ON: Broadview Press, 1992), 33.

29. David Dilks, *The Great Dominion, Winston Churchill in Canada* (Toronto: Thomas Allen Publishers, 2005), 101.

30. Gordon Robertson, *Memoirs of a Very Civil Servant, Mackenzie King to Pierre Trudeau* (Toronto: University of Toronto Press, 2000), 65.

31. C.P. Stacey, *Canada and the Age of Conflict*, Volume 2. (Toronto: University of Toronto Press, 1981), 298.

32. Ibid., 298.

33. Robert Bothwell, *Canada 1900–1945* (Toronto: University of Toronto Press, 1987), 341.

34. Ramsay Cook, *Canada A Modern Study* (Toronto: Clarke, Irwin & Company, 1963), 86.

35. Richard Gwyn, *John A., The Man Who Made Us: The Life and Times of John A Macdonald*, Volume 1 (Toronto: Random House Canada, 2007), 434.

36. Glen Frankfurter, *Baneful Dominion: The Idea of Canada in the North Atlantic World, 1581–1971* (Don Mills, ON: Longman Canada, 1971), 173.

37. W.L. Morton, *The Critical Years, The Union of British North America 1857–1873* (Toronto: McClelland and Stewart, 1963), 212.

38. Though the term had been used briefly before to describe early New England.

39. Kenneth McNaught, *The Penguin History of Canada* (Toronto: Penguin Books, 1988), 130.

40. Charles Dickens, *Pictures from Italy and American Notes* (London: 1859), 205.

41. In return, Canada presented clerk's table made of Canadian oak to the restored House of Commons.

42. Ged Martin, 288.

43. Oscar Douglas Skelton, *The Life and Times of Alexander Tilloch Galt* (Toronto: Oxford University Press, 1920), 410.

Walk 4: Westminster and Lambeth

1. D. Creighton, *John A Macdonald: The Old Chieftain* (Toronto: Macmillan, 1965), 279. A term to describe a representative of the pope.
2. Roy MacLaren, *Commissions High, Canada in London* (Kingston/Montreal: McGill-Queen's University Press, 2006), 40.
3. Ibid., 39.
4. Ibid., 229, quoting Peter Larkin in *Saturday Night*, September 15, 1923.
5. Donald Creighton, *John A. Macdonald: The Young Politician* (Toronto: Macmillan, 1952), 443.
6. Oscar Douglas Skelton, *The Life and Times of Alexander Tilloch Galt* (Toronto: Oxford University Press, 1920), 408.
7. Donald Creighton, *The Young Politician*, 454.
8. Alan Gowans, *Looking at Architecture in Canada* (Toronto: Oxford University Press, 1958), 113.
9. Ibid., 115.
10. Franklin Toker, *The Church of Notre Dame in Montreal* (Montreal: McGill-Queen's University Press, 1970), 77.
11. Roy MacLaren, 41.
12. Edmund Burke to the British House of Commons, 1870, quoted in David Bercuson et al., *Colonies: Canada to 1867* (Toronto: McGraw-Hill Ryerson, 1992), 130.
13. Kenneth McNaught, *The Penguin History of Canada* (Toronto: Penguin Books, 1988), 71. One of these was Henry Dearborn (1751–1829), nicknamed "Granny" by his troops.
14. Castlereagh to Liverpool, 1815, quoted in Kenneth Bourne, *Britain and the Balance of Power in North America 1815–1908* (London: Longmans, 1967), 53.
15. Christopher Hibbert, *Wellington: A Personal History* (Reading, MA: Perseus Books, 1979), 238.
16. Clive Holland, "McClintock, Sir Francis Leopold," in *Canadian Dictionary of Biography*, Volume 3 (Toronto: University of Toronto/Université Laval, 2003), www.biographi.ca/009004-119.01-e.php?BioId=41016.
17. William Whiteley, "Saunders, Sir Charles," in Dictionary of Canadian Biography, Volume 4 (Toronto: University of Toronto/Université Laval, 2003), www.biographi.ca/009004-119.01-e.php?BioId=36283.
18. Stephen Brumwell, *The Paths of Glory: The Life and Death of General James Wolfe* (London: Habledon Continuum, 2006), 304.

19. McNairn, A., *Behold the Hero, General Wolfe & the Arts in the Eighteenth Century* (Montreal: McGill-Queen's University Press, 1997), 69.

20. G.R. Elton, *England Under the Tudors* (London: Metheun, 1974), 42.

21. Christopher McCreery, *The Order of Canada: Its Origins, History, And Development* (Toronto: University of Toronto Press, 2005), 13–14.

22. Donald Creighton, *The Old Chieftain*, 272.

23. Fred Anderson, *Crucible of War* (New York: Knopf, 2000), 113.

24. W.S. Kennedy, *Henry W. Longfellow: Biography, Anecdotes, Letters, Criticism* (Cambridge: Moss King Publishers, 1882), quoted in Cecil B. Williams, *Henry Wadsworth Longfellow* (New York: Twayne Publishers, 1964), 155.

25. C.P. Stacey, *Quebec 1759* (Toronto: Robin Brass, 2002), 134–36.

26. Alan Taylor, *The Civil War of 1812* (New York: Alfred A. Knopf, 2011), 47.

27. John Campbell, *F.E. Smith: The First Earl of Birkenhead* (Cape, 1983), 266, quoted in Anne Chisholm and Michael Davie, *Beaverbrook, A Life* (London: Pimlico, 1992), 113–14.

28. Village of Rexton website, www.villageofrexton.com/bonar.php, updated 04/16/2014.

29. June Purvis, *Emmeline Pankhurst, A Biography* (New York: Rutledge, 2002), 332.

30. Ibid., 331.

31. The name given to syphilis by the Italians. The French called it the Italian Disease.

32. June Purvis, 323.

33. Ibid., 329.

34. Alan Taylor, 51.

35. *National Post*, January 6, 2001.

36. I. Vincent, "Paintings Raise Blunt Questions," *National Post*, December 14, 2000.

37. Robert F. Legget, "By, John," in *Dictionary of Canadian Biography*, Volume 7 (Toronto: University of Toronto/Université Laval, 2003), www.biographi.ca/009004-119.01-e.php?BioId=37404.

38. Angus McLaren, *A Prescription for Murder: The Victorian Serial Killings of Dr. Thomas Neill Cream* (Chicago: University of Chicago Press, 1993), 34.

39. Lynn Macdonald, *The Collected Works of Florence Nightingale* (Waterloo: Wilfrid Laurier University Press, 2001), 23.

40. A.N. Thompson, "Smithurst, John," in *Dictionary of Canadian Biography*, Volume 9 (Toronto: University of Toronto/Université Laval, 2003).

41. William Anthony Styles, *Unusual Facts of Canadian History* (Toronto: McClelland and Stewart, 1947), 112; Vivienne Smith, "Preacher Carried a Torch for Florence," *Derby Evening Telegraph*, September 28, 2004, www.stjohnselora.ca/index.cfm?page=FlorenceNightingale.

Walk 5: Fleet Street to St. Paul's

1. Peter Ackroyd, *London: The Biography* (London: Vintage, 2001), 404.

2. *Drawings of John Soane*, Volume 42/55: John Soane (1753–1837): Government House, York, Upper Canada, November 13, 1818, www.soane.org.uk/drawings.

3. "Passed Legless Air Hero Now Posted to R.C.A.F.," Canadian Press, October 15, 1940, http://acesofww2.com/UK/aces/bader.

4. Brereton Greenhous et al, *The Crucible of War, 1939-1945: The Official History of the Royal Canadian Air Force*, Volume III (Toronto: University of Toronto Press, 1994), 40.

5. Brereton, Greenhous et al., 54.

6. Peter Burroughs, "MacDonnell, Sir Richard Graves," in *Dictionary of Canadian Biography*, Volume 11 (Toronto: University of Toronto/Université Laval, 2003), www.biographi.ca/009004-119.01-e.php?BioId=39794.

7. James E. Hendrickson, "Cary, George Hunter," in *Dictionary of Canadian Biography*, Volume 9 (Toronto: University of Toronto/Université Laval), www.biographi.ca/009004-119.01-e.php?&id_nbr=4341.

8. Ged Martin, *Britain and the Origins of Confederation* (Vancouver: UBC Press, 1995), 282. See footnote 249.

9. Stephen Eggleston, "The Myth and Mystery of POgG (Peace, Order and Good Government)," *Journal of Canadian Studies*, Winter 1996–97.

10. Ged Martin, 110; Donald Creighton, *Road to Confederation*, 282.

11. Brereton Greenhous, "Billy Bishop — Brave Flyer, Bold Liar," *Canadian Military Journal*, Autumn 2002, 61–64.

12. James Boswell, *Life of Johnson* (Boston: Carter, Hendee and Co., 1832), 194.

13. "The Mill Founder, His Descendants and Their Canadian Tax Crusade," *Globe and Mail*, February 17, 2009.

14. Alan Cooke, "Frobisher, Sir Martin," in *Canadian Dictionary of Biography*, Volume 1 (Toronto: University of Toronto/Université Laval, 2003), www.biographi.ca/009004-119.01-e.php?&id_nbr=230.

15. Tom Bower, *Conrad and Lady Black: Dancing on the Edge* (New York: Harper Press, 2006), 127.

16. Ibid., 112–13, quoting R. Siklos, *Shades of Black*.

17. Ibid., 170.

18. "All over at the Black Lubianka?" *Sunday Telegraph*, February 2, 1997, 8.

19. Anne Chisholm and Michael Davie, *Beaverbrook: A Life* (London: Pimlico, 1992), 135.

20. Ibid., 163.

21. "Daily Express, A Chequered History," *BBC News*, 25 Jan 2001; http://news.bbc.co.uk/2/hi/business/974835.stm.

22. Anne Chisholm and Michael Davie, 200.

23. "A Century Later, was Dr. Crippen Really Innocent?" *Daily Express*, November 27, 2010.

24. Fred Anderson, *Crucible of War* (New York: Knopf, 2000), 12.

25. Brendan Simms, *Three Victories and a Defeat: The Rise and Fall of the First British Empire, 1714–1783* (London: Allen Lane, 2007), 64; Richmond Bond, *Queen Anne's American Kings* (Oxford: Clarendon Press, 1952), 4; and Fred Anderson, 20. The paintings of the four kings are now in the possession of Library and Archives Canada.

26. Alan Taylor, *The Civil War of 1812: American Citizens, British Subjects, Irish Rebels & Indian Allies* (New York: Alfred A. Knopf, 2011), 188–89.

27. James Morris, *Heaven's Command: An Imperial Progress* (London: Penguin Books, 1979), 350–55.

Walk 6: Mayfair

1. F.H.W. Sheppard (general editor), *Survey of London: Volume 40: The Grosvenor Estate in Mayfair Part 2*, British History Online, Institute of Historical Research, University of London, www.british-history.ac.uk/source.aspx?pubid=298.

2. Richard Gwyn, *John A., The Man Who Made Us: The Life and Times of John A. Macdonald* (Toronto: Random House Canada, 2007), 258.

3. C.P. Stacey, *A Very Double Life: The Private World of Mackenzie King* (Toronto: Macmillan of Canada, 1976), 213.

4. Francis Parkman, *Half Century of Conflict*, Volume I (Boston: Little Brown & Co., 1898), 178.

5. Kevin O'Brien, *Oscar Wilde in Canada, An Apostle for the Arts* (Toronto: Personal Library, 1982), 146.

6. Ibid., 79.

7. Ibid., 44.

8. Ibid., 119.

9. Paul Martin, *The London Diaries 1975–1979* (Ottawa: University of Ottawa Press, 1988), 374.

10. Donna McDonald, *Lord Strathcona* (Toronto: Dundurn, 1996), 489.

11. Tom Bower, *Conrad and Lady Black: Dancing on the Edge* (New York: Harper Press, 2006), 399.

12. Ben Pimlott, *The Queen: Elizabeth II and the Monarchy* (London: Harper Press, 2012), 3.

13. See www.niagaraparks.com/attractions/sir-adam-beck-history.html.

14. Pierre Berton, *Niagara: A History of the Falls* (Toronto: McClelland and Stewart, 1992) 215.

15. Howard Schneider, "A Statue of Limitations Not Fit for a King," *Washington Post*, May 18, 1998.

16. W. Kaye Lamb, "Vancouver, George," in *Dictionary of Canadian Biography*, Volume 4 (Toronto: University of Toronto/Université Laval, 2003), www.biographi.ca/009004-119.01-e.php?&id_nbr=2195; Stephan Ruttan, "The Vancouver/Camelford Affair," Greater Victoria Public Library, http://gvpl.ca/using-the-library/our-collection/local-history/tales-from-the-vault/the-vancouver-camelford-affair.

17. P.B. Waite, "Bernard, Susan Agnes," in *Dictionary of Canadian Biography*, Volume 14, University of Toronto/Université Laval, 2003, www.biographi.ca/en/bio/bernard_susan_agnes_14E.html; Louise Reynolds, *Agnes: The Biography of Lady Macdonald* (Toronto: Samuel Stevens, 1979).

18. P.B. Waite, "Stanley, Frederick Arthur, 1st Baron Stanley and 16th Earl of Derby," in *Dictionary of Canadian Biography*, Volume 13 (Toronto: University of Toronto/Université Laval, 2003), www.biographi.ca/en/bio/stanley_frederick_arthur_13E.html; "Blimey, it's Stanley; Lord Stanley's Cup makes its First Visit to its Birth Place," *Hamilton Spectator*, April 21, 2006; Kevin Shea and John J. Wilson, *Lord Stanley, The Man Behind the Cup* (Bolton, ON: Fenn Publishing Company Ltd., 2006), 383.

Walk 7: Greenwich

1. Peter Ackroyd, *London: The Biography* (London: Vintage, 2001), 548.
2. Leslie Roberts, *There Shall Be Wings* (Toronto: Clarke, Irwin and Company Ltd., 1959), 137.
3. Peter Foster, *Towers of Debt* (Toronto: Key Porter Books, 1993), 201.
4. Ibid., 199.
5. Ibid., 287, see footnote.
6. Stephen Hume, "Sir Francis Drake, not Captain James Cook, was the First European to set Eyes on the B.C. Coast," *Vancouver Sun*, February 19, 2009, A17.
7. Frank McLynn, *Captain Cook, Master of the Seas* (New Haven and London: Yale University Press, 2011), 350–51.
8. Ibid., 278.
9. Derek House and Beresford Hutchinson, *The Clocks and Watches of Captain James Cook 1769–1969*, reprinted from four quarterly issues of *Antiquarian Horology* (London: 1969), 194.
10. K1 and K3 are the only timekeepers associated with Cook.
11. Derek Hayes, *Historical Atlas of Canada: Canada's History Illustrated with Original Maps* (Vancouver and Toronto: Douglas & McIntyre, 2002), 158.
12. Jean McGill, *The Joy of Effort: A Biography of R. Tait McKenzie* (Oshawa, ON: Alger Press, 1980), 125.
13. Clark Blaise, *Time Lord: The Remarkable Canadian Who Missed His Train, and Changed the World* (Toronto: Vintage Canada Edition, 2000), 86–90.
14. Francis Parkman, *Montcalm and Wolfe: The French & Indian War* (New York: Da Capo Press, 1995), 415.

IMAGE CREDITS

Unless noted all images are from author's collection.

27: © 1897 Canada Post. Reprinted with permission. Library and Archives Canada.

39: © 1939 Canada Post. Reprinted with permission. Library and Archives Canada.

41: Library and Archives Canada/3036-134.

54: Library of Congress Prints and Photographs Division, LC-B2-5213-13.

66: Library and Archives Canada/C-000999.

70: Canada Patent and Copyright Office/Library and Archives Canada/PA-029035.

80: M15885 | Bust | *Head from a Bust of George III, 1765* © McCord Museum. Reprinted with permission.

82: Topical Press Agency/Library and Archives Canada/PA-126948.

91: © Government of Canada, Canadian Conservation Institute, 2001, CCC 73456-0003.

127: © 1966 Canada Post. Reprinted with permission.

146 (bottom): Glenbow Archives NC-6-1746. Reprinted with permission.

154: Archives of Ontario/Thomas Connon (Connon family fonds). C 286-3-0-11.

173: Library and Archives Canada/C-011413.

177: Canada. Dept. of National Defence/Library and Archives Canada/M-263B.

208: William James Topley/Library and Archives Canada/PA-026376.

232: © 1977 Canada Post. Reprinted with permission. Library and Archives Canada.

ACKNOWLEDGEMENTS

Like countless others who have written on London, I am indebted to the multivolume *Survey of London*, which made me want to write more about this wonderful city than was ever practical. Many an evening was lost reading it. I am even more indebted to the *Dictionary of Canadian Biography* from whose pages emerge so many colourful characters that it will disprove anyone who thinks our history is boring. "There's nowt so queer as folk," the Welsh might say of us. The fact that both of these sources and so much more can be consulted online is an inexpressible luxury, especially for anyone writing during a long winter in Ottawa. Certainly I am not the first to look at the Canadian connections in London. *The Canadian Guide to Britain, Volume 1: England*, by Jeffrey Simpson and Ged Martin, blazed that helpful trail in the 1980s. My walks in London would have been much shorter but for their research.

Separating historical fact from fiction is not always the best recipe for storytelling. Part of a tour guide's value is sometimes the local lore he or she imparts. Thus, while I have tried to be accurate as possible, at times the unsubstantiated might have been too tempting to pass up. Readers, I think, will have the good sense to know the difference.

There are several people to whom I owe thanks. For place to stay in London and a home cooked Marks & Spencer meal whenever I returned, Richard Hallas; for advice, help, and encouragement Randy Allan, David Blewett, John Fraser, Beth Gorham, Veronique Nguyen, Arthur Sheps, and Eric Enno Tam. If there are glaring errors, omissions, or outright transgressions in the text they are entirely mine.

For my parents, Lois and Ray Walters

INDEX